A regular presenter on BBC television, Dan Cruickshank is an architectural historian best known for his popular series *Britain's Best Buildings* and *What the Industrial Revolution Did For Us*.

His most recent television series include *Marvels of the Modern Age*, *The Lost World of Friese-Greene* and *Around the World in 80 Treasures*, which was accompanied by a bestselling book of the same title.

He is an active member of the Georgian Group and has been a visiting professor in the Department of Architecture at the University of Sheffield.

His previous books include *Life in the Georgian City* and *The Guide to the Georgian Buildings of Britain and Ireland*.

He lives in London.

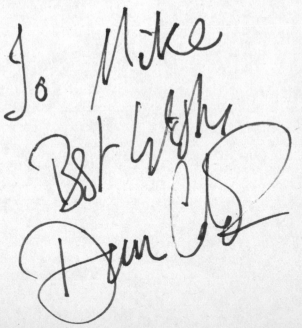

Adventures in Architecture

DAN CRUICKSHANK

PHOENIX

A PHOENIX PAPERBACK

First published in Great Britain in 2008
by Weidenfeld & Nicolson
This paperback edition published in 2009
by Phoenix,
an imprint of Orion Books Ltd,
Orion House, 5 Upper St Martin's Lane,
London WC2H 9EA

An Hachette UK company

1 3 5 7 9 10 8 6 4 2

Printed and bound in Great Britain by
Clays Ltd, St Ives plc

The Orion Publishing Group's policy is to use papers that
are natural, renewable and recyclable products and
made from wood grown in sustainable forests. The logging
and manufacturing processes are expected to conform to
the environmental regulations of the country of origin.

www.orionbooks.co.uk

Contents

Introduction

This book is the result of a journey around the world that started in Sao Paulo, Brazil in October 2006 and finished in the remote centre of Afghanistan in August 2007. The journey embraced over 20 countries in five continents of the world, ranging from the icy vastness within the Arctic Circle and of north Russia in the winter, to the baked deserts of the Middle East, the steaming rainforest of the Amazon, and the teeming cities of India and China.

The object of the journey has been to discover and chart the history of humanity, its aspirations, beliefs, triumphs and disasters, by exploring buildings and cities around the world. This quest has embraced truly dramatic juxtapositions and contrasts in cultures, climates, and in scales and types of building. I have looked at entire cities including the oldest continuously inhabited city in the world, Damascus in Syria, and the first new capital city to be completed in the 21st century, Astana in Kazakhstan, to see how people live together and how architecture can define and reflect communities. I have also explored individual structures including temples, churches, castles, palaces, a skyscraper, a brothel and harem, a gaol and, in Afghanistan, the finest early minaret in the world – the enigmatic 12th-century Minaret at Jam. I have sought the origins of architecture by helping make what is, in a sense and paradoxically, the oldest structure in the world. In Greenland I joined an Inuit to construct an igloo, an ancient and ingenious structure – an object of pristine beauty – that reveals how architecture evolved at the dawn of time as man used his intuitive engineering genius and available materials to create shelter from the elements and defence from beasts.

The discoveries made during this quest, shown in a series of programmes on BBC2 entitled *Adventures in Architecture* and now recorded in this book, tell a very personal history of architecture. Compiling this history has been exhausting, but nearly always exhilarating and exciting. Architecture is man's most pressing and arguably most consistently demanding and creative activity when many seemingly competing needs have to be reconciled, have to be made to coexist in happy harmony. For example, architecture reveals how the potentially hostile forces of nature have to be overcome through design, how nature must be used to tame – to defy – nature; how potential problems can be turned to advantage. Buildings have to withstand the force of gravity but immensely robust engineered structures such as domes and arches are strong precisely because they harness natural forces such as gravity. We also see how, through the ages, architecture has utilised the potential offered not just by natural forms and materials – such as clay, stone and timber – but also how the products of nature have been transformed and strengthened by art to create new and ever stronger building materials such as iron, reinforced concrete and steel. Architecture is, at its best, the inspired and inventive marriage of art and science or, as the Roman architect Vitruvius explained over 2,000 years ago, architecture must possess 'commodity, firmness and delight'. These are the potentially conflicting forces that architecture has to reconcile. Simultaneously a building must fulfil its functional requirements, must be structurally stable and must be poetic, possess beauty, meaning, inflame and engage the intellect and imagination – and if a sacred building evoke the spiritual through material means. A construction that fulfils just the first two of Vitruvius's requirements is a mere utilitarian structure, the possession of the third – structurally non-essential but spiritually uplifting delight – transforms a structure into architecture.

The locations discussed in this book are grouped under eight themes that relate to the forces that create architecture and reflect the reasons why humans build: to create shelter and in response to disaster, to express worldly power, to honour and commemorate their gods, to create images of paradise on earth and give tangible expression to idealistic dreams, to mark the mystery of death and reflect the speculations about life beyond death, to create communities that realise the potential and benefits of shared living, for sensual pleasure and the spiritual and visual delights of artistic beauty.

I've learned much during this epic journey – and been reminded of much. Architecture is the great adventure open to all because architecture surrounds us, it's the great public art. Like it or not we all live in, work in or merely walk through or around architecture. Buildings are privately owned or occupied but they also have a powerful public life – great architecture belongs to all of us. To see it properly, to understand architecture even a little, to unravel the stories locked in its stones, is to be enriched, to have daily delight. I hope this book helps any who read it to love and understand architecture a little more.

I fear that some of the locations I've included will shock and puzzle but also, I hope, intrigue, delight, inform and entertain. The absence of any locations in Britain and Ireland does not mean an absence in these islands of architecture of quality and of world importance. Far from it, but I have already written elsewhere about most of the locations I would have included in this book and rather than covering them again, I have chosen to focus on architecture and locations of immense interest that have long intrigued me but which, in many cases, I have not visited before or investigated in detail.

Most of the locations in this book can be visited with relative safety and ease, but given the environmentally damaging consequences of travel many readers might prefer to read about remote and fragile architectural treasures rather than visit them. But greater and more immediate danger comes from conflict and poverty. The world is becoming an increasingly hostile and divided place, with ever more of its monuments threatened by war and neglect and historic sites ruined by looting. This book does, I hope, act as a reminder of the cultural and artistic treasures potentially at risk and, at the very least, documents those that may soon change forever.

1

Beauty

The origin of architecture in the land of ice and snow

Igloo, Greenland

I fly into Greenland. Below me is deep blue water, speckled with floating ice, then in the distance I see a white curving cliff – it's the beginning of the pack-ice that embraces the coastline. There is no sign of any living being – no towns or tracks. I feel I'm gazing at a landscape as old as earth itself.

I've come to find the origin of architecture. I hope to help make a structure which is an example of man's earliest exercise in the creation of shelter. I'm here in quest of the igloo. For me the igloo – the domed house of snow and ice – is the perfect building. It seems so simple yet demonstrates how functional buildings, when brilliantly and logically conceived and executed, can achieve pure beauty and become architecture. Particularly impressive is the inspired use that's made of snow, the region's only readily available building material, and the way in which this weakest of natural materials is given immense strength through design, by being fashioned into blocks and stacked to create one of the strongest forms in nature – the dome. Yes, this miniature-engineering marvel has long fascinated me. How did the igloo evolve, when and where? No one knows for sure, but traditionally igloos were built by specific Inuit communities in relatively small areas of Greenland and Canada, and were used for temporary accommodation in winter or by Inuit on hunting expeditions. I can't wait to find out more.

We are heading for an airfield at Scoresbysund, on the east

coast of Greenland. Contemplating this remarkable landscape it's easy to be deceived, to be lulled. Greenland from the air looks limitless and unchanging. But this land mass is now in the front line of global change. Temperatures in the Arctic Circle are rising twice as fast as in the rest of the earth, and ice-floes in Greenland have receded by 40 per cent in the last 30 years. Much of what appears to be land mass – the pack-ice and glaciers – is melting as a result of global warming. If this continues – the result of human misbehaviour elsewhere on the planet – this land faces catastrophic change, which will also spell catastrophe for much of the planet as melting ice inundates low-lying areas around the world. I realise that I may be arriving just in time to see what remains of traditional Inuit life, a life dictated by the cold climate and icy land. In a few years it might not even be possible to build houses made of snow and ice in areas inhabited by the Inuit.

The Inuit live several miles away from the airfield on the coast, in the town of Ittoqqortoormiitt. The town looks picturesque from afar – a scattering of gaily painted one- and two-storey, pitched-roof timber cabins placed on land which falls steeply down to the coast. But a brief walk through the town reveals that all is not well. There's real poverty here and a sense of desperation, even alienation. I study the houses more closely. Pretty they might be, but they are sinister harbingers of things to come and they signal the cultural end of the Inuit. The houses are virtually all the same, frames clad with timber panels. Clearly they arrived as flat-packs, no doubt from Denmark, of which Greenland is a dependency. These mass-produced cabins are easier to build than traditional Inuit houses made of animal hide, driftwood, snow and ice, so people prefer them. But of course this means that the methods of constructing traditional buildings – including the igloo – are being forgotten.

The Inuit of Ittoqqortoormitt belong to one of the last genuine hunting communities in the world. They range out on their hunting sledges to kill – not for sport or fun, but to live, and for them this remains a most honourable vocation. The boys I see frolicking in the town don't aspire to be lawyers or doctors – they want to be hunters. The girls, I suppose, want to be nothing other than hunters' wives. I ponder the ice-dried pelts of polar bears. Such hunting is now at odds with the sensibilities of the larger world and I'm shocked by what I see. But if we want to protect what survives of genuine Inuit culture, such as their snow-built architecture, then we must defend their right to hunt. It's what defines them and gives them pride and identity.

I am going to meet the man with whom I'm to build the igloo. Andreas Sanimuinaq is 65 years old, the son of a famous Ittoqqortoormitt hunter and one of the few men in town who has actually built an igloo. We talk and he tells me that the first step is to find the right snow and the right site. The snow mustn't be too hard or too soft. It has to have the right density – compacted by the wind – so it can be cut into building blocks and act as an insulator to help keep the interior of the igloo warm.

As we prepare to depart I tell Andreas that I feel lucky to have one of the town's few igloo builders to help me. He smiles. There is no one else, reveals Andreas ruefully. No one else in the town knows how to build an igloo and he adds that no one cares, the children don't want to know. My goodness, things are more desperate than I thought. We came here merely to build an igloo but it seems we are in fact to document a nearly dead tradition. Andreas tells me that he was taught to build an igloo by his grandfather and father, and he has not been able to pass the mystery on. When he dies the Ittoqqortoormitt igloo dies with him. This is becoming a serious mission. We leave the house, board Andreas's long hunting sledge, pulled by a pack of ten beefy hounds, and off we go to find the right snow with which to construct the perfect building.

We glide, at speed, on the surface of the frozen fjord, hugging the coastline. Andreas suddenly halts the sledge and prods the snow with the handle of his whip. Yes, we've found a location where wind, blowing along and around the rocky coastline, has compacted the snow to the right consistency. But the site of the good snow is on falling land, on the beach flanking the fjord. Can we really build an igloo on the slope? Andreas sees my puzzled expression and strides onto the flat ice and declares that we will cut the snow blocks over there, on the sloping bank, and build the igloo on the flat frozen sea water of the fjord. He uses the whip to stamp the outline of an accurate circle in the snow. It's the plan of our igloo and bigger than I expected, with a diameter of about four and a half yards. This is going to be some task. But more worrying is the choice of site or rather the choice of two sites – one for the quarry and one for the igloo. Already the theory of my perfect building is being challenged by reality. A corner stone of the theory of igloo construction is that the pit from which the snow blocks are dug should also form the basement of the igloo – an elegant solution that reduces double-handling of the snow blocks and contributes significantly to the ideal igloo's heating and ventilation system. Hot air rises while cold air sinks so, according to the theory, cold air will sink into the basement while the warm air – created by the body heat of the igloo's inhabitants and seal-blubber lamps –will rise into the dome where it will be trapped and enjoyed by the inhabitants.

In addition, if the entrance to the igloo is below ground level, and leads first into the basement, then the entrance tunnel will act as an air trap, preventing cold air from entering, since it can't rise, and warm air from escaping, since it can't descend. All very clever, revealing the igloo to be a fascinating machine for living in which heat is balanced delicately against cold, and in which nature is harnessed to tame nature. Warm air not only excludes cold air but also helps to seal the igloo and make it draughtproof, for as the warmth from bodies and lamps heats the interior it causes the inner surface of the snow blocks to melt. The water trickles down, fills the joints between blocks and then, during the night, refreezes and acts as a sort of grout. If snowflakes fall on the outside, the relative warmth of the igloo's outer surface causes them to melt and also trickle into the cracks where they also refreeze during the night and so complete the job of sealing the joints. This constant thawing and refreezing, through internal heat and the actions of the sun in the day and the cold at night, rapidly transforms the igloo from a house of snow into a far stronger house of ice. Any ventilation needed can be achieved by poking a couple of small holes through the surface. In some regions, the Inuit made the process of transformation from snow to ice speedier and more dramatic by throwing buckets of water over the igloo.They knew that it would initially melt the surface of the snow blocks, which would then refreeze to give the structure a hard veneer – indeed, turn the igloo into a beautiful little crystalline ice-house.

I ask Andreas about the wisdom of separating the ice quarry from the construction site and about building on the ice, which is only about eight inches below the surface of the snow and so prevents the creation of a basement and an air-trap entrance tunnel. Surely this will doom the interior of the igloo to perpetual cold? Andreas smiles and gets on with digging for the good, compacted snow, which he finally finds about 18 inches below the more powdery surface snow. Well, I suppose many igloos must have been built on ice so perhaps there's no need for alarm. Andreas isn't building me the perfect theoretical igloo. He's building a real igloo that responds to the potential of an actual site. This thought consoles me somewhat.

Andreas has already extracted and roughly shaped a block of snow. He hands it to me to carry to the building site. It's about 30 inches long, 18 inches high and just over a foot deep – and incredibly heavy. As I wilt under the load I ask Andreas how many of these monsters we will need. He smiles again, and says he doesn't know. Doesn't know! I suddenly fear this chap hasn't constructed an igloo for a very long time – if ever. I insist that he must have some idea. Fifty – maybe, says Andreas who turns back to cut another block.

After cutting and carrying about a dozen blocks we start to build. Andreas flattens the surface of each one, using an old bread knife as a tool, and then selects one and cuts a slight bevel on its top. I watch closely as Andreas lays the first couple of blocks. He carefully flattens and shapes all the surfaces that will abut each other and then, just before placing the blocks in position, runs the teeth of his knife over the surfaces about to be joined. The careful shaping has ensured that a large area of each face will actually be touching while the final sawing causes friction that momentarily melts snow crystals on the surfaces about to be abutted. Before this surface moisture freezes, the blocks are rammed together and held in place until the moisture on abutting surfaces turns to ice and unites the blocks. So that's the secret of the construction, without supporting scaffold, of a large domed structure in this particular climate. The individual blocks are bonded, frozen together, by ice acting as mortar. But I'm worried. I can see how this system works when the blocks are laid almost vertically, but what happens when the wall start to incline more to the horizontal? Can just a thin veneer of ice really hold such heavy blocks in place? I'll soon find out.

The first three courses of the igloo, which consume nearly 50 blocks, create a four-foot-high, more or less vertical wall. But that fits the theory. An igloo is not meant to be a hemispherical dome but should take the profile of a massively strong catenary arch, which means its lower portion slopes inwards only slightly, while its upper part is cone-like and shaped to resemble the pointed end of an egg. The shape is immensely strong, forming a dome that it is possible to construct without scaffold, and – most important – the weight of the heavy snow blocks thrusts mostly downwards to the ground and not outwards as would be the case with a more rounded arch.

Now, as we reach the fourth course of the igloo, comes relief. Andreas is at last doing what I've been hoping for. He starts to build the igloo as a continuous spiral. He does this simply by shaping a block into a wedge shape so that it acts as a ramp when the time comes to build above it. This happens at the moment when construction starts to get a little more difficult because the wall begins to slope significantly inwards. The spiral is an ingenious answer to the constructional problem. It means that from here on each newly laid block will have the support of the block beside it as well as the blocks below it, and they can, if required, all be wedged together.

And so up we go, theory and practice working happily together. But all is not smooth. Blocks are being laid with a bevelled upper surface, implying that soon the blocks will have to be laid almost horizontally. I just can't understand how this will be possible. Andreas picks up a block of snow, studies the place it is to go, ponders the angles that the new block has to match and then slowly cuts it to shape. He cuts and re-cuts, sometimes discarding a block and starting again. He has to create angled faces that fit together as closely as possible to maximise the areas that touch, that can be frozen together. When he's happy with his efforts, Andreas and I lift the block into place and look to see how closely the often crazily angled surfaces fit together. If the fit's not bad, Andreas does a little tailoring in situ, roughs-up the surfaces to create some moisture and we gently push the block into position. Then we hold it – and pray. We look at each other. Andreas smiles and whispers, 'One minute.' When the time is up we slowly remove our hands to see if the precariously perched block has – seemingly in defiance of the laws of gravity – frozen into place. Mostly it has. After about eleven hours we have two thirds of the igloo complete.

We are back at the building site early in the morning. I contemplate yesterday's work. This is the moment of truth. I simply don't see how we can make blocks stay on the upper bevels we have cut on last night's blocks. The bevels are too acute, the next blocks will have to be almost horizontal. Andreas appears unconcerned. He cuts the first block of the day and puts it in place. He ignores the bevel that promised a near horizontal block and places the new block in a near vertical position. It works, but this igloo will have a distinctly strange shape. As we work I wonder. Our dome may be odd of shape but I admire it greatly. Indeed I admire domes. The dome is regarded as one of the high points of architecture and engineering. It is beautiful, the universal symbol of the vault of heaven, and although tricky to build is immensely strong if firmly constructed. We toil on for the rest of the second day of construction. Thank goodness we're not building it in earnest for shelter. This is a hostile world and we'd be dead by now.

And so the third day begins. It's well into the afternoon before we are ready to fit the last block in place. And once again theory is questioned by practice. The last block is meant to be the keystone, the block that stops the dome from collapsing because, as it is pressed down by the force of gravity, it locks all the lower stones in place. But Andreas's keystone is very slight, just a capstone, and is really locking nothing in place. In fact, he cuts it in half so that he can put it in place, half at a time, from below the igloo. Surely, I say, the keystone should be a large block, with bevelled sides, rammed in place from above. Andreas is shocked and warns me of the foolishness of the idea of climbing on the outer surface of the incomplete igloo. It could collapse, he says. I ask when the structure will be strong. Soon, soon. I suppose when the blocks, after a few days melting under the sun in the day and freezing in the cold of the night, have more fully turned to ice. The finishing touch is the entrance tunnel – really just a porch roofed by two enormous blocks of snow. Since this is by no means the air-lock of my theoretical igloo, I ask how the cold winds will be kept out and warm air kept in. By a snow block door, explains Andreas. Not quite as scientific as a tunnel, but I suppose it will work.

We stand outside and contemplate our work. The igloo is much more of a cone in shape than I'd expected, but it looks heroically strong and timeless, like the first building in the world. We crawl inside and build a high bench made from snow blocks, and place a musk ox hide on it. It's most satisfying. The sun shining through the thick blocks of snow and ice creates a wonderful soft, luminous light. And so the task is complete. I have helped make a building that is new but feels ancient. Andreas's determination to make the igloo not just functional but also a thing of beauty – an ornament – shows how a merely utilitarian building can turn into a work of architecture, a work of expressive art.

To celebrate the completion of the igloo we go fishing. We drop a large hook and line through the nearby hole in the ice and attempt to catch passing fish. As we rhythmically sink and haul up the line Andreas tells me about his life and the Arctic. His direct experience confirms what I already know. The climate is changing – warming – at an alarming speed. Hunters have to curtail their expeditions now because the pack-ice forms later and melts earlier than in the past times, and game is disappearing because of changing migration routes and habitats. He is angry that his people are powerless, that their world and traditional way of life are being destroyed by the irresponsible actions of remote nations such as the United States and China. The increasing difficulty of hunting in the region seems to be illustrated by our little experiment. We stand around our hole for over an hour, and no luck. I ask Andreas what we should do.

He flashes me a smile, reaches in his haversack and pulls out a frozen fish. Supper. It's the wrong time of year to catch fish like this he now informs me. This fishing expedition was, it seems, just to humour me.

We cook the fish in front of the igloo and as the sun goes down a lamp inside starts to make the odd-looking little structure glow. It's stunning. The igloo is an admirably functional object, but what now strikes me most is its perfect beauty. It's beautiful because of the pure logic of its design and construction; beautiful because it seems so simple, yet is complex in its functions and, of course, beautiful because of its form. The igloo's dome is not only the supreme example of a structure in which form is the rational expression of function and materials but it is also powerfully, and movingly symbolic. The igloo's dome is celestial, an image of the heavens, the Inuits' symbol of the life-giving sun in their icy world. Yes, the igloo is more than just a shelter, more than architecture – it's a world in itself.

Breathtaking Baroque masterpiece

Catherine Palace, St Petersburg, Russia

St Petersburg is beautiful, bitterly cold and covered with a veneer of snow when I arrive in early spring. The River Neva and the canals encircling the city centre are streaks of ice, and in the streets huddled figures struggle against the icy blasts. All this arctic activity is taking place against an architectural backdrop in which details and colours are Mediterranean – pink, warm yellow ochre, blue-green – in contrast to the snow and leaden skies. As always, St Petersburg – perhaps the greatest classical city in the world – astounds.

I've come to see a building which in many ways tells the story of the city and embodies its architectural aspirations. The Catherine Palace, 25 kilometres to the south of the city in the royal park of Tzarskoje Selo, was built by the woman who was largely responsible for the establishment of St Petersburg as a great city. Empress Elizabeth, daughter of Peter the Great who founded St Petersburg in 1703, put her heart into the realisation of her father's dream – to create a great capital in the barren land around the Baltic that he had just, with great effort, reclaimed for Russia from the Swedes. After Peter's death in 1725, the capital of Russia was returned from the remote wastes of the Baltic to Moscow. But Peter's successor – his niece Anna – moved the capital back to St Petersburg before she died, and Peter's daughter, Elizabeth, when she came to the throne in 1741, committed herself to making the city work. During the 1750s nobles and courtiers built palaces in the city centre, near the queen's own rebuilt and enlarged Winter Palace. Many were the work of the same architect, the man who gave mid-18th-century St Petersburg its distinct look – its powerful architectural beauty.

Bartolomeo Rastrelli was born in Paris in 1700. The son of an Italian sculptor, he came to Russia in 1716 with his father to work for Peter the Great. In the following years Rastrelli travelled extensively in France and Italy while also working for the Russian court and, thanks to his talent and training, was made court architect in 1738. He was commissioned by Elizabeth to build a vast palace – one of the most impressive structures of its kind ever created. Elizabeth named the building after her mother – Catherine – and made its design and construction the focus of her life. This palace was intended as the main summer residence of the royal family. It was to be the Russian equivalent of Louis XIV's Versailles – the very epitome of power, of imperial order. In this building beauty was to be used as a political weapon, as an expression of divine majesty.

I arrive at the Catherine Palace and in front of me is a hot-blooded Baroque masterpiece. All is brightly coloured – turquoise walls, white architectural trim, with various details picked out in yellow ochre. The palace packs the visual punch of a great and emblematic painting, and originally the impact would have been greater still, for what is now ochre was then gold. All is enhanced by the masterful manipulation of scale. The form of the palace is extraordinary. It's thin in plan – essentially only two rooms deep – but incredibly long, 350 metres from end to end. This is because the interior is organised to present a formal route along which visitors would progress on a journey to the heart of the imperial court.

The sheer length of the elevation could easily lead to monotony. So the architect has used devices to break it up, to balance the composition by introducing a constant counter-play of vertical features. The long elevation is broken into a series of pavilions, each with a centre emphasised by groups of giant columns supporting pediments. Giant columns also whip the slightly lower linking elevations into a frenzy of vertical movement, so that they appear to rise and fall, advance and recede in a stately manner. Everywhere there are rich details – masks above windows, elegant mouldings – to ensure that this sublime composition not only possesses presence when seen from afar, but also interest when viewed from close to.

I walk to the south end and reach the location of the original main door. Rastrelli's main staircase was removed in the late 18th century, when a new principal staircase was created in the centre of the palace. This revised arrangement may have been more convenient but it compromises the original and ruthless logic of Elizabeth's creation with its formal route – an enfilade – stretching from the south end of the palace to the north, all the door openings aligned to create a spectacular internal vista. This was, in a sense, to be an interior version of St Petersburg's long and straight Nevsky Prospect. It was to be a parade of power and beauty with Elizabeth, the empress, as its focus.

Despite the drastic interior alterations I find a route of entry at the south end of the palace and make my way to the first floor – the piano nobile or main floor on which are arranged all the principal rooms. Now I pursue the journey envisaged by Elizabeth. The first thing I observe is that there are in fact two parallel south–north routes through the palace. The one to the west links all the larger staterooms and so is clearly the more important route, to be followed by high-born courtiers, nobility and diplomats. The route to the east links the smaller and more private rooms. This must have been the route leading to the heart of Elizabeth's private world – the route for her intimates. But both are subject to the same basic rule: they were intended to reveal the hierarchy of the court and of the land, and those she most favoured would penetrate deepest.

For the first portion of the progress from the main entrance at the south end of the palace to the private suite at the north end, the two routes pass through the same rooms, each of which is furnished with two pairs of doors. Those to the west look north to the larger rooms in the distance while those in the south look to the smaller rooms in the distance. It's all most subtle and intriguing, no doubt reflecting accurately the complex atmosphere and constantly shifting balance of power in Elizabeth's court. I follow the route to the west – the route of state that looks directly towards the sequence of main rooms to the north. This southern end of the palace has been much rearranged but there are still three large rooms set in a row and each stretching the full width of the palace. These are various ante-rooms and guard-chambers, the most relatively public parts of the palace interior. Here the less exalted would gather, merely being allowed a glimpse into the wonders of the world beyond. I look through the rows of open doors, the vista receding into the distance. It's astonishing. The door openings are framed by lively Baroque and light-hearted Rococo decorations, all gilded. Only the privileged could have walked the route I now tread. I pass from this sequence of rooms into one of the most magnificent interiors in Europe – the Great Hall. It is vast and sparkles with gold, glass and shimmering light. Both the public and the private routes lead into this hall – the 'Gallery of Light' – and it seems to have been a fusion of all the aspects of Elizabeth's world. Architecturally it's breathtaking. Light floods in from both sides through tiers of windows; placed between these, and at each end of the hall, are huge areas of mirror set in gilded Rococo frames, drooping with luscious detail. The artistic intention was to baffle and overwhelm the senses. It is high Baroque theatre. The combination of windows and mirrors breaks spatial boundaries. It's almost impossible to see where the room starts and ends, to see what is real and what illusion.

The space seems limitless, and in all four corners of the room are doors leading to receding vistas.

From the Great Hall northwards the two routes divide. Following the one to the west brings me into a gold-sprinkled dining room intended for courtiers in attendance. This was a gathering place for members of the court who were in some degree serving the empress. The room is furnished with a massive stove, which rises from floor to ceiling and is clad with blue tiles – although this was intended as a Summer Palace, each of the main rooms is heated by at least one of these stoves. With their beautiful tiles, often showing amusing and characterful Russian scenes and fashions, the stoves are at once ornamental and functional and are among the chief glories of the palace. Beyond this dining room was a hall decorated in Chinese style, but this was replaced in the late 18th century by the new main staircase. Then there is Elizabeth's formal dining room, followed by a reception room and then by a larger room called the Portrait Room. The original function of these rooms is revealed by their ornament. Each door is topped by a huge gilded crown signifying a formal place of entry for Elizabeth when she, in all her imperial grandeur and glory, arrived for an interview with a foreign prince or ambassador.

Elizabeth's appearance on these occasions is suggested by a painting that hangs in the Portrait Room. It was painted by Heinrich Buchholz in 1768, six years after Elizabeth's death, but it shows her in her prime. It's fascinating. It's all to do with power and wealth – expressed through beauty. She stands against a backdrop of massive classical architecture and around her are placed expensive objects of fashion – gilded Baroque furniture and a huge oriental vase. Elizabeth is clad in a vast and luxuriant ermine-trimmed cloak of a rich golden fabric, embroidered with the imperial insignia of the double-headed eagle. This majestic cloak is wrapped around a formal court dress. It's an amazing piece of work – low cut and with wide panniers that emphasise the hips. Elizabeth is said to have possessed 15,000 dresses when she died – what consumption! She carries a sceptre and before her is placed an orb – both traditional symbols of royal rule – and she wears the blue sash and star of the Order of S. Andrew, an exclusive chivalric order founded by her father and awarded only to nobility. I peer at the painting. Yes, I see the power, but what was she really like as a woman? I study the face – the human being behind all this pomp. Elizabeth looks homely, and far from arrogant. I feel I could trust her and I know she loved architecture and created one of the most exciting buildings in the world. I must admit it – I like her!

I move along the enfilade and enter a room with almost magical qualities, a room that's haunted the imagination of the western world. It's been described as one of the most beautiful ever created – the Eighth Wonder of the World. This is the Amber Room, and it is really a hymn to the power and beauty of nature. It's extraordinary – the texture and colouring is like tortoiseshell, for each wall panel in the room is a veneer of hundreds of small pieces of amber. Each is slightly different in colour, ranging from yellow to deep red-brown. Much of the amber is carved with intricate Baroque detail, including fine but tiny cameos, and glows with a warm, honey colour. It's almost hypnotic to look at – the rich detail and colours are intoxicating.

The work here is fine and beautiful, but this isn't the Amber Room that was made in the 18th century. This room – a near perfect copy – was completed only five years ago! Its splendid and spirited recreation is emblematic of the story of the Catherine Palace, much of which was reduced to a fire-blackened shell in the Second World War. So here, as in all the rooms in the palace, virtually everything is a post-war recreation. The communist regime undertook the reconstruction of these Tsarist interiors because it recognised that they were a source of great national pride and identity. They had been created by Russians, or by foreigners working for Russians, for the glory of Russia. They were great national treasures and works of art and their loss was an intolerable blow. A great wrong had to be put right, lost beauty recovered, and for the last 50 years reconstruction has been underway.

I leave the Amber Room, with its almost supernatural glow, and enter the Picture Gallery. This is a large room that stretches the full width of the palace and so unites the pair of enfilades. Its walls are covered with 130 oil paintings. Elizabeth purchased most of the paintings in the 1740s (and all but a dozen or so of her purchases survived the war), and some are very fine – they include Dutch and Flemish land- and seascapes and mythical and Biblical scenes – but Rastrelli hung all for purely decorative effect. He ignored subject matter, artist and style and took account only of size and colour range to create a roughly symmetrical and tonally balanced display. It's a triumph of decoration over art.

I walk back along the enfilade, to see restoration in progress. In one gaunt room is a man busily regilding a screen. He is bearded and long-haired and looks like an Orthodox priest. I'm told he is the longest serving member of the current restoration team. We talk about his work in the palace and I ask him why he believes it worthwhile to recreate something that was once beautiful but has been destroyed. Is it really possible, I wonder, to bring dead beauty back to life? He is silent, I fear I have offended him. Then he replies, quietly but with utter conviction: God creates beauty, it is His gift. Man destroys it and it is our duty to regain God's beauty. As he offers me this explanation, virtually a justification of his life, a tear comes into his eye. It's a good answer. I leave him to his holy work, and return to the magnificently restored rooms. They are the vindication. They were utterly destroyed just over 60 years ago and now are utterly alive once more and surely feel as compelling, authentic and vibrant as when first completed in the 1750s. Everywhere there are details to feed the mind and imagination, to inflame the senses. Both emotion and intellect are engaged.

It all says so much about Elizabeth. The palace is an astonishing work of art and an almost shockingly personal portrait of a most unusual woman. The palace is beautiful but there is also something sinister, terrifying, in its remorseless and colossal scale. The palace seems to carry an unsettling message – it's a fist of iron wrapped in a glove of beauty. But as well as being an exercise in power the palace is also a monument to Elizabeth's deep love of Russia – a love that she expressed through architecture. It shows in a most spectacular way, how the creation of beauty can give a nation cultural identity and artistic pride.

The power and the glory
of Gothic architecture

Albi Cathedral, Languedoc, France

Albi is an historic city perched above the wide River Tarn. The centre is a maze of red brick-built structures dating mainly from the late Middle Ages and 16th century. Rising high above the tiled rooftops is a vast and surprising structure. Also built of brick, it looks austere, powerful and strangely modern, with its array of towered forms. It could be mistaken for a mighty fortress – in fact it's the city's cathedral, Ste Cécile. Its extraordinary story reveals the history of Languedoc and chronicles the struggles of the people of the region and the life of the man who was almost single-handedly responsible for the creation of this most unlikely house of God. Languedoc is now a peaceful land, but during the 13th century it was the site of one of the most vicious episodes in medieval history. It was invaded and there was a bitter battle for the soul of the people of the region, a battle in which beauty was used as a political weapon.

Before the 13th century Languedoc wasn't part of France but a semi-independent state ruled by the Count of Toulouse. Culturally, ethnically and spiritually, it was closely associated with neighbouring Catalonia and Aragon. In this area there evolved a powerful religion that was eventually to bring catastrophe. It now seems extraordinary that one of the most fanatical and bloodthirsty crusades undertaken by Roman Catholic Christians in the Middle Ages was not against Muslims in the Middle East but in Europe – against a people who venerated Christ. The people who were the target of the crusaders' rage were known as Cathars. Their beliefs were entirely admirable, pacifist and rational, but they did challenge the worldly might, power and very purpose of the Roman Catholic Church. Inevitably, they were accused of heresy and had to be suppressed.

The Cathar belief seems to have arrived in southern Europe from the Middle East in the 8th or 9th century and represented a pure and idealistic view of creation. The sect not only questioned the materialism and secular power of the Roman Catholic Church but also pointed out that such power was bound to corrupt – or at least confuse – spiritual intentions. Inspired by the mysticism and non-materialism of the early Church and Christ's teaching, the Cathars renounced the sensual snares of the material world and argued that each individual, as potentially carrying the spark of the divine within them, had no need of priests as intermediaries, or the complex rituals of the Roman Catholic Church. Instead each human must develop a personal and direct relationship with God. Cathars also questioned the conventional Biblical texts, and their world view was startling. Essentially, they argued that the entire material world, including the Roman Catholic Church, was a parody of God's spiritual creation and a great delusion set up by Satan to beguile and entrap souls.

Naturally the Roman Catholic Church viewed the Cathars' criticism of its temporal power and wealth as intolerable. Things came to a head during the first decade of the 13th century and coincided with mounting French ambitions to expand from the north and obtain a foothold on the Mediterranean and a jumping-off place for trade and conquest in the east. The Cathar church was to be destroyed for religious reasons and much of the region was to be conquered by the forces of the north. An unholy and familiar alliance was forged, and a war of conquest was clothed in the garb of a religious enterprise. The Cathars were duly declared heretics and the Roman Catholic

Church offered indulgences and pardons to all who agreed to participate in their suppression. Initially the Dominican Order went through the motions of persuasion and threat to get Cathars to recant, and then in 1208 Pope Innocent III launched the Albigensian Crusade, named after Albi, which was seen as a centre of the heresy.

The purpose of the crusade was to force the Cathars to renounce their faith and join the Catholic Church, or die. The agencies of the crusade were to be the French and other northern European forces – this was to be in effect an invasion of the south from the north. The Count of Toulouse perceived the crusaders as invaders, pure and simple, and initially resisted them, as did his feudal overlord the King of Aragon. But the French, under the command of Simon de Montfort, soon triumphed. The King of Aragon was killed and the count was forced to compromise. His religious beliefs were ambiguous – for reasons of policy and politics he had to appear a Roman Catholic, but he had links with the Cathars and prominent Cathars among his supporters. But after his military defeat the count could do little to help the Cathars – they were at the mercy of the crusading northerners and their best defence was secrecy. The crusaders proved as bloodthirsty in Languedoc as they had in the Holy Land when fighting Muslims. The Cathar religion was driven deep underground, with survivors forced to retreat to remote regions or even exile beyond French power. The Roman Catholic Church and the French were triumphant, but the Cathar faith was not dead; it lived in the heart of the people. The enemies of the Cathars, who now occupied their land, knew this and they were suspicious – and fearful. The distrust and fear felt by the occupying forces and the Catholic authorities led to decades of suppression and brutal inquisition.

One of the leading members of the inquisition was Bernard de Castanet, the Bishop of Albi, and it was he who initiated the construction of Albi Cathedral. In 1282, when work started on a new site adjoining a smaller Romanesque cathedral, the Cathars had been suppressed for decades. But the design and construction of the cathedral reveals that the Roman Catholic French still felt fear and uncertainty. Albi, like no other cathedral built in Europe, proclaims itself an interloper in a foreign and occupied land. Its massively powerful, fortified appearance declares the dominance of the established Church, and makes it clear that it and the French were in Languedoc to stay.

The walls are immensely thick, built of hard, well-fired brick made from local clay and thickened at their base to stop them being penetrated by battering rams. The cathedral itself was really a mighty redoubt set within a well-calculated network of outer fortifications. There were high walls, towers and gates defining baileys or courts around the cathedral, and to its north, on the steep river bank and within the fortified enclosure, was the bishop's palace. This dated back to the early years of Cathar suppression and had been built using treasure seized from persecuted families. It was massively enlarged and strengthened by De Castenet to form an almost independent fortress, connected to the cathedral by a deep tunnel. This really was an architecture bred out of terror and designed to instil terror.

I arrive outside the cathedral on a summer afternoon. The raking light emphasises the pleasing texture of the mellow red brick, casting strange shadows and throwing the rows of buttresses into dramatic relief. The cathedral may be a sinister presence but it's not without a striking sculptural, if terrible, beauty. I stand and wonder. The Cathars saw material beauty as the snare of Satan, intended to confuse and inflame the senses. They practised honest, puritanical simplicity. They despised the Catholic Church and its lavish ritual, but this great cathedral, although beautiful, is also incredibly simple. It possesses an honesty that would surely have appealed to the Cathars. It openly expresses its materials and means of construction and all its superfluous decoration – such as its ornate porch – are much later additions. What was De Castanet up to? Was he trying to beat the Cathars at their own game, appropriate some of their principles in his new cathedral, demonstrate that the material world could represent a pure and almost spiritual beauty? No one now knows the name of the master mason who designed the cathedral. Some think he was a Catalan named Pons Descoyl – a man steeped in the cultural and Cathar traditions of the south, not of the Catholic north – and certainly the building possesses the bold simplicity found in much of the ancient architecture of Languedoc. Also, unlike virtually all Gothic cathedrals in France, Albi has no transepts; its plan is not in the form of a Latin cross. Cathars abhorred the symbol of the cross because they claimed Christ was not crucified. I fantasise – perhaps the designer was at heart a Cathar? Is this cathedral ironically a Cathar building?

The main door to the cathedral is not, as is usual, at the west end but in the centre of the south side. Its position and its small size reveal that its location and design were determined by the need to make the cathedral secure, to place its entrance within a fortified courtyard. I go inside and discover a strange world. Small windows mean that little light penetrates but, more surprising than the gloom, are the rich wall decorations. Virtually every surface is covered with painted ornament, most of it executed in the early 16th century in Renaissance style. There are also very ornamented later Gothic additions – particularly a 15th-century screen that defines the choir and at the west end a huge, spectacular and somewhat lurid mural showing the Last Judgement. Originally the interior of the cathedral was strikingly simple, like its exterior. It was essentially one sublime, barn-like space, defined by thick and strong brick walls.

The determination to make the cathedral a fortified building made it unlike contemporary ecclesiastical building in France.

Most French cathedrals of the late 13th century are skeletal in their principles of construction, with walls that are largely non-bearing. This highly engineered Gothic style relieved the walls of much of their structural role so they could be pierced with large windows and so allow for the creation of a light and open interior. But the cathedral at Albi is different. Here the major buttresses helping to support the weight of the nave vault are located inside the building rather than outside, and form stout walls which connect the high piers in the nave to the outer wall. The visual and spatial consequences of this decision are striking and most unusual for a medieval Gothic building. Typically, French medieval cathedrals have a central nave flanked by at least one row of aisles. But here the central nave is flanked not by open aisles but by a series of recesses that now house chapels. The reason for this structural peculiarity is simple. It was feared that external buttresses, connected to the outer wall of the cathedral by flying buttresses, could easily be demolished by attackers and lead to the collapse of part of the cathedral vault and wall. So the internal buttresses, expressed externally as brick half-cylinders, are part of the cathedral's system of fortification.

In the 13th century one of the ways in which the Church expressed God's power and omnipotent presence was through Gothic architecture. Inspired by Biblical texts, and responding to the laws of nature, cleverly engineered Gothic churches – in which materials gained strength through ingenious design – revealed the wonder and wisdom of God's creation. They were the word of God rendered in stone – elegant stone structures that are minimal, precisely tuned like musical instruments in their forms and proportions. In essence, a Gothic cathedral was a carefully wrought crucible of the transformation of the soul. But Albi, with its massive walls and small windows, is essentially an anti-Gothic structure. Little of God's energising and illuminating flight floods in here.

The interior of the cathedral is disturbing, not least because of the Doom painting at the west end. This is one of the largest and best preserved of its kind anywhere in the world and its artistic quality is very high indeed. It was painted between 1474 and 1484 and, as with all Doom paintings, it shows the dead rising from their graves at the end of time, ready to be judged for their conduct when living and consigned to the pleasures of heaven or to the perpetual torments of hell. But here the rewards of paradise hardly feature, while the punishments for the wicked explode in huge images of appalling suffering. This is essentially a massive painting of naked human beings being tortured by hideous and grimacing demons in most alarming ways. The tormented are divided into seven groups, each reflecting the punishments thought appropriate for those who commit one of the seven deadly sins. The Proud are being broken on wheels with bloody spikes protruding through their bodies, a naked women is being forced to swallow something horrid – clearly she was a glutton – and the avaricious are being boiled in large cauldrons. I stare in disbelief. What a strange religion Christianity is. Christ preached love and forgiveness yet here – in the house of God – there are these gruesome images of the dead calculated to terrify, alarm and intimidate the living.

The unusual and graphic imagery of this vengeful and unforgiving Doom surely reflects the atmosphere in Albi in the late 15th century. The Roman Catholic Church must still have feared that Catharism lived on, in secret, and that the people of Albi needed a permanent warning of the punishments in store if they lived in sin, as heretics. Another oddity of this vast Doom is that it shows no image of Christ and the Apostles judging the dead, an omission that makes the painting appear simply like a secular catalogue of sadistic torture. In fact, a later bishop cut a large door through the central image of Christ, and so removed the focus, the redeeming image – almost the meaning – of the painting. Extraordinary men, these Albi bishops. De Castanet appears to be the mould of the perfect medieval, hypocritical, ecclesiastical villain who, in his behaviour, fully justified the Cathars' suspicion of the Catholic Church. He was greedy for worldly power and wealth and for the pleasures of the flesh, and, it seems, would stoop to any corrupt means to satisfy his cravings. According to his enemies, his tastes included abusing and murdering young female prisoners. As his reign become more ruthless the cathedral grew taller, financed by funds extorted or confiscated from local people. No wonder De Castanet was held in fear and loathing and the cathedral must have been seen as no more than an emblem of his power – an emblem of evil.

Long before the cathedral was completed the people of the diocese rebelled against their hated bishop and petitioned the King of France and even the pope to investigate and punish De Castanet. These forces – also enemies – were clearly regarded as lesser evils than De Castanet. But justice was not seen to be done by the king or Catholic Church. De Castanet was finally removed from his seat at Albi in 1308, but he was never publicly punished for his appalling abuse of power. In 1316 he was even elevated by Pope John XXII to the position of cardinal. If the Catholic Church forgave De Castanet it did not forgive the people of Albi. Even after De Castanet was removed the inquisition was maintained to keep the population in order. Property continued to be confiscated for the completion of the cathedral – which took over 100 years – and even the bodies of the dead, if the inquisition decided they had been heretics in life, were exhumed, then hanged or burnt. Some of the gruesome images shown in the cathedral's Last Judgement had, in fact, taken place in the streets of Albi.

I walk across the River Tarn to contemplate this vast, sculptural object by evening light. The cathedral may have been built on suffering and blood and intended as a mechanism of terror and oppression, but its architecture speaks of other things. Whatever De Castanet thought he was doing, a masterpiece has been created. Its sculptural and abstract forms possess a spiritual power – a beauty – that deals with the very essence of things and so transcends the history of its making. It is a sublime creation by man that echoes the power of the works of nature. God does indeed work in wondrous ways.

Monument to the divine power of sexual energy

Sun Temple, Konarak, India

I have come to Orissa in northeast India to see one of the country's most magnificent and richly decorated temples, which for generations has dominated the Bay of Bengal coast where it stands. Despite its architectural glories, this temple has had a bewitching and dramatic effect on many observers – it has puzzled, shocked, even appalled. It's been called one of the most beautiful buildings in the world but also one of the most obscene. But one thing is certain – it's a sensational monument to the power of sex. The temple was built in the mid-13th century by King Narasimhadeva I, a powerful Hindu monarch famed for bringing stability and prosperity to the throne of Orissa and for keeping Muslim invaders at bay.

As I approach the temple after a long road journey I see a massive pyramidal and richly carved stone form rising above the trees. This is the main hall, or mandapa, of the temple and, big as it is, it represents only part of the temple as originally built. Next to the mandapa, on the same high base, once stood a 70-metre bulbous tower placed over the main sanctuary. It was the form of this tower – only the base and a few fragments of which now survive – that prompted the temple's first European visitors to call it the Black Pagoda. But even when Europeans first recorded this temple, more than 300 years ago, it was already in ruins, a victim of the changing fortunes of the Orissa throne, natural calamity and the prolonged struggle between Hindus and Muslims for domination in northeast India. The earliest European accounts of the temple register little beyond shock and outrage – these visitors were intimidated, confused and challenged by what they saw. They rose to the temple's exquisite beauty but couldn't comprehend or tolerate what it seemed to be saying. When G. F. Cockburn, a commissioner of Orissa, saw the ruin in 1858 he suggested that, 'The beastly representations with which it is covered makes it...desirable that the whole of the remaining building should be levelled.'

Some of the beautifully wrought images still retain the power to shock – they show couples, or groups, engaged in varieties of sexual union which suggest, at the very least, that the creator of this monument had a very fertile, indeed positively red-hot and stimulating, imagination! It is often assumed, for superficially obvious reasons, that this erotic sculpture is an attempt to illustrate the sexual acts described in the *Kama Sutra*, the aphorisms of Love, compiled by the Hindu sage Vatsyayana, in around AD 100. In fact, few of the scenes illustrated tally with those described by Vatsyayana. So what is the message of this astonishingly powerful sacred building? Few now agree – the temple remains a place of mystery and it is this, as much as its exotic images, which makes it so popular with tourists.

I enter the temple grounds and walk from the east towards the pyramidal mandapa. First I come upon a substantial structure set in front of, and on an axis with, the mandapa. It's a detached Dance Pavilion and Hall of Offerings – the Bhogmandir – consisting of a platform, set on a high base and framed by wide, oblong-section piers and originally covered by a now entirely missing stone roof. All is made of stone, and the base and piers are embellished with tier upon tier of beautifully carved figures of dancing girls and musicians. Clearly the ritual of dance – no doubt both sacred and profane – was all-important to the function and purpose of this temple. To the south of the Dance Pavilion were the temple kitchens – essential to its role as a pilgrimage site – and immediately to its west rises the mandapa with, originally, the towering spire behind it. I climb the steps to the mandapa and look back towards the Dance Pavilion. What a mystery this place is. What's obvious is that nothing here is quite as it appears. The temple buildings enshrine a code – they contain a secret. I have to discover clues to its meaning and here's one. As I look from the mandapa to the Dance Pavilion, I find myself looking towards the rising sun, towards new life, to the birth of a new day. This is most revealing. The temple is dedicated to Surya, the sun god. I walk around the platform to the remains of the sanctuary. Images of Surya survive and show him in his various manifestations – in his youthful glory and as the morning sun. Surya is the god of heat. He generates passion in humans and animals, is the source of nurturing warmth in plants and leads to birth and growth, to regeneration and fruitfulness. He vivifies and infuses energy into all things. So all here must be to do with fertility – the images are symbols of fertilising and the creative power of the rays of the sun. One explanation for the multitude of erotic images on the temple is that they celebrate the means by which humans create life – sexual union, the action through which humans achieve the creative power of the gods.

But this, if partly correct, is far too simplistic a solution. Many of the scenes show acts that clearly do not lead to procreation. There is much more going on. Another clue is the temple complex itself. The main section of the temple, the platform on which stands the mandapa, is conceived as Surya's mighty chariot – his Ratha – which is the means by which he moves through the sky from dawn to dusk. To make this point the platform is furnished with huge wheels and is drawn by prancing steeds. The platform possesses 24 wheels and seven horses, and number is all-important in Hindu theology. The wheels are arranged in 12 pairs and it has long been established that in accordance with Hindu custom they represent the 12 new moons and 12 full moons of the year, and the 12 months of the year, while the seven horses represent the days of the week. In addition, each wheel has eight large spokes to represent the eight divisions of the Hindu day, with the large hubs of the wheels on the south side of the platform acting as gnomons marking the passing hours on small stone balls carved on the rims of each wheel. Each wheel is a mighty sundial that in turn marks the passing of time as the sun moves across the temple. They are charkas, wheels that mark the cycle of life. This temple is not only a representation of Surya's celestial vehicle, but also a time machine, or rather a magic machine outside time, which rolls through eternity. And all is organised around the sun which during the day moves around the temple, energising the images carved on it.

The cosmic quality of the temple is confirmed by a series of carvings which once embellished the collapsed tower. These are now in a small shrine on the northern perimeter of the site. I go to see it and, entering a small room, find a stunning array of 13th-century sculptural images. They show personifications of the nine planets of the Hindu universe. There is Mars, Mercury, Jupiter, Venus, Saturn, Rehu or Neptune (who holds a crescent Moon and the Sun in his hands), Ketu or Pluto (holding a sword and pot of fire), the Moon or Chandra – and the Sun, not actually a planet, holding a lotus in each hand. The symbolism and meaning of some of these images is debatable, but it is generally accepted that Rehu and Ketu are the 'demon' or dark planets and that Rahu, with his fanged face, is the god of the eclipse, for he devours the Sun and the Moon that he holds. The pot of fire that Ketu holds is the sacred kalasha – the pot that represents the womb of birth and that contains Amrita, the nectar of immortality, while the sword probably represents male power, virility. The lotus blossoms held by the Sun are, by Hindu tradition, emblematic of female genitals – the vulva, the yoni – and so symbols of fertility.

The meaning of this temple is becoming clearer – it's to do with the heavens and the planets and with their gifts of fertility and the creative power of sexual energy. I walk back to where I started, to the Dance Pavilion, and once again climb the steps to the top of its platform. It's square in plan, but with only a small central area on which the girls – the Devadasis – could dance. These temple dancing girls had an extraordinary role in the function of Hindu sacred buildings. Generally, they were brought to the temple when children, acquired by Brahmins or given by their usually impoverished families, to serve both god and man. They were essentially married to the gods they served, but were also to serve the priests. When they danced, they danced to put the earth to rights. And this is what the carved images on this structure show – the girls dancing, striking magical and sacred postures and gestures as they stamp and gyrate in accord with the rhythm of the planets. The presence of dancing girls or priestesses in temples is as old as recorded religion, and from the start there has always been an overlap between the sacred and the profane, and between sacred and sexual energy. From the earliest documented civilisations in Babylonia and Sumer in Mesopotamia, in present-day Iraq, evidence has been found from as early as 18,000 BC that describes or depicts priestesses engaged in ritualistic sex in the Temple of Love. The idea was simple – sexual energy was a wonder, the power of orgasm tremendous and strange and the creative consequences of sexual union divine. In the ritual the priestess would assume the power of the goddess, experience the quintessence of female energy and bring the feminine bounties of love-making from the heavenly realm of the Great Goddess – passion, joy, emotion, insight – to the world of humankind. The male partner would, in this communion with the goddess via her priestess, be transformed, would be regenerated. It was the 'spiritual union of the divine with the mortal'. (See 'Sex in the Temple: the tradition of the Sacred Prostitute', Nancy Qualls-Corbett, in *Secrets of Mary Magdalene*, edited by Dan Burnstein and Arne J. De Keijzer.) Something similar seems to have taken place at Konarak, as is revealed in the famed erotic imagery that abounds on the walls of the temple. It is only necessary to observe these images to understand that this place has to do with female power – with shakti, the active and energetic power of god that is always embodied in the feminine aspect of creation.

The female power on display here is another clue to the meaning of this place, but to understand more it is necessary to consider aspects of the Hindu faith 800 or so years ago. It was a time when certain Tantric practices were gaining strength within Hinduism, and this involved the vision of the body as a microcosm of the universe – an image of the cosmos – and the conviction that sensation and emotions were not barriers to be overcome by devotees but the most powerful of human forces. If channelled and controlled, they had spiritual potential that could benefit individuals and the world. Tantrics venerated female power as the great giver of life, and the female goddess Vajra Yogin who personified female wisdom and energy. Quite simply, Tantrics believed that sexual bliss was akin to spiritual ecstasy and, as in Mesopotamia thousands of years before, were convinced that orgasm, and the force it unleashed, opened a window onto the divine, that oneness and unity with god was achieved, that two fuse into one. For the purposes of the rites of this temple the dancing girls must have become the embodiment of the goddess Vajra, and so made magic with the priests and holy men, the wandering sadhus. Children born of these encounters must have entered the service of the temple – as dancing girls or attendants.

There were two schools of Tantric thinking that influenced Hinduism 800 years ago and one was radical indeed. It was called the 'left hand school' and it challenged most established Hindu conventions, eschewed tradition, argued that the highest dwelt in the lowest and promoted five means of worshipping its deities. One of these was sexual union. It also continued an ancient belief that phallic and sexual images had supernatural power and offered protection from evil – from demons, disease and famine. If this relatively unusual form of Tantric thinking is behind the scheme carved on the temple walls, then everything here begins to make sense and the temple starts to reveal its secrets.

The Tantras combined ancient religious practices – including animism and magical formulae – with Hindu beliefs and had much in common with the rich and esoteric world of Tibetan Tantric Buddhism. One of these beliefs was to do with the sacred nature of bodily fluids. These seemed divine, the stuff of life. Children were born in liquid, from the mixing of male and female liquids – and in some ancient rites the consumption of certain bodily fluids was an important means of spiritual transformation. To consume bodily fluid was to undergo a new birth, it was the way of joining a family, a clan, a means of initiation into a religious sect. Liquid also plays a central role in the Hindu creation story. By a great churning of an ocean of white creamy milk, some gods came into being and the primal battle between good and evil was resolved. The churning was achieved by a mighty tug of war between gods and demons, pulling on a huge and somewhat phallic snake, with the prize an elixir of immortality that the churning would produce. One by-product of the churning was the creation of celestial maidens who, upon emerging from the milky ocean, displayed their charms so that the demon team was distracted, faltered and consequently lost the contest. Significantly this Hindu story celebrates female sex appeal and power for it is seen not as a temptation to the good but one of the means by which evil is defeated.

Once the Tantric belief in the sacred nature – the transformative power – of bodily sexual fluids is understood then many of the perplexing images on the temple make perfect sense. They are not simply people gratifying each other, but they are feasting on or distributing ambrosia – divine nectar, the very stuff of life. It's through sexual fluids that life is passed from generation to generation – they are truly the nectar of immortality.

I study the startling images carved on the temple. Some on the upper tiers of the pyramid are life-size or larger, while those on the sides of the platform are a metre or so high with many being much smaller, miniatures really. The means by which the precious nectar was extracted or distributed can only leave you lost in wonder at such admirable invention, not to say gymnastics. Some show three people engaged in sexual activities, but most show couples and in Hindu terminology these images of the powerful and balanced pairing of male and female aspects are called maithunas. They are like highly charged amulets. Animals, which according to Hindu beliefs contain souls on a journey, are not left out. I discover a thoughtful young lady who's giving a dog a divine meal – she's clearly helping a soul on its way. And then I find an image of a woman offering bodily fluids to an altar in which burns a sacred fire. This was a vital offering to a Tantric deity. A recurring theme is a girl entwined by a massive snake or naga that may – or may not – be her own lower body. This must refer to Kundalini energy, the 'coiled fire-snake' located at the base of the spine that passes through six chakras or centres in the body to the Vishuddha chakra located in the neck. It's an image of the transforming power of controlled sexual energy which, when released in the correct way, is a path to spiritual enlightenment. Some of the figures seem to be composed to form yantras – magical diagrams used in meditation – while in others the women make Tantric gestures – called mudras – that are still used in sacred dance.

Yes, this temple is strong meat and now remote from what most people regard as sacred – but even in the age that created it many misunderstood its intentions. A 15th-century edition of the sacred Hindu text of the Mahabharata observes indignantly that the temple at Konarak 'makes all obscene – all obscene episodes from the puranas told before the Sun' (Sarala Das, quoted in *Konark*, Thomas Donaldson, 2003). This was to a degree intentional. The priests who ordered and embellished this temple did not want its secrets known to all, they preferred to conceal them under layers of confusion. Only the wise and the initiated were to have access to its power, to the beliefs enshrined in its stones that Tantrics realised were open to misinterpretation. As they explained: 'Everything is pure to a pure man and lust is to be crushed by lust. Do strenuously that which is condemned by fools, unite with your chosen deity – enjoy all the pleasures of love without fear. Do not fear, you do not sin.' (See James Hastings, *Encyclopaedia of Religion and Ethics*, XII, 1928, p. 196.) The Hejavra Tantra is explicit: those who are able can be liberated from bondage to the material world through the very thing by which wicked people are bound. The world is bound by lust, and you can be released by the same lust. This temple very neatly expresses the Tantric theory of opposites, the belief that the highest lurks in the lowest, that unrestrained sex was a route to spiritual liberation and enlightenment, that the potential of the body and the emotions were to be used to the utmost to achieve spiritual bliss.

One of the many mysteries of this temple is its end. By the early 17th century it was already a desolate ruin – no doubt damaged by typhoons and abandoned as inauspicious, perhaps rejected by its people. By the early 19th century much of it was buried under sand and the pyramidal mandapa – now supported by a massive internal structure that has obliterated its interior volume – was near collapse. All this is made more poignant because the temple at Konarak was to be the last of its kind ever built. The king had constructed it after a military triumph over invading Muslims, but here Islam was finally to prevail and such creations – embellished with images of living beings locked in life-giving embrace – were viewed by Muslims as idolatrous and an affront to decency. So this spectacular temple represents both the high point, and the end, of a great culture.

I sit in the temple garden and gaze at the huge structure before me. It's extraordinary this temple – a mighty, slumbering giant. The huge stone pot, the kalasha, that stood on the top of its pyramidal roof – the symbolic container of the ambrosia of immortality – has long gone. The structure is sadly battered and the sacred power of the place has been reduced, but it is far from lost. People are drawn to its wonderful architecture and beautiful if puzzling sculpture. What people make of it must reflect their own nature – to those of evil intent all is evil, to the pure all is pure. I watch visitors scrutinising its dazzling array of art. All appear enthralled by this temple of joy, this vast demonstration of the belief that sexual power not only offers physical delight and new life but also spiritual release, a path to salvation.

A vast stone Buddha evoking the beauty of nature

Giant Buddha, Leshan, China

Leshan lies within land that is culturally and spiritually between worlds. It's in the Sichuan Province of southwest China but within the great cultural pale of India and the Himalayan state of Nepal. Trade routes – known collectively as the Silk Road – ran through Sichuan and not only connected China commercially with India and the West but were also the arteries along which ideas and religion circulated through the ancient world. It was along the Silk Road, during the 1st century AD, that Buddhism entered China, spread by merchants and wandering monks. Buddhism, with its beautiful ideas about the power of nature, its commitment to non-violence, and its practice of meditation, meshed easily with the Chinese belief in nature-orientated Taoism, and so a composite religion started to evolve. I've come to Sichuan to see an object which is a product of that fusion, an object that forms a bridge between the physical world and the spiritual, and which uses beauty and scale to stimulate the imagination and overwhelm the senses.

But first I investigate the pleasures of the city of Leshan. It lies on the confluence of the Dadu, Qingyi and Min rivers and is a large, thriving place. I go to one of the open-fronted street restaurants with great expectation because the delicious spicy food of Sichuan – itself, I suppose, a fusion of Himalayan and Chinese culture – is world-famed. I sit in a tiny plastic seat designed for a child, and loom over a table that rises only a couple of feet from the floor. Most odd – like being at the Mad Hatter's tea party. While puzzling over the reason for this strange practice – the people here really are not that small – I'm offered a menu. I ask for the most interesting local dishes and hope for the best.

First comes a plate of baked chicken feet and small skulls. I inquire what they are. They are rabbit heads. Then comes a dish loaded with red chilli, sliced garlic and bits of flesh. I taste it – delicious, spicy, almost numbing, packed with punch. What can it be? Snails, I discover. Then a similar-looking dish arrives, but this time the meat is rabbit stomach. This is followed by barbecued ducks' tongues and baked chicken combs. I sample all, then tackle a rabbit's head. The jaw muscles are succulent and the tongue clearly a delicacy. This spicy food is meticulously prepared and most creative in its use and mix of ingredients. It certainly overwhelms the senses. A crowd has been gathering on the street as I eat. They look on approvingly as I devour the food. They nod to one another. Perhaps I'm not such an uncouth barbarian. I thank the kindly restaurant owner and off I go. Yes, my imagination has been stimulated – and this is just the beginning.

I pass over a bridge and below me waters thunder as the three rivers meet. Ahead are tree-covered hills of dramatic profile sporting a spattering of temples. This is holy land. I have a target – a theme park with a difference. As I approach, the theme is written clearly across the cliff face in front of me: it's a huge carved image of a reclining Buddha, so large in fact that it is, bizarrely, quite easy to miss it. At a casual glance the massive head could be mistaken for a natural feature, and it's separated from the feet by clumps of trees. This park was created in the late 1980s soon after the state permitted the return of religion, and contains over 3,000 images of the Buddha, large and small, carved and painted. Superficially, the aim of this place is tourism pure and simple. Or at least it was when the park opened in 1994. But the images of the Buddha here are beautifully wrought and many are of heroic scale and movingly integrated with the dramatic landscape. I watch my fellow visitors – they obviously love the place, which is not surprising since representations of the Buddha, with their benign and smiling faces, have an innate spiritual appeal and beauty. They are pleasing, calming, serene – joyful. This may have been launched as a theme park for tourists, but many of the people coming here are Buddhist believers; they are here to worship. This park, this museum of Buddhist art, is slowly being transformed. It's becoming the real thing, the largest Buddhist shrine in the world. It seems that religion is returning to the Chinese people by stealth, in the guise of a tourist attraction.

But this theme park – strange and dramatic as it is – acts only as the prelude to the real star of Leshan! Adjoining it, and looking out across the wide waters of the turbulent river, is one of the great monuments to Buddhism. It's the largest stone-carved Buddha from the ancient world – the Giant Buddha of Leshan. It was started in 713, for reasons now lost in myth, took 90 years to complete and rises 71 metres in height. But the scale is larger than the height implies because the Buddha is seated, carved out of an entire cliff face of the sacred mountain it adorns. I approach by boat for my first view. The image appears, looming above me, hands on knees, and the face with a solemn and compassionate expression, staring patiently to the west, towards the setting sun. It certainly has a sublime beauty – tantalising, enigmatic. With a sculpture that took so much time and trouble to create, everything – proportion, composition, details – will have a specific meaning. But what? I land and walk towards the Buddha's feet; he rises vast and mighty above me, his head literally disappearing into cloud because this is a misty day. It's breathtaking.

At the time this mighty image was created Buddhism had evolved greatly since the death of Siddhattha Gotama – the Buddha or the Enlightened Being – in around 2450 BC. Through self-sacrifice, ascetic living and meditation he achieved enlightenment – an explosive state of realisation or sudden awakening – that, it is said, allowed him to see the past, present and future, to understand himself, the nature of mankind and of the cosmos. He realised all humanity had the potential to achieve enlightenment. All could be Buddhas, with the power to create positive energy, the power to help the cosmos. Having achieved wisdom and power through enlightenment, the Buddha started to teach and attract followers who organised themselves into religious communities. He taught that it is not necessary to go in quest of enlightenment, all you have to do is realise the divine potential inherent in humanity and discover how to use it.

The Buddha formulated his message in simple terms. He pointed out the 'Four Noble Truths', which characterise man's current condition: life is suffering, this suffering is caused by unrealisable worldly desires, and to escape the suffering that causes misery and blocks spiritual development you have to remove desire. This is possible, said the Buddha, by following the 'Eightfold Path' that includes correct attitude, action, livelihood and meditation. This path leads to liberation from the law of karma, which states that all actions ultimately have appropriate consequences, and from Samara, the eternal cycle of birth, death and rebirth of the soul in one of the six worlds of Buddhist belief. Rebirth, determined by karma and during which the consequences of actions finally resolve, can be unpleasant, since three of the six worlds – those of ghosts, animals and hell – are undesirable places in which to find yourself. Good karma allows for rebirth in one of the three positive worlds which includes that of humans, and from these worlds it is possible to attain nirvana, the final extinguishing of all worldly connections, or what is called moksha in the Hindu faith. This brings release from the cycle of rebirth and the unity of the divine soul with the cosmos, the creator.

Mystery not only surrounds the circumstances of the creation of this giant image but also its precise meaning. It is supposed to have been initiated by a monk called Haitong, who fought hard to secure funds for its completion. Why he felt it necessary to create a colossus Buddha here is not certain. Some say he had seen the sufferings of the local fishermen community in the dangerous waters here and wanted Buddha to still the local, vicious water spirit. No, I don't think so. Some other greater scheme is at work here, but what?

As I walk, I study the figure that is like a piece of architecture in its scale and constructional technology. I know the basic dimensions of this sculpture: 71 metres high, 32 metres wide at the feet, 28 metres wide at the shoulders. The head is 15 metres deep, the ears – with their huge lobes – are 7 metres deep. I look and ponder. Yes, ears are important. Large lobes reflect an oriental ideal of beauty and denote a refined and developed soul. Of course, the ear is the basic module of the composition. The head is about twice the depth of an ear, the shoulder width is roughly twice the depth of the head, while the depth of the whole body is roughly two and a half times the width of the shoulders. I see that the composition fits within a rectangle of 5:2 proportion – a rectangle formed by two and a half squares, and that the head forms one fifth of the depth of the entire body and the ear one tenth. This proportional system was intended to give the Buddha the harmonious beauty of an ideal form, with all parts proportionally related. The geometry of its composition must have defined a mandala – a sacred diagram to aid meditation; it's a mantra, a divine incantation. I'm beginning to understand. This huge image is starting to speak, to reveal its purpose – a dramatic voice from the past. It's a window onto enlightenment, a door to nirvana.

But why this obsession with scale? From the start of the practice of rendering Buddha in human form there has been a tendency to make him vast. Clearly size mattered and, it seems, the bigger the better, the more beautiful. In a faith that focuses on the spiritual, not the material, this preference for the gigantic seems odd, out of character. No one is now quite sure what it signifies, but it seems safe to bet that, in one way or another, largeness of image was intended to reveal the all-embracing, cosmic scale of the Buddha. He is vast beyond comprehension, a power without limit. These vast images were meant to evoke this sense, to convey an idea of the cosmic to the devotee. Various Buddhist texts support this interpretation, as does the Mahayana vision of the three bodies of Buddha. One is an earthly body, like that of any mortal, then there is his 'heavenly body', located in paradise, and lastly, his cosmic body, as large as all the worlds. This must be the heavenly or cosmic body that I'm confronting. I get nearer the head and study its telling details. The eyes have a look of transcendental bliss and compassion, looking down at the devotees at his feet, at fishermen toiling on the waters. His hair is arranged in little coils, each like a stupa or shrine, each a focus of meditation. Just between and above his eyes is a small red disc denoting wisdom, and on the top of his head is a bump – the Ushnisha – a sign of cosmic consciousness, it's the portal by which the soul departs for nirvana.

When pilgrims reached this point they must have believed themselves in heaven, and before descending, they would have gone to the nearby temple. I do the same. It's a beautiful place, and there is a service in progress, with monks chanting sacred texts and sounding simple percussion instruments – shell, cymbals, bells. I seek out the abbot, who is warm and willing to talk. But I am aware that religion in China is a political subject and that abbots are, ultimately, political appointees and subject to political control. So I proceed delicately. I ask him about the posture of the Buddha, what it signifies? It means, he says, that the Buddha is standing by, waiting to return to this world. Really? What form of Buddha is this? It's Maitreya, he answers, the Buddha of the future, a Buddha to come. I'm puzzled. Usually Maitreya is shown as a smiling fat man, laughing at adversity. Why is this image so different? I ask. The abbot smiles, almost the image of Maitreya. I realise it's a silly question, Buddha is full of surprises. When will the Buddha return? I ask. When the world is ready, when the present age of Buddhism has degenerated, when it's almost forgotten, then the Buddha will come again to usher in a new age. All this is rather like the millenarian vision of Christianity, with Christ returning at the end of days to defeat Satan and usher in the New Jerusalem. I now remember something I was told by a Tantric Buddhist in Bhutan. All giant Buddhas are depictions of the Buddha of the future to make the point that when he returns men will have shrunk not only spiritually but in physical stature. Where is this Buddha now and when will he return? I ask the abbot. He is in heaven and will return in about 5.6 billion years, I'm told. Ah, another example of the Buddhist love of mind-bogglingly large concepts. One last question – I ask the abbot what he sees when he looks at the Buddha. A living being, he replies.

I leave the abbot and temple and return to the cliff face. So this particular Buddha is all about the future – it's a declaration of intent to return when this world is coming to an end! And to judge from the state of the Buddha's head this will be sooner rather than later. He was given a facelift in 2001, but is already badly soiled again. His face looks tear-stained. The problem is that China burns a huge amount of coal, mostly mined in Shanxi province, to get cheap energy. The result is pollution on a staggering scale, and the resulting acid rain is leaching minerals from the sandstone from which the Buddha is carved, slowly eroding him. As I contemplate his mighty image men appear and descend a rope ladder which leads to his shoulder. They've come to try to scrub some of the dirt away, and start brushing the tear-stains. All their exertions do little obvious good. But, despite his disfigurements, the scars inflicted by the modern world, the Buddha does not look less beautiful, less spiritually powerful – just sadder, more resolved. And as I look, I realise that the real beauty in this figure is not to do with the human body; this creation is no conventional work of art. The beauty here is more elemental, more cosmic. Carved from the entire cliff face, confronting the thundering river, framed by lush trees, this figure creates a sense of awe – it's all to do with the beauty of nature. The Buddha is all-embracing, vast in scale – and also the personification of the force, the breathtaking beauty, the wisdom of nature. This fantastic creation is emblematic of the world – a world which, through pollution, global warming, the thoughtless exploitation of natural resources, is now at risk. I understand the brooding and solemn image of the Buddha of the future – he's a warning from the past to the present about the future. And as I look and wonder, the puny figures continue to scrub away at the tracks of his tears, and still they do no good.

2

Connections

Optimism survives in one of India's most crowded cities

Dharavi, Mumbai, India

Mumbai on India's west coast is one of the most fascinating and teeming cities in the world. The origins of this city are peculiar – it sprawls next to the sea over an ancient site which was holy to Shiva, on an area once made up of wide beaches, small islands and swamp. For thousands of years the area was the home of fishing communities and then in the 16th century annexed by the Portuguese. But they found little use for this largely aquatic and exposed possession and presented it to England as part of the dowry of the Portuguese princess Catherine of Braganza when she married King Charles II in 1661. The English saw the commercial potential of the place and during the following 100 years made Bombay, as the city was then called, one of the main urban bulwarks – along with Calcutta and Madras – on which they constructed what was ultimately to be a British-controlled empire in India. Although a mighty city and port by the late 18th century, Mumbai was to enjoy its Golden Age during the second half of the 19th century. Land was gradually and remorselessly reclaimed from the sea and the city expanded rapidly to make it one of the most beautiful, successful and important ports in the world.

The wonder, grandeur and wealth of Mumbai attracted many to the city – both rich and poor, Indian and European. When the poor arrived they discovered an economy that fascinated them but which they were – initially at least – ill-equipped to join. It was a vicious circle: until regular employment was secured the price of accommodation proved too high, but until accommodation was found it was hard to get a job. So the poor had to fend for themselves by possessing, often illegally and secretly, those parts of the city and its immediate environs that were empty, unsavoury or generally regarded as unusable, such as the creeks and swamps that drained the city centre. Mumbai's slums started to grow in the very shadow of some of the wealthiest and most architecturally spectacular communities in the world – rich and poor side by side, each supporting the other while living in worlds that could hardly be more different. Quite simply, without these low-paid slum dwellers the city could not function – they serve and service it, they keep it a living and breathing proposition. One of the most dramatic consequences of this pattern of living is Dharavi, once a collection of small fishing villages on the edge of one of Mumbai's islands. It started to grow in earnest in the 1950s as people came seeking work in the city and is now one of the most densely occupied places on earth and known, probably erroneously but memorably, as the largest slum in Asia. I'm fascinated to see how people live in extreme conditions and how – when left to their own devices – they create their own architecture and sustain their own communities.

I arrive in the centre of the area that is a city within a city. Most buildings seem to be constructed out of rubble and waste – recycled, corrugated steel for roofs and walls, old planks or refrigerator doors for window shutters – and many buildings sit on narrow and choked drainage ditches that are plainly nothing other than open sewers. But nothing here is quite what it seems. This square mile or so of ad hoc building that makes up Dharavi houses somewhere between 600,000 and one million people. Yet, virtually everyone I see as I travel through the area looks industrious, clean and cheerful. Dharavi may appal most outsiders, but to those who live here it is clearly home.

The sprawling, largely self-built and mostly organic mass of buildings is generally organised into a series of distinct quarters or wadas reflecting the geographic or ethnic origins, religion, caste or occupation of their occupants. These often distinctly different portions of Dharavi are divided by two government-built and roughly straight roads that slice through the area and meet at a crossroads near its southern corner. These two main roads are called Ninety Feet Road and Sixty Feet Road and were built during the 1980s when the city government belatedly recognised the fact that Dharavi was a place of urban and economic significance. I drive slowly along Ninety Feet Road, locked in dense traffic, and see images that are spellbinding and strangely beautiful. Set against the generally drab and dusty colours of the buildings and streets are the fresh and bright colours of people's clothing and the goods they carry – chillies, bright red tomatoes, exotically patterned cottons. And I catch glimpses of extraordinary vignettes of Dharavi life. A row of ad hoc houses stands above a high wall that embanks a wide water channel. On the edge of the wall I see a row of girls sitting, all brightly attired; they are laughing, chatting, combing each other's long black hair. They look happy – and beautiful. But just below them I see a vast rat climbing slowly in their direction – then another and another. The water is full of them, and of unspeakable debris – it's a ghastly and stagnant sewer. The triumph of the human spirit over the waste of the material world perhaps, but it's best not to get too romantic. I suppose these girls are merely making the most of a difficult situation – accepting the reality of their position with a true Hindu resignation. Their karma obliges them to live this life in Dharavi, perhaps to atone for sins in past lives, where there are lessons aplenty for their souls to learn.

As I suspected, the social, economic and architectural structure of Dharavi is complex; it has grown to accommodate diverse communities but just as some have gained by its expansion others have lost. And all is now in transition. As Mumbai has expanded during the past decades the square mile occupied by Dharavi has not only become relatively more central but also, in an ever-expanding and wealthy metropolis with limited building land, increasingly valuable. Now, ironically, the land occupied by this shanty-city is some of the potentially most valuable urban development land in India – indeed in the world.

I long to know more about Dharavi and make my way through its crowded streets. The experience is exhilarating – everywhere I see colour blossoming among squalor, active, smiling and immaculately turned-out people living in the most cramped and primitive accommodation. I peer through open doors straight into single-room houses and see interiors that are neat and clean. As I pass through narrow alleys people are washing and cleaning the few square feet in front of their doors, even while mountains of debris quietly rot a few yards away. Some of the structures I pass hint at the origins of architecture. They appear as merely utilitarian structures created to achieve shelter from the elements and security – basic and functional building. But then many have something extra added, such as a garland of flowers over the door, a coat of bright paint, an image of a god – something that's non-functional but calculated to add beauty or symbolic meaning. And at a stroke a functional hut is transformed into a work of architecture – something that is more than mere structure. It's a delight to see these humble yet powerful works of art, each a wonder in its way, an expression of hope that seeks to give delight.

I find myself in an area where the streets are relatively wide and regular – it's a small section of gridiron city. I'm told it's called the Transit Camp area and was built by the city during the 80s when it accepted the reality of the squatter communities settling in Dharavi and provided accommodation. This area is occupied by Tamils, Kashmiris and Gujaratis. I pass a large Tamil temple and school packed with smartly attired and cheerful school children – and soon arrive at my destination. It's the Kumbharwada – the home to a community of potters, originally from Gujarat, who were among the first people to move into Dharavi when their ancestors arrived in the Mumbai area during the 1930s. There are now around 2,000 households here and this district is an amazing spectacle with narrow alleys connecting a series of courts, each dominated by a communal open kiln, and pot-making and storage areas. Some of the kilns are stacked with pots and fuel and are quietly smoking, in others the fired pots are being removed – and many of them are of traditional form and beautiful. This is an amazingly industrious and well-organised place in which each family makes and decorates pots in and around its own small house but has access to, and splits the cost of, the kiln shared by all who live and work around its court. The buildings I see are remarkable – mostly two-storey chawls with living accommodation above ground-floor workshops. One in particular catches my eye – clearly home to a large family. Outside it, the grandmother and her grandchildren stack pots in a kiln, while their menfolk toil at pot-making and younger women bustle around the house and court. I ask the family if I can visit their house. They gladly agree. I take off my shoes and climb the steep and narrow stairs to the first-floor room. It is spotless and with only a pelisse on the floor, on which sits a young child. It is on the walls and on shelves that the family's history and pride reside. There is an ornate shrine, next to it an array of pictures of family and of gods, a television set, a large clock – and, of course, rows of pots. Adjoining this room is a far smaller kitchen – again very neat and clean with metal pots stacked and shiny cooking implements hanging from the wall. And that's it. In these two rooms a family of a dozen people lives and sleeps.

I continue my odyssey through this strange land and come upon other peoples and ways of life – with all communities housed in different manner. Most areas are orderly and maintained but some of the peripheral areas that are recently squatted are more chaotic – roads are no more than mud tracks and I pass a garbage-choked creek whose banks are in use as a communal latrine – it's desperate.

The tall, modern buildings I see rising among the densely packed acres of metal-roofed chawls are my last destination. I want to see the new Dharavi – what could be the Dharavi of the future. A few of these high-rises have been built as private apartments by optimistic developers, but most were built by the government-sponsored Slum Rehabilitation Authority (SRA) and date from the 1990s. But rents are relatively high and the sort of accommodation offered is hard to reconcile with most Dharavi trades that demand ground space, like the potters. Some fear these high-rise blocks will become high-rent ghettos for interlopers; others that they will simply and rapidly become high-rise slums. I enter the walled courtyard around a group of slab blocks built by the SRA little more than a decade ago but already in a state of far from picturesque decay. I talk to a young woman who lives here. She is bright, full of laughter and speaks fine English. I ask her if she likes living in Dharavi. Yes, she says, mainly because it's very safe: 'there is always someone on the streets, all the people are very helpful, that's why I'm comfortable here.' She smiles and then adds, 'Eid, Dhivali and Christmas – all the Muslim, Hindu and Christian festivals are celebrated in this building; all are Muslims here but all celebrate these festivals. I'm Indian so I celebrate all the festivals of India, all the people of Dharavi do, that's why I'm happy here.'

I head for my last meeting, with a Mr Jockin who heads the National Slum Dwellers Association. I want to find out more about the long-term government plans for this remarkably industrious and harmonious self-made city. Mr Jockin is a charismatic, articulate and well-informed man. He must be in his late fifties and was born and has always lived in Dharavi. I ask him what should happen to Dharavi and its people. Whatever is decided, he says, it should be through full consultation and agreement of the communities of Dharavi. 'This place was built by the people, they created today's high land value – it's by the people, of the people and so Dharavi's future should be for the people.' Strong stuff. Mr Jockin has conjured an extraordinary image – Dharavi is no slum but a kind of Utopia, a place created by people, for people and in which human values and commercial values live in harmonious balance – despite the general absence of sewers or running water!

I leave Mr Jockin and re-enter the lanes of Dharavi. Walking through this place has been an astonishing experience and since cities around the world are expanding rapidly and many of the new city dwellers will be impoverished – Dharavi does hold lessons. It shows how communities can survive, indeed thrive, in extremis, how wealth can be created. It's a complex organism born out of desperation but which, through the energy and enterprise of its population and the mutual support of its communities, has created a viable and vibrant society – even beauty. Dharavi may be poor, but not in spirit or in soul. This is a city of joy – a place of warmth and welcome. The people who live and work in Dharavi have given it meaning and value – I only hope that they can reap the rewards of their own industry.

High life in a city within a city
Rockefeller Center, New York, USA

The skyscraper is the building of the modern age. It was born in the late 19th century – the product of man's ancient dream to build towering structures aspiring to the heavens – and came of age in the early 20th century. Its realisation was the result of many pioneering technological developments coming to maturity at the same time, including wrought-iron and steel-frame construction, the fast and reliable lift, electric power, strong plate glass and finally steel-reinforced concrete, and the skyscraper offered not just new architectural forms but a new way of living in cities.

I've come to New York City to see not the first or tallest of its skyscrapers but certainly one of its best – one of the first to realise the artistic, urban and social potential of building high, and one that New Yorkers and generations of visitors to the city have taken to their hearts. The Rockefeller Center was designed in 1931 with construction not completed until 1940. It was conceived and created in changing and potentially disastrous circumstances, but the result is the rebuilding of six blocks of midtown Manhattan, north of 48th Street and between Fifth and Sixth Avenues, to create an architecturally cohesive community of 14 buildings. The blocks, of varied heights but symmetrically disposed, are each embellished with specially commissioned art integrated with the architecture. Together they contain a rich mix of uses, all calculated to make the Center an important and vibrant part of the city. The project was to a degree experimental – it was the first to include a skyscraper as part of a group of related buildings – and depended on the lead financier, John D. Rockefeller Junior, keeping his nerve while he risked his family fortune on something that was far from being a certain success. But the investment paid off, not just commercially but in the creation of a self-contained community located in and around a set of buildings and spaces that many now regard as the heart and soul of Manhattan. Rockefeller and his lead architect – Raymond Hood – had a vision of a better way of living and working together in a crowded modern city and the extraordinary Rockefeller Center is the result.

The skyscraper is now seen as the quintessential building of New York. But in the early years of the 20th century this was far from the case and the city's pioneering skyscrapers were regarded with mixed feelings. The high-rise building – serviced by lifts, with metal frame construction, an open and flexible floor plan and in which much use was made of glass and fire-proof materials such as terracotta for external cladding – first appeared in the United States in Chicago in the late 1880s. Two epoch-making and pioneering examples, both designed by Burnham & Root, are the Monadnock Building, started in 1889, and the Reliance Building, constructed between 1890 and 1895. Within a few years the new building type arrived in New York where it was rapidly pushed to daring extremes.

At first New Yorkers appear to have been intrigued, even delighted, by the occasional tower that seemed to make their city so distinct and avant-garde, the very symbol of progressive and successful American architecture in the service of equally dynamic American capitalism. When the Flatiron Building, designed by Daniel H. Burnham, was unveiled in 1902 it caused a generally agreeable sensation. Then in 1906 a builder called Theodore Starrett captured the heady excitement of the moment. He proposed a 100-storey mixed-use building that would include industry at its lower levels, then offices, apartments and a hotel.

Each section was to be divided by public plazas which would serve theatres and shops. At the top of the structure was to be an amusement park, roof garden and swimming pool. This was a visionary scheme that even Starrett did not seriously envisage happening, but other towers were rising in quick succession – and they provoked a backlash among New Yorkers who suddenly saw their city changing rapidly, irredeemably. Soon the high-rise was seen by many New Yorkers as a social and artistic evil that threatened to blight the city by putting much of it in perpetual shade and by overloading its streets and public transport system. Of particular concern to the richer city centre residents was the way in which their areas were transformed almost overnight into commercial enclaves the moment a high-rise office block opened nearby. Towers were soon seen as no more than expressions of individual greed, as a novel means by which real estate agents and landowners could make fortunes at the expense of the rest of the citizens of the city. Henry James captured the cynical mood in 1907 when he wrote in *The American Scene*, 'Skyscrapers are the last word of economic ingenuity… the thousand glassy eyes of these giants of the mere market.'

In 1908 the newly founded Committee of Congestion of Population in New York decided enough was enough when the plans were unveiled for the 909-foot-high Equitable Life Assurance Building sited on Broadway. One member of the committee told the *New York Times* that 'to accommodate such a crowd, the people would have to walk in three layers, one above the other, while the roadway would not hold the delivery wagons, automobiles and carriages of people using the structure.' The committee proposed that the city should revise its building codes to limit skyscrapers and consider an absolute height restriction, a limit of tall buildings to certain districts, or a special tax on skyscrapers.

These conservative views did not prevail; indeed how could

they, since the opposing force was as powerful as nature itself –
the manifest destiny of New York to thrive. The rapidly growing
commercial importance of the United States and of New York,
the fact that the city's central portion and financial quarter were
constrained by being located on a rocky island surrounded by
wide expanses of water, made the rise of the tower inevitable. It
was the obvious and economically sound way of increasing the
ground area of Manhattan – if the city couldn't easily expand
outwards, it had to expand upwards – into the sky

Although these early campaigners against the New York
skyscraper didn't stop its rise, they did influence its form and
design. The Equitable Life building was constructed – although
reduced in height to 36 rather than 40 storeys – but when
completed in 1915 its height, form and the way it blocked the
light of its neighbours did send a chill through New York. It
was resolved that such a massive and block-like building would
never again be constructed in the city, and in 1916 the first
Zoning Ordinance in the nation was passed. Among other things
the ordinance limited the bulk, and by implication controlled the
form, of new buildings by stating that a skyscraper's floor area
could not be greater than 12 times the size of its plot area – the
plot ratio of the Equitable Life building was a greedy 30 to one!
If a building were to rise more than 12 storeys the developer
had to build on only part of the potential building plot or had
gradually to reduce the area of the floors as the skyscraper got
higher – this approach led to the creation of the tiers of set-backs
that give many American skyscrapers of the 1920s and 30s such
a distinct profile.

I arrive at the Rockefeller Center on a winter morning, just
a few weeks before Christmas. This is the season when the
Center comes into its own and functions most efficiently – and
affectionately – as the heart of New York City. The Center erects
a massive Christmas tree for the delight of New Yorkers and the

surface of the sunken plaza at the core of the Center is turned into an ice-rink that is now one of the great traditions of the city. I've come to explore this complex of buildings, to see how they work. I turn into the Center from Fifth Avenue and immediately meet the full architectural force of the place. In front of me is a narrow pedestrian street framed by uniform and relatively low-rise buildings, and with planting and a channel of water running down its centre. This street terminates in the sunken court of Rockefeller Plaza and immediately above this plaza rises a tower that, seen from this position, is almost terrifyingly slender and tall. I stare at the ensemble. It's magnificent and all is united by the spare detailing and stone-face walls. The low buildings framing the pedestrian street contain shops at ground level and, when completed in 1940, were to house French businesses and cultural interests on one side and British on the other, so naturally this little pedestrian street is called Channel Gardens. There were also to be buildings dedicated to German and Italian concerns. Giving the Center a sophisticated international flavour was a clever commercial move on the part of Rockefeller, and helped to inspire much of the art, such as sculpture, metal doors and carvings integrated into these buildings – but the timing was bad. The build-up to war put paid to the German and Italian connections – but the French Building and British Empire Building struggled to life and even now retain a lingering flavour of their respective countries. As I walk along Channel Gardens I'm delighted to see a French bookshop – the Librairie de France – still in occupation. But it's the 70-storey, 850-foot-high tower that intrigues me. Its simplicity is modern, yet it's clearly rooted in history – all the buildings of the Center, with their implied pilasters, Art Deco ornament and rigid symmetry – have a distinct, if abstract, classical feel. What I find most compelling about the tower is its powerful sculptural presence, its cubist, machine-like beauty achieved by the modelling and layering of its form through the cascade of 'set-backs' – inspired by the 1916 Building Ordinance – that reduce the bulk of the building the higher it rises. This regular reduction in width creates a sense of false perspective and works a visual trick to make the tower seem impossibly tall. It's beautiful, and also surprising, for the tower changes its character entirely when seen from the side – now it's a mighty slab-like ziggurat, its surface etched by tiers of set-backs that step down the elevation.

Looking at the massive development of masterly, mature and well-balanced design, it's almost impossible to imagine its chaotic and near-catastrophic origin. The roots of the story stretch back into the late 19th century when business entrepreneur John D. Rockefeller founded the family's fortunes by more or less inventing the oil industry. But the ruthless manner in which he ran his main company – Standard Oil – made Rockefeller not only one of the richest men in America but also one of the most hated. When Rockefeller retired from Standard Oil in 1897 he devoted much of his time and money to philanthropy. As a committed Christian he knew he should put something back into society – but he would decide who would benefit and in what way. This autocratic approach to philanthropy and the mix of money-making with very selective money-giving, became one of the distinguishing traits of the Rockefeller dynasty, so it's not surprising that in 1927 Rockefeller's son – John D. Rockefeller Junior – agreed to help the New York Metropolitan Opera Company build itself a new home in the city. He bought the lease of a huge midtown site on which the opera company would relocate itself and for which it would, in due course, reimburse Rockefeller. He also took responsibility for organising the commercial development of the periphery of the site to raise money to subsidise the Opera's operations. Plans were drawn up but before work got underway disaster struck. In 1929 the Wall Street crash plunged the United States into complete financial meltdown and nearly a decade of economic depression. Almost overnight much of the population of what had been the richest country in the world was forced to queue at breadlines and soup kitchens and labour at any meagre task that might raise a few dollars.

In these desperate circumstances it's not surprising that the Opera pulled out of the deal, declaring that it was unable to afford the project. But it was too late for John Rockefeller Junior. He had the lease on the site and faced a loss of $5 million a year for the 24-year term of the lease. A lesser man would have quailed, even thrown in the towel, but not Rockefeller. He decided he could turn disaster in success by developing the site himself – a proposition that many at the time thought insane since the nation was still reeling from the disastrous consequences of the crash. By 1931 Rockefeller had organised a team of architects – with Raymond Hood as lead consultant – and came up with enough potential tenants – including Standard Oil – to allow the development to proceed, although its successful completion was far from certain.

With a brilliant leap of the imagination Rockefeller had seen that this development – it was the nation's first high-rise, large-scale, mixed-use urban development project – would be attractive to innovative tenants. The radio and television industry was young, pioneering and fresh in its business attitudes and Rockefeller got RCA, RKO and NBC as primary tenants. The development was named Radio City, with an entire block becoming the 'Radio City Music Hall', while the Center's dominating tower was christened the RCA Building. Detailed designs were drawn up and, with Rockefeller taking direct and personal control of the project, the scheme went ahead. It became one of the greatest generators of employment and wealth in the city during the Depression – around 75,000 people worked on the Center's construction – and when completed in 1940 it was, and remains, the greatest real estate enterprise ever undertaken by private capital in the United States.

Although the Rockefeller Center contained no apartments or hotel it did house a wide range of shops, restaurants and bars – notably the glamorous Rainbow Room and Grill on the top floor of the tower. This rich mix of convivial uses with office space, combined with the high quality of its architecture and art, made the Center an immediate success and a central location for New York life. Gertrude Stein, the charismatic catalyst of modern art and friend of Picasso, declared that her first view of the Rockefeller Center was 'the most beautiful I have ever seen, ever seen, ever seen'. The Modernist architect Le Corbusier, who didn't much like the chaos and dark canyon streets of New York, found virtue in the Center, which he thought 'rational, harmonious' and the embodiment of 'architectural life'. The development had cost $102 million to build and given Rockefeller almost a decade of worry but it was, in the end, a triumph. He was vindicated. During the 60 years since its completion the Center has evolved, it has gone through bleak moments, and has changed ownership on several occasions. The current owner, Tishman Speyer, has recently repaired the Center and takes great pride in running and maintaining a much-loved New York institution that nearly a hundred million people pass through every year.

I enter the tower, now called the GE Building, through the main door off Rockefeller Plaza and below a low-relief panel showing a huge bearded figure rendered in a stylised but appealing Art Deco manner by the artist Lee Lawrie. The figure holds a huge pair of compasses and so must be the image of God, the great architect of creation, and presides over a passage from the Old Testament: 'Wisdom and Knowledge Shall be the Stability of thy Times.' It's a reminder to all entering this building that their actions will be judged by a higher power, and that wisdom is the creative force of the universe. Golly, this place is not just a temple to Mammon but clearly Rockefeller believed it had a moral and improving role to play in the life of the city. The entrance lobby is a truly stupendous space – not merely the way into a commercial tower but a public thoroughfare through the city, containing shops and staircases to a subterranean shopping mall. This entrance lobby is the scene of Rockefeller's great battle with one of the 20th century's most curious artists, a place where the conflicts that run through this mighty enterprise came to a bitter and destructive head; it's where Rockefeller revealed his soul.

It's a commonplace to observe that the Rockefeller Center is a great paradox, a unity of contradictions – it is a private commercial development that feels like a great public building; its architecture is modern and functional, yet also romantic and packed with traditional and historic reference; it's the marriage of hard-headed capitalism and idealistic philanthropy – the creation of a mighty merchant prince, yet seems almost socialist in some of its aspirations. This sense of paradox can be confusing and it certainly seemed to confuse Diego Rivera in 1933 when he was commissioned by Rockefeller to paint one of the murals in the entrance lobby. Rivera chose a theme that applauded Soviet Communism, condemned capitalism and showed workers being persecuted by the police. It's a remote possibility that Rockefeller could have tolerated all of this in the name of artistic freedom of expression, but what he couldn't tolerate was the portrait of a saintly Lenin clasping, as Rivera later explained, 'the hands of a black American and a white Russian soldier and worker, as allies of the future'. The idea of this image presiding in the entrance of the RCA Building was too much for Rockefeller and he asked Rivera to replace Lenin's face with that of an anonymous man. Rivera refused and the stand-off turned ugly, with the artist being dismissed and his work finally destroyed in May 1934. Rockefeller was heavily criticised by elements of the artistic community for his 'vandalism', but most New Yorkers seem to have felt that Rivera had really gone too far with this act of provocation. Rivera himself never forgave Rockefeller, lambasted him in his biography and when he later painted a version of the mural in the Palace of Fine Arts in Mexico City added a portrait of Rockefeller that, Rivera explained, 'I inserted into the night-club scene, his head but a short distance away from the venereal disease germs pictured in the ellipse of the microscope'.

Following this distressing experience Rockefeller quickly commissioned other artists to decorate the walls of the entrance hall and these are the works that now enthral me. Particularly powerful are those by José Maria Sert – they are patriotic, idealistic and illustrate medical, political and social progress, and venerate advances in technology. Yes, this is much more what Rockefeller had in mind. Particularly didactic – not to say amusing – is the mighty mural that rises high above the receptionist's desk. It's entitled 'American Progress' and shows the development of America through the unity of brawn and brain. In the centre is a portrait of Abraham Lincoln – the 'man of action' – resting his hand on the shoulder of Ralph Waldo Emerson – the 'man of thought' – while behind them looms the Rockefeller Center itself, the epitome of these American virtues.

I want to meet the denizens of this world and plunge first into the subterranean shopping mall. It's full of activity, its shops and restaurants buzzing with life. I'm attracted by one shop in particular – it seems so much of the city. It's a shoeshine business and presents a most memorable image – a row of sharply suited and booted executives sitting on high chairs, their heads buried in their newspapers, while shoeshine boys crouch and toil at their feet. I enter and take my place on one of the high chairs and receive the buffing of a lifetime. My goodness, I come down from my pedestal one very satisfied customer. I seek out the owner of the place. His name is Hugo and he's Uruguayan. I ask him how he likes having his shop in the building. Hugo's delighted to answer, 'What I like about the Rockefeller Center is that it's a community, we all know each other. Customers, clients, we have a good relationship, it's a very good place to be.'

I ascend to an upper floor. I have a date with a partner from one of the large firms of corporate lawyers that perch in the tower. The chap's name is Whitney Gerard and he's worked in the Center for over 20 years. We meet in his corner office. I admire the view. Whitney muses, 'Well, that's actually it. Everybody likes to have a corner office, makes you feel important. In normal buildings you have four corners but because of the set-backs here there are eight corners on every floor, we have nine floors so 72 happy partners.' Ah, an additional benefit of the set-back. Whitney has more to say: 'Most of the people who work here are aware that this is a different place. They get benefits, aesthetic in part, and practical because it's accessible to everyone. You get every kind of service here, from having your shoes shined downstairs to having an elegant meal in the Rainbow Room.'

I leave the lawyers and continue my journey up the tower. I'm on my way to see David Rockefeller, born in New York City in June 1915 and the last living son of John D. Rockefeller junior. We meet on the 56th floor, in the offices the family have occupied since the building opened and still retain. David Rockefeller is small, dapper and with the quiet and immaculate manners that come from an old and now sadly lost world. I ask about his earliest memories of the site and of the construction. 'We lived at 10 West 54th Street, and I had a bedroom on the fifth floor. I could see St Patrick's Cathedral on the edge of the site, and where we are now was covered with relatively low buildings, tenements, inexpensive housing.' I ask about his father's vision for the Center and what it's done for New York. 'He wanted to build something that would be beautiful and not just an office building. He wanted a place that people could come and enjoy with open areas. It was a very wise and good thing. And there's no doubt that in terms of providing employment it was a very important thing for the city.' How, I ask, did your father hold up under the pressure? How did it affect family life? 'He was strained financially and emotionally, worried how it would all turn out being built in the middle of a depression. I remember he would have these damn headaches and he would go to bed and I would visit him. He was very courageous but those headaches were very hard to take. They were an added problem.' Yes, financing and building the greatest real estate enterprise ever undertaken in the United States by private capital during the nation's greatest financial depression must, indeed, have been something of a headache.

I complete my journey through the Rockefeller Centre by going to the Rainbow Room at the top of the tower. It's a splendid Art Deco extravaganza and remains one of the most glamorous bars and restaurants in the city. I sip my dry martini and gaze through the window at the dazzling city of towers that surrounds me. High buildings have been much maligned during the last 40 years but the Rockefeller Center shows how it should be done. It's a private and commercial enterprise but with many public benefits. It combines utility with beauty and ennobles rather than diminishes New York – it's a solution to modern city living, not part of the problem. For me, with its mix of uses, its vibrant life and fine details, the Rockefeller is just about the best high-rise development in the world.

An oasis of harmony in a troubled world

Damascus, Syria

Damascus is arguably the oldest continuously occupied city on earth, with a history dating back at least 7,000 years. While other great and ancient cities – Persepolis, Babylon, Jericho, Petra – are now just ruins or have shrunk into mere villages, Damascus thrives. I have always found Damascus an intoxicating place – a city full of warmth and welcome which appeals to all the senses. I've come here now to discover how the city works, the secret of its success and what it can teach other cities about the creative ways in which people can live together. To start this quest I go to where the city started, to find two of the main reasons for its being – the oasis and the river.

Damascus is now vast and spreading, but at its heart survives the old city, still within its ancient walls. And there are the remains of the fertile oasis – the Ghuta – that nurtured the city in its earliest times. In rich and mixed profusion I find pomegranate trees, oranges and lemons, date palms, vines and olive trees. It seems an image of paradise and plenty. Indeed, the ancient and unexpected delights of this oasis in the desert explain the tradition that Damascus is the location of the Garden of Eden.

After the oasis I make my way towards the old city. I press through the traffic and find the long stretch of city wall that runs unbroken along its north side. Below this is a cutting that was the site of the once mighty River Barada – the life-giving artery that allowed Damascus to thrive in the desert. But now the great river is no more than a trickle of dirty water. I walk towards the wall. Here it is superb. The lower courses are formed by massive stones, and these are the remains of the city wall built by the Romans soon after they took Damascus in 64 BC. Damascus was then a frontier city on the edge of the Rome-dominated world; touching these massive stones – rough and impregnable – I sense how secure the inhabitants of Damascus would have felt within this powerful fortification.

Prominent among these inhabitants were the merchants, as Damascus was the focus for a number of the great trade routes between east and west and the south. Silks, spices, incense, dyes and precious metals from China, India and Arabia swelled the city markets and eventually made their way to the Mediterranean ports and on to western Europe. Along with this trade came art, culture and ideas which, combined with the treasures of the world, made the Damascus of 2,000 years ago not only one of the richest but also one of the most cultured, diverse, beautiful and fabulous of cities.

The Roman city had seven gates. Most of these, along with the upper portion of the city wall, were rebuilt in medieval times, but one Roman gate survives. The gate stands on the eastern side of the city and is now called Bab al-Sharqi but was originally known as the Gate of the Sun – I suppose because the rising sun would cast its rays between gate's portals. It's much rebuilt but essentially dates from around AD 100 and it's probably now the oldest structure to survive above ground in Damascus. I enter and I'm confronted by a wondrous sight. Ahead of me, stretching into the distance, is a narrow but distinctly straight street. It is the oldest trading street in the world still in use – it's the Straight Street mentioned in the New Testament. First there are the stalls. The western half of Straight Street turns into the Midhat Pasha Souk and this connects, via the winding alleys of the spice market, to the other great market street of al-Hamidiyeh. I plunge into the bowels of the Midhat Pasha Souk, a dark and cavernous place in which shafts of sunlight unexpectedly penetrate its arched and iron-clad 19th-century roof. Here is a wonderful array of narrow, open-fronted shops selling spices, tea, coffee, dyes, nuts, sweets in endless variety. The aroma is overwhelming; you can taste it.

I discover my money is no good in the market. No one will accept it. I'm given soap, sweets, spices. Arab hospitality is legendary and I've enjoyed it many times before. But now it's particularly reassuring. As events get uglier in neighbouring Iraq, with thousands of Iraqi refugees flooding into Damascus, I feared the city's customary warm reception might well be chillier, especially given Britain's role in Iraq. But no. I was silly to worry. The people here are sophisticated and cultured. They do not hold individuals responsible for the political actions of their country. I feel genuinely welcome. I walk on. A chap is pressing lush pomegranates to produce a deep red juice. The pomegranate is a timeless image of fertility; the fruit of the oasis. I order a glass. The juice is sweet and strong – delicious.

With my sense of taste and smell satisfied, at least temporarily, I go in search of more visual and mental stimulation – architecture, pure and simple. The khans of Damascus, where merchants could store and display their goods and locate their counting houses, are among the architectural wonders of the city. Just off Straight Street is one of the best – the Khan Assaad Pasha. It was built in 1753, during the centuries of the Ottoman domination of Damascus, and is a geometrically precise and optically stunning palace of commerce, more like a mighty mosque than a merchants' assembly. The khan takes the form of a large, double-height open space that is square in plan, defined by two-storey blocks of merchants' offices. The open space contains four free-standing piers that help support nine domes. The central and largest one collapsed years ago in an earthquake and below where it once stood is a basin of water. The walls of the khan are banded with black and white stone that, with the cool perfection of the composition of the domes, gives it a striking, abstract, perfection.

But this khan is empty! I must see one that still functions. I dash back to Straight Street and see one, much smaller but loaded with goods and full of merchants using their small offices just as they were intended. It is called the Khan al-Tutun – the tobacco khan – and, like most of these buildings, originally accommodated one product. I walk back towards the Khan Assaad Pasha because right next door to it is one of the most attractive and useful buildings in Damascus. It's the Hammam Nur al-Din, a bathhouse which dates from the 1150s. A modest entrance leads to a large domed vestibule, an Ottoman period rebuilding, off which are the steaming and massage rooms. Beneath the dome sit swarthy moustachioed fellows in various states of undress – admirable Damascus merchants, some smoking narghiles or drinking coffee.

Nur al-Din, who originally built the hammam, is one of the key figures in the history of Damascus. He took control of the city in the mid-12th century and, through skill and military prowess, achieved decades of peace and prosperity. Among Nur al-Din's other legacies were the public buildings he created in Damascus. The hammam is one, but the architecturally most significant to survive is the Bimaristan Nur al-Din – a mid-12th-century hospital. Entry is through a beautiful arched gate that incorporates a re-used Roman classical entablature. This leads to a court around which are series of tall and wide recessed niches called iwans, and various rooms and wards. When this hospital was constructed Arab science and medicine were by far the most advanced in the world, and the 11th-century writings of Ibn Sina make it clear that Arab doctors appreciated the relationship between the mind and the body and realised that emotional ailments can have physical symptoms and respond to physical treatments. All this is reflected in this hospital; here treatment is administered via the senses. The symmetrical and beautiful architecture creates visual delight and evokes a sense of order and harmony. Herb plants and orange trees in the court create a pleasing fragrance, and the murmur of the fountain in the central court creates a calming sound.

I leave the hospital and wander the narrow and winding streets just to the south and east of the Great Mosque. I pass from the Jewish Quarter into the Christian Quarter where I have a date to look around one of the buildings for which Damascus is famous. It's a courtyard house that dates from the Ottoman period and is now occupied by the Kabawat family. I arrive outside the house, which has a simple, discreet exterior. The door is opened by a woman who leads me into the main courtyard, with a central pool and fountain, orange trees, wisteria and vines and a marvellous pavement of inlaid marble. Hind Kabawat tells me her family has occupied the house – built in 1836 – for five generations. Courtyard houses like this, she says, are an oasis in the city. Outside all is noise, and congestion. Within there is tranquillity, scent from the plants mixed with the aroma of coffee and cardamom, the soothing gurgling of the fountain. We talk about life in Damascus. Hind, whose family is Christian, says there is no tension with her Muslim neighbours, in fact they are among her best friends. She loves her city and she sees it as a place of beauty, warmth and tolerance.

The greatest building of the old city I have left until last, the single building that tells so much of the history of Damascus – the Great Mosque. For at least 3,000 years, one site has functioned as the sacred heart – the soul – of the city. As far as anyone now knows the site was first occupied by a temple dedicated to the local deity called Haddad. Then, with the coming of the Romans, the Temple of Haddad was replaced, in the 3rd century, with a Temple to Jupiter. When Christianity finally became the state religion of the Roman Empire in the late 4th century the Temple of Jupiter was adapted to serve as a cathedral dedicated to St John the Baptist. In 636 Christian Damascus surrendered to a Muslim force and the cathedral was rapidly adapted to serve both Muslims and Christians. At this point Damascus became one of the key locations in the Muslim world. The first governor of the city, and the man who allowed Christians to continue to use part of their cathedral, was Mu'awiyya who within a few years of the death of the Prophet Mohammed was at the centre of the struggle for the leadership of the nascent Islamic world. But in 705 al-Walid – a successor of Mu'awiyya – resolved to remove the Christians from their cathedral and rebuild on the site in spectacular style. He wanted to do nothing less than build the greatest mosque in the world. It's al-Walid's creation that now confronts me and the most striking thing is that although he removed the Christians from the site, al-Walid did not remove all the older buildings. A fragment of portico from the Temple of Jupiter survives, as does virtually all the handsome masonry outer wall of the temple complex that now forms the perimeter wall of the mosque.

I walk up to the main gate, take off my shoes and enter the court. It's a stupendous space but is now only a shadow of its former self. Originally, all the external surfaces of the courtyard were covered by a vast mosaic, sparkling with gold. It must have looked sensational. Some fragments, much faded, survive. One, within an arcade on the west side, shows the River Barada, houses, mosques and palaces, fragments of the oasis with trees and plants – clearly a scene of paradise and reference to the legend of Damascus as the Garden of Eden.

Although most of the mosaic has gone, the vast court still sparkles as the sun shines on its polished marble pavement. It is an extraordinary place – arcades on three sides in which visitors stroll or sit to chat and in one corner rises the Tower of Jesus, the place where, according to Islam, Christ will descend at the end of days to fight the antichrist. But the most striking structure to look into the court is the mighty prayer hall that stretches along its entire south side. I enter – it's a powerful and beautiful space. It is divided into three wide aisles by two colonnades that clearly reused columns and capitals from the Christian cathedral. The floor is carpeted, the atmosphere is relaxed – almost more secular than sacred. People stroll and chat, family groups loll on the carpets, pilgrims process through. It's like the theatre of life. At its eastern end the hall contains a small, domed building that reaches up to the very roof timbers. This is the shrine of St John and is said to contain, at the very least, the Baptist's head. I sit on the carpeted floor and observe. There are wonderful sounds, the soothing murmur of prayers, the music of the call to prayer. Sitting here you feel that, within these ancient walls, still resides the soul of Damascus. I reflect on my day and the city. There's the sense of the eternal about the place. Damascus – with its rich diversity – offers lessons on how people can live together in friendship. It's highly appropriate that the oldest city in the world can teach younger creations how to live harmoniously.

It's time to eat. I go to the early 18th-century Jabri House, a splendid courtyard house that's now a restaurant. I want to meet the chef to discover some of the secrets of Damascus food. He prepares one of my favourites – baba ganoush. He gets baked aubergines, cuts up tomatoes, onions and peppers, adds olive oil, pomegranate syrup, lemon and salt and all is ready. This and other dishes – tabouleh, fattoush, mutaba, stuffed vine leaves – are loaded on a table and I set to work. Yes, the old city of Damascus satisfies all the senses. There's visual beauty – beautiful buildings, the scents of spices and incense – and now the food. It's obvious really, but it only now strikes me. Food is emblematic of the city – delightful to look at, to smell, to taste. And the food – some the produce of the local oasis, some the result of the city's long-honed trade routes – attracts people, makes and cements social connections. Here I am in a convivial gathering, with people of all types – locals and visitors, Christians and Muslims – sitting down in friendship to eat together. The atmosphere is intoxicating. It's easy to see this jolly restaurant as Damascus in miniature, maybe – an oasis of hope in a troubled world.

The facts of life
in a Modernist dream

Brasilia, Brazil

We fly into Brasilia in late October, in between mighty storms. The sky is overcast and moody, but as we drive into the city shafts of bright sun burst through the dark clouds. Brasilia is a city I have longed to see. It has a strange and compelling history and such huge aspirations. A capital city built from scratch in an impossibly remote location, it was intended to express the pride and spirit of the nation, evoke its character, and define its future – and to achieve all this by employing revolutionary, avant-garde architecture and planning. What a place! As we drive along the wide freeways that form the arteries of the city I'm agog to discover whether I'll be truly moved by this heroic creation – at once an heroic piece of contemporary art and a would-be utopian model of an egalitarian modern city – or bitterly disappointed. As I stare around, striving to get my first glimpse of the city, I realise I'm in its very heart. So huge is the plan that I've arrived almost without warning. This is disconcerting; there is no sense of arrival, no dramatic sense of presence. Will this mighty creation – with its bold artistic and social pretensions – be a visual let-down?

We pass rows of identical-looking government ministries and the elemental Congress Building incorporating a huge white bowl of a structure and closely set twin towers that soar into the menacing storm clouds. Brasilia does indeed appear the very dream of the modern city, with vast public buildings set like huge abstract sculptures in expansive squares and lush green parkland. The emblematic buildings are left behind, the freeway continues into what appears to be the country and suddenly an extraordinary building comes into view. It's long and low with minimal white arches wrapped around the glass façade of the building and supporting its boldly projecting flat roof. It's the Presidential Palace. We sweep past it, crossing what appears to be a huge car park. All is eerily deserted. Then our journey abruptly ends. We are at our hotel, the Blue Tree Park. It's startlingly modern – low, curving with a glazed façade and flat roof. We have arrived at the future – or at least the future as conceived in the 1950s. This is heroic Modernism without irony or apology. This is an attempt to build a new capital city for a new nation.

Brasilia is one of the most audacious architectural projects ever realised, not least because this great city, built in remote brush many miles from the inhabited coast, was effectively completed in five years. But its history stretches further back, indeed to the origin of Brazil as an independent nation. Brazil was colonised by the Portuguese in the early 16th century, when African slaves toiled for a small elite of Europeans who owned and ruled the land. In 1815 Brazil was made a kingdom with John VI becoming king of both Portugal and Brazil, and in 1822 his eldest son, Dom Pedro, declared Brazil an independent nation. In 1831 Pedro abdicated and handed over rule to his son Pedro II, who clearly had a moral conscience. He freed all his slaves, but others did not follow suit and it was not until 1889, when the nation was declared a republic, that slavery was finally abolished.

Through all these years the fledgling nation was haunted by a compelling idea – the creation of a new capital city, a place free of associations with the old colonial regime, a place that would express national identity, and where the citizens of the new Brazil would live together in peace and with pride. The name of the city was agreed as early as 1823 – it was to be called Brasilia – but what was not so easy to determine was where the city should be and what it should look like. The ideal city became a Shangri-La for all Brazilians. It was, in a sense, Brazil's promised land, the place in which the nation's hopes and destiny would be made manifest. The dream was compelling but for decades that's all it remained – a dream.

Traditionally Brazil's cities had grown along its coast or along the Amazon, and one of the agreed aims was that the capital should open up the country. Expeditions were mounted and sites in the remote centre located, but no decisions were made until 1955 when a location was at last agreed on. The project would probably still have continued to slip if not for one man. In 1956 Juscelino Kubitschek de Oliveira was inaugurated as president and he had a burning desire to build the city the nation had dreamed of for over 130 years. For Kubitschek a new capital would not only realise a long-held nationalistic vision but would also be a powerful and contemporary political statement. To speed things along Kubitschek approached Oscar Niemeyer, old friend, architect and fellow communist, for assistance in developing a plan for the city. Niemeyer agreed to begin designing buildings but insisted that its plan be determined through a competition. So in September 1956 all architects, engineers and urbanists licensed in Brazil were invited to offer their ideas for the creation of the ideal city.

The competition was won in the spring of 1957 by Lucio Costa. He conceived the city in terms of two major intersecting axes, each formed by wide freeways divided by well-planted central reservations – almost linear parks. One axis was to be straight and wide and was to be lined with government and ministerial buildings with the collection of congress buildings at one end. The other axis was to curve, with the form of the terrain, and was to be lined with residential and shopping blocks. The image, when seen from above, was of a cross with a curving cross-bar, commemorating the cross planted in the land by Portuguese explorers in the early 16th century. Or, perhaps more in the futuristic machine-age spirit of the project, the plan could be seen in the form of an aircraft with the congress buildings at its head, ministries along its fuselage, housing and shopping along its wings and, where the engines would be, offices and commercial buildings – the driving force of the economy!

Despite spiralling costs and increasing scepticism from the press Kubitschek kept his nerve and, by sheer force of will, managed to complete enough of the city by 1960 so it could be inaugurated while he was still in office. The construction process had been termed an act of insanity, a waste of public money, and Kubitschek dismissed as Brazil's megalomaniac pharaoh, but at last the nation had its visionary city.

I leave my hotel and head to the Congress Building that forms one side of what is termed the Square of the Three Powers. The buildings around this square – all designed by Niemeyer – form one of the most iconic images of Modernism. The Congress Building itself is long, low, generously glazed and spans a wide cutting, its flat roof acting as a sort of bridge between two flanking freeways. In front is a lawn and lake, behind is the Square of the Three Powers. I contemplate the Congress. It is strange indeed; on its roof are two huge, white-painted, abstract sculptures – a massive flat-topped bowl and a saucer dome. Between the two is a pair of tall thin towers – administrative offices – linked in their centres by a bridge so they form a huge, elongated letter H. As I look I begin to understand. The Congress Building is, at first glance, a bold Modernist composition – simple, sculptural, functional and bold. But now I see that it is more complex and more ambiguous in meaning. The flat roof is the key. The whole building is a sort of Acropolis, a sacred mound. It can be approached by a long ramp or from narrow bridges linking to the freeways. So, if this is an Acropolis then the buildings on top – the bowl and the dome – are temples, Brasilia versions of the Parthenon. The bowl-shaped structure houses the Chamber of the Deputies, its form suggesting that debate here is open to all ideologies. The domed structure roofs the Senate, suggesting that reflection and balance are all-important. So one part of the Congress is open and receiving and the other closed and nurturing. All is rich in meaning – modern yet antique in its associations, patriotic and rational but also almost religious – even esoteric.

I'm reminded of alternative stories about Brasilia's creation – some say the real reason the site was chosen is because it stands at the symbolic heart of South America. Other stories are weirder still. Strangely, Brasilia is now popular with members of fringe, even wacky, religious movements. They say it's a great centre of natural energy and a gateway to the heavens – an idea that seems to be reinforced by the soaring, indeed thrusting, forms of the twin towers. What's more certain is that Niemeyer is a curious fellow – an artistic radical and communist but also open to the potential of ancient and mystic forms. He was also not without wit. This is revealed by the vast and somewhat arid Square of the Three Powers – the governmental heart of the nation. On one side is the Congress Building – the centre of legislative power – while on two other sides squat buildings that represent the executive power of the president – the Palácio do Planalto – and of the Judiciary – the Palácio do Supremo Tribunal. These two buildings face each other across the square, both are architecturally similar and both make the point that Niemeyer's Modernism was not machine-made and placeless in its forms. Niemeyer explained that he wanted his architecture to reflect the nature of Brazil – the curves of its mountains, of the clouds, of, as he put it, 'the lover'. He also admitted a predilection for the curvaceous form of the 'Baroque buttocks' of a Brazilian beauty. So both these buildings have glass-faced façades framed by elegant, minimal and curving columns that taper to support flat roofs, also support the raised floor slab, and that reach the ground on points. The consequence is that the buildings are light in appearance and seem to hover above the ground. All most satisfactory.

What is most obviously omitted from this epicentre of national power is a church – strange in this great Roman Catholic country but predictable since Kubitschek and Niemeyer were both communists and atheists. But Niemeyer did soon after design a cathedral and it stands near the junction of the 'wings' and 'fuselage' in the city plan – in the commercial area. Symbolic, I wonder. I arrive – the image is familiar, a circular structure formed by soaring concrete ribs that gather to form a spiky pinnacle that looks vaguely like a crown of thorns. I plunge inside, into darkness. It's like entering an Egyptian tomb, and then suddenly there's an explosion of light as I enter the body of the cathedral. The tomb – symbolically Christ's tomb – suddenly becomes a womb, a place of resurrection, of rebirth bathed in sunlight. Now I see what Niemeyer is doing. He's creating a quintessential, an elemental sacred space. This building is not just about Christianity; it's about all religions. It's making a statement about the multi-cultural character of Brazil – Africans, indigenous people, Europeans. The cathedral's doing nothing less than trying to define – to represent – the nature of the nation. It's ambitious and – in many ways – it works. Most surprised, I leave. Nothing here is turning out quite as I expected.

The next thing to discover is what it's like to live in the city. To get a feel I must visit the housing blocks located along the curving axis that crosses the Monumental Axis. These are some of the most famous, and controversial, aspects of Brasilia. In designing these Costa remained very true to Modernist orthodoxy. The housing takes the form of a series of six- to eight-storey slabs organised into squares of well-planted land with each square defined by freeways or wide roads. Each square is called a superquadra – a 'super square' – and the roads that divide each square are lined with shops and restaurants. In addition each superquadra was intended to contain a crèche and other facilities that were to make it into a self-supporting community, each with its own identity. Also, more radically, each was to house a mix of Brasilia residents – they were to be models of egalitarian living with, for example, a judge living next to a plumber. This was the ideal of modern urban living in the 1950s – how has the theory worked in practice? I go to superquadra number 105, the first completed. The slabs appear in good repair, the gardens they sit in are well maintained. I have come to meet Olga Bastos, who has lived here from the start. How does she like living here, I ask, would she move if she had the chance? She tells me she loves her home and loves Brasilia. She sees herself as one of the pioneers who helped shape the city. So, for the professional class the Brasilia dream appears to have worked.

I go next to meet a person who works in the city. I want to discover what's happened to Kubitschek's egalitarian dream for Brasilia. Brazil is a country that is full of vitality, of joy. But it is also a nation crippled by poverty, crime and inequality. To discover how life in Brasilia measures up I go to one of the uniform set of ministries along the central Monumental Axis. It houses the Orwellian-sounding Ministry of Cities. I've come here not to meet a bureaucrat or politician but Francisca Vieira, who works in the ministry as a cleaner – a woman who lives not in Brasilia, but in one of the notorious 'satellite' towns that sprawl in the country around the city, outside the scope of its architectural and social vision. As we talk she starts to sob quietly. Why? I can only guess it's because no one has bothered to ask her story before, or documented the hard life she lives, typical of the majority of working people in Brasilia. Her wages are abysmally low, the time and cost of travelling by bus to work at the ministry are daunting. She struggles to survive and support her family in a self-built house in a satellite town an hour's drive from the capital. She says that Brasilia is nothing to her.

I return to my superquadra to visit one of its restaurants, to see if there is indeed a convivial nightlife, if a sense of community exists. As I drink my caipirinha I am, in a way, living the Modernist dream. I'm surrounded by local residents, happily chatting, in a park-like setting with the housing slabs rising nearby. Indeed a self-sufficient community. But, despite this, Brasilia is a social failure – it has not lived up to the dream. It has not become a vibrant capital, the cultural as well as the administrative hub of its nation, and – a far worse betrayal of its egalitarian vision – it is a true reflection of the unequal Brazilian society. It has no place for the poorly paid workers like Francisca. They make long journeys to service the city but simply can't afford to live in it, and feel like outsiders when they walk through its array of Modernist masterpieces.

Paradoxes abound. When I dined in a smart restaurant I was prepared feijoade – a tasty medley including beans and pork served in various ways. This, traditionally, was slave food, made of cheap ingredients and left-overs, but, in city centre restaurants, even this slave food is now too expensive for Francisca. The city is still an infant – not one of its buildings is older than I am – but it's hard to see how it can mature into a compelling capital city that is a centre of culture and commerce as well as of government administration. In Brasilia, I fear, creative connections between the people who use it and who maintain it will never be made.

Greenland Clockwise from top left: Having found snow of the right consistency, we begin to quarry large, heavy blocks; after scribing the igloo in the snow and dedicating the first block to the life-bringing sun, we start to build; the blocks are laid to form three horizontal courses that slope slightly inwards; a wedge-shaped block acts as a ramp for the following block so that the igloo rises as a continuous and self-supporting spiral of blocks to form a dome; blocks can be cut to wedge together, but mostly stick because their surfaces are melted through friction from the blade of the saw – when the water refreezes adjoining blocks are cemented together; the igloo nears completion; the keystone is in place and we rest on the sleeping platform; the complete igloo: strong and most pleasing in its purity.

Catherine Palace, St Petersburg, Russia Looking along the enfilade of staterooms on the first floor of the palace. The richness of the gilded detail is almost overwhelming.

Languedoc, France Albi Cathedral dominates the city and surrounding countryside. On the river bank are the walls of the fortified bishop's palace with its dominating squat central tower. The group of structures, most of which were started in the late 13th century, has more the appearance of a mighty castle than a house of God.

The nave of the cathedral looking east. The rich, painted Renaissance decoration dates from the early 16th century.

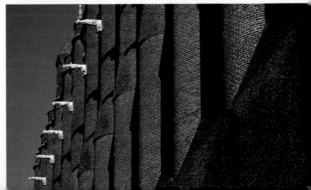

Buttresses, looking like an array of towers, sprout gargoyles.

One of the sacred wheels on the Sun Temple at Konarak, India. There are 12 pairs of wheels that symbolise the months of the year and work as sundials to mark the passage of the life-giving sun and passing of time.

Sun Temple, Konarak, India Clockwise from top left: Four of the nine Hindu planets shown in human form. The Sun is on the far left, holding lotuses – symbols of fertility; inside the remains of the Dance Pavilion, or Offering Hall, with the main mandapa behind; the sun god Surya, as the personification of the Morning Sun – the god of heat, regeneration and fruitfulness; the stairs to the Dance Pavilion are guarded by ferocious mythical beasts; on the base of the mandapa a considerate young woman offers a dog a divine meal.

Giant Buddha, Leshan, China Maitreya – the Buddha of the future – has a most solemn expression, full of compassion.

Mumbai, India
Dharavi covers one square mile and is said to be the largest slum in Asia. Most of its houses are ad hoc constructions of brick, timber and metal.

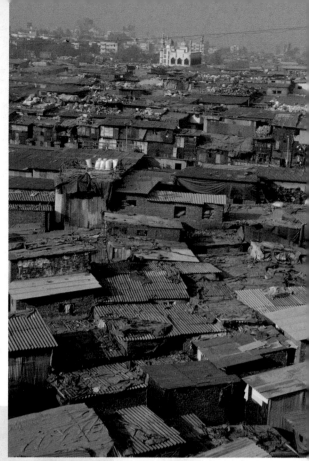

New York, USA
The 70-storey Rockefeller Center was the first Manhattan development to include a skyscraper as part of a group of related buildings with a mix of uses, creating what was virtually a city within the city.

Syria The court of the early 8th-century Great Mosque in Damascus. Here people not only gather to pray but also to meet, talk and relax – a most inclusive and convivial place.

Brasilia, Brazil Public buildings of extraordinary form – really giant abstract sculptures – loiter around the edges of the Square of the Three Powers.

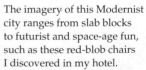

The imagery of this Modernist city ranges from slab blocks to futurist and space-age fun, such as these red-blob chairs I discovered in my hotel.

3

Death

Eternal life
through artistic beauty

Staglieno Cemetery, Genoa, Italy

Genoa is an ancient port and trading city which has survived many tribulations over the centuries. But in the early 19th century it faced a potentially catastrophic threat – a threat that came not from the living, but from the dead! I've come to this wonderful city to see the artistic consequences of the way in which this particular threat was dealt with.

During the early 19th century Genoa thrived and expanded as a result of ever-increasing industrial activity, and as its population grew so, of course, did the number of its dead. Throughout Europe burial practice had changed little since the late Middle Ages. The Christian belief that all human bodies should be preserved and buried after death as an essential prelude to resurrection, judgement and consignment to heaven or to hell, meant that the centres of expanding cities like Genoa were being engulfed by corpses. By tradition, the dead were buried in the graveyards or vaults of city churches, but even with the regular removal of skeletal remains to charnel houses room was running out. Bodies were piled on top of bodies and graveyards seeped with decay – and decay bred disease. In most European cities in the early 19th century the dead were, quite literally, killing the living. It had been clear to medical men for decades that there was a direct link between putrefying city-centre burial grounds and diseases such as cholera, even though the exact route was hotly debated, but it was not until 1854 that cholera was proved to be a water-borne disease. Long before this date, however, all agreed that no matter what the means of transmission, the only solution was to remove the cause. Burials in city centres were to stop.

In 1832 the city had passed a Regie Patenti (royal patent) that moved responsibility for the bodies of the dead from Church to state and stopped most church burials, while confirming extramural interment. In 1835 Genoa took the momentous step to acquire, construct and maintain a large cemetery. Located well away from the city centre, this cemetery was intended to become a parallel world – a world where the dead could repose without being a risk to the health of the living, and be honoured and commemorated. This was a cemetery that would also be a work of art, a national shrine that would pay homage to the great of the city and engender a sense of pride and identity. And the pride, the act of memory and commemoration, would come through the creation of beauty. This cemetery was to be one of the most glorious sculpture galleries in the world, with the exhibits being sculptural monuments commissioned by the leading families of the city. The grander and more glorious your monument, the greater your family and the more likely that the name of the dead, through association with high art, would live on through the years.

The Cimitero Monumentale di Staglieno opened on 1 January 1851. It was laid out on rising ground well away from the city centre, but now it's been engulfed by urban sprawl, while retaining a splendid sense of isolation. I arrive at sunrise and I'm confronted by a long, arcaded but windowless wall, with a great classical three-arched gate set in its centre. Behind, on hills richly covered by trees, are tall monuments and chapels in a dazzling array of architectural styles – Italianate, Gothic, and I even spy a Hindu or Buddhist-inspired stupa. This really is a world in itself, an almost unbelievably large and noble city of the dead.

I walk through the central arch in the gate and enter a world of shadow. As I walk, I glance to left and right – there is a succession of long, gloomy, vaulted galleries which seem to stretch into the shades of infinity. Each I can see is packed with memorials to the dead of Genoa, and some of these take the form of dramatic sculptural compositions. It's an astonishing vision, but I press on. I find myself in a massive, well-planted court, which, as the sun's rays stream from the heavens, seems like a paradise, a symbol of rebirth, of the Christian belief in life after death, and the everlasting life that's Christ's gift to the righteous.

I stop and look around. All is ordered, almost urban. There are paths, squares and, instead of houses for the living, there are tombs and mighty memorials for the dead. Right in front of me is a huge statue by Santo Varni and behind it, atop a high flight of steps, is a huge porticoed and domed building. I drink in the extraordinary vistas. All of this was conceived by a Genoese architect called Carlo Barabino, and he was obviously determined to give death dignity through Grecian- and Roman-style classical design on an heroic scale. He clearly believed in honouring the bodies and memories of the Christian dead, which I suppose was fortunate since, just after work started here, he was carried away by a cholera epidemic (no doubt caused by one of the city's pestilent old cemeteries) and so became one of the first inhabitants of this city of shades.

The Santo Varni statue, classical in style and pretty stolid, represents Christian faith, crowned by the rays of the sun, the image of life. The statue also perhaps symbolised the faith that the people of Genoa had in this vast cemetery when it first opened; they believed that by providing hygienic repose for the dead it could save Genoa from the blight of contagious disease – from death itself. Beyond the statue is the Rotunda, which was inspired by the ancient Pantheon in Rome and serves as the cemetery's main chapel. I pass between its Grecian Doric portico into its fine, domed interior. The Roman Pantheon was the temple of all the gods and, appropriately, this temple is where the city's great have their monuments – yes, there's Barabino's name emblazoned on a stone near the main entrance.

I leave the Rotunda and enter one of the pair of vaulted and classically detailed galleries adjoining it. It is packed with huge, artistically breathtaking monuments. There may or may not be life after death, but there certainly is competition. Here the families of the departed vie with each other to proclaim their taste and wealth. They are creating family monuments which will honour them, and their descendants, through the ages and grant them immortality. As I pass along this gallery I realise that in Staglieno fame – and wealth – secured you the best locations. This necropolis is a true reflection of the social hierarchy of the city it served, for in the galleries adjoining the Rotunda and its memorials to the city's luminous heroes are grouped the graves and monuments of many of the leading members of 19th- and early 20th-century Genoese society.

Passing through these galleries, which are several storeys high and deep, it soon becomes clear that Staglieno captures, with piercing exactness, changing artistic and religious convictions in European society. The earliest monuments, from the mid-1850s, are of conventionally neo-classical design, boasting the usual paraphernalia and symbols of death, such as urns, cherubs and angels. But during the 1870s everything got more interesting. It was the period of Realism. Now the dead are shown as they were in life – or perhaps in the moment of death; they glory in their worldly attributes and achievements, and display the means by which they made their wealth – some monuments have machine parts entwined with wreaths. Many of these tombs are embellished with images of crouching, grateful orphans and beggars, emphasising the dead's charitable and philanthropic deeds. And in these monuments mourners are shown in incredible and life-like detail: they are real people, not symbols, even if the mourning scenes in which they participate are conventionally sentimental, showing mourners wandering out of tombs or kneeling tearfully in front of biers. All of this speaks of faith and certainty in Christian values, in resurrection and the afterlife – a conviction that heaven is not unlike affluent society on earth.

The master of this art was Lorenzo Orengo, and standing in a corner of one of the arcades I see what is perhaps his masterpiece. It's an extraordinary work – the tomb of a woman named Caterina Campodonico with a life-size statue of the deceased. She was a hawker who sold nuts and bread at local fairs, and during her life she saved money for this funereal work, which was carved before her death. She is shown in her finery, festooned in nuts and bread – the means by which she made the money to commission this powerful, commemorative monument. Her face is dignified, almost defiant, and all she wanted has been attained. In death she achieved, through art, a semblance of middle-class respectability and, perhaps more important, she has a foothold in eternity. Through this much admired sculpture, won through honest toil, her name and memory live on and she now stands forever among the ranks of Genoa's rich and powerful families.

Life-size and highly realistic marble figures with an almost photographic precision of detail are something of a specialty of Staglieno. You can walk through these galleries and meet the dead, get to know their mourners, embrace them and almost share their grief. The Piaggio tomb of 1885, created by Giovanni Scanzi, has a splendidly attired and spectacularly life-like young woman walking down its steps, while on another Piaggio monument (this time by Giuseppe Benetti of 1873) a young, beautiful and tearful widow, head bowed and clutching a Bible, totters from the tomb's door to the gallery floor. It's quite impossible not to embrace her. Perhaps the most strangely moving of these Realist monuments is the Pienovi tomb of 1879 by Giovanni Battista Villa. It shows a widow, holding the shrouded hand of her dead husband while she pulls back the cloth covering his face. It is, I suppose, a last farewell, but her face is not tormented with grief. Instead, she seems intensely inquisitive; she's about to confront the great mystery of death, to see the familiar face of a loved husband when life has fled.

The Queirolo family tomb is far more theatrical. It incorporates busts showing husband and wife – wealthy tradespeople I would guess – but above these busts is something extraordinary. A skeleton – the scythe-carrying grim reaper no less – is being struck by a lightning bolt and flames are leaping from its ribcage. This is an image of death itself being killed, and the action is orchestrated by a heavenly body, a prim and proper angel, which, as the tomb itself explains, is ensuring 'the eternal rule of the kingdom of life'. This tomb shows what the middle class of Genoa believed in – immortality through art and the Christian faith.

But in the 1880s there was a change. What you see in the monuments in Staglieno was happening throughout Christian society – solid belief was being replaced by doubt and uncertainty. The best of the monuments produced during this period are beautiful, often utterly surprising in their imagery and, above all, deeply and sometimes almost breathtakingly erotic. Death now became a mystery, something to be feared, as the Christian faith and old certainties were challenged, and as new scientific discoveries and psychological insights created an air of scepticism and pessimism. It was not only the fate of the soul at death that was now debated, but also whether there was a soul at all. If death was now a thing of terror and a door to the unknown it was also, it seems, strangely arousing – the ultimate sensual emotion. From the 1880s, the forms of the sculpture became increasingly organic, the mood often orgasmic – strange indeed for a cemetery.

This, in art historical terms, was the age of the Symbolists – a revolutionary art movement which blossomed in the 1880s and attacked Realism and false sentiment. It sought instead art that liberated the imagination, was fuelled by dreams and expressed ideas and ideals. Often, as the century came to a close, these ideas were dark, even decadent, and by the conventions of the age often shocking and perplexing. This was the avant-garde art movement of the 19th century – one that threatened all middle-class and Christian conventions. What is extraordinary is that this socially revolutionary, even subversive, art movement found so many patrons among the merchant and capitalist middle class of late 19th-century Genoa. As I walk through the galleries I see astonishing examples of Symbolist sculpture of the highest quality, which seems to ignore all conventions. What was in the mind of these respectable Genoese families when they commissioned monuments incorporating erotic and far from holy angels, stalking spectres of triumphant death, and sprawling and seductive female forms? I suppose, as before, they wanted to be remembered through art so they bought the artist's poetic vision, even if they did not really quite understand, or even like, his art.

This was perhaps true of the wealthy banker Francesco Oneto's family, who commemorated him by one of the most peculiar and enigmatic angels ever made by man. In 1882 the artist Giulio Monteverde designed a tomb dominated by a large and exquisitely beautiful being, which defies interpretation. It bends its head and looks, it seems, into eternity, but is this look mean and moody or compassionate and offering consolation? Is this an angel of salvation or simply an angel of death, a bringer of eternal life in paradise or of eternal suffering in hell? And what sex is this angel? This seems a relevant question since this sculpture is far from asexual – it's sexually charged. Its face is boyish, its body feminine – what on earth did Monteverde have in mind? I stand and contemplate this strange, somewhat sinister image. It seems a creature from the subconscious, a sensual angel for a post-Christian world, almost an angel for unbelievers, which seems to promise that death could be bliss.

Another sculpture by Monteverde is less ambiguous. It was created in 1894 for the rich Celle family and shows the dance of death, the traditional clash between life and death, in which the living writhe and pirouette in their futile attempts to escape the inevitability of death. Here death is shown as a shrouded skeleton while life is represented by a beautiful and nearly naked girl. The upright and remorseless image of death has a bony grip upon life's wrist and she seems to be succumbing to death's imperious demands. It's extraordinary – here death seems synonymous with sexual assault. It's a terrifying figure, this potentially violent and certainly triumphant image of death. The tomb offers no consolation, no assurance of eternal life after death in a Christian paradise. It's a dark but beautiful work and its evolution was not without difficulties. There was no censorship in Staglieno, but in this case the family stepped in. Monteverde had intended to show life entirely naked, but he was obliged to veil the lower part of her body by the swirling shroud worn by death. Inevitably this tantalising partial concealment only makes an already hot statue even steamier.

As I walk the galleries I'm continuously assaulted by these sensational Symbolist images. The Delmas tomb of 1909 by Luigi Orengo, the son of Lorenzo, shows a nearly naked young woman – in the sleep of death – being held in a most intimate manner by a naked young man. The composition is familiar – it's the Christian pietà, in which the naked and dead body of Christ is shown cradled by his grieving mother, the Virgin Mary. But in a shocking reversal of tradition, a Christ is replaced by a woman, and Mary by a muscular young man. The kiss he is bestowing is, I suppose, meant not to be sexual; it's the last kiss from the living

to the beloved dead. Here all hope of an afterlife seems absent
– there's just loss. Hopeless grief is the forte of these Symbolist
artists. The Ribaudo tomb of 1910, by Onorato Tosso, consists of
a shattered stone block sporting Egyptian hieroglyphs on which
sprawls a disconsolate young woman dressed in a skimpy vest.
Only the crumpled wings on which she lies reveal that she is an
angel lost in grief for the dead. More peculiar still is the 1920s
tomb of Luigi Burlando, by Pietro de Verona, on which lies a
languid and naked girl collapsed on her back, as if recovering
from an excessively emotional event. She has no wings, and is
clearly no angel.

Around the galleries and Rotunda are the extensive grounds of
the cemetery, rising into the wooded hills. As the city has grown
over the decades so has the cemetery, acquiring ever more tombs
and monuments, and once-open fields have been used for more
modest burials. These graves only last ten years, after which the
bodies are removed to make way for new burials. The bones
are put in storage beneath the Rotunda, but effectively these
humble dead are forgotten. It's a sobering thought that here in
death, as in life, money matters. In Staglieno only the expensive
and artistically impressive monuments stand in perpetuity. It's
as simple as that. If you can afford a grand tomb your name
will live forever; if not you get no more than a ten-year lease
on eternity. This alone explains why so many families spent
so much on their monuments – and some of these tombs were
colossally expensive.

I walk up winding and picturesque paths; all around are
tombs and chapels. This is like a garden city, and as you wander
through the beauty of nature you feel peace; the intention was
to make death seem less ugly, less fearful. Here the monuments,
unprotected from the weather, have an even more romantic
appeal as they lurk in leafy glades and emerge among vigorous
blooms and bushes. I come upon one particular work that takes

my breath away – it's a Symbolist tomb of the Chiarella family, again by the talented Luigi Orengo, and dates from 1910. On one side of its portal stands a naked woman carrying what appears to be a huge and roughly carved garland, a strange and ecstatic smile on her face. Above are other carved figures, also with enigmatic smiles –here death seems a friend, a thing of beauty to be welcomed as you would welcome the embrace of a lover. Death is the blessed release – whether to eternal life or oblivion.

This is one of the most astonishing sculpture museums on earth. The work is of the highest quality and preserves not only the names and likenesses of the dead, but also captures their very souls, reveals their hopes, beliefs and desires. Here people believed that if commemorated by the best art money could buy, their names and deeds would live forever.

Rituals and Mayan monuments in honour of the dead

Yaxha, Guatemala

Automatic gunfire. Where am I – Baghdad? No, I instantly remember, Guatemala City. It's 2.15 in the morning and I have to leave the hotel and be on the road to the airport by 4.30 for a flight to Flores. I hope the eruption of violence on the street has died down by then. It does, and all goes according to plan. We arrive at the northern Guatemalan town of Flores, a picturesque place located on an island set in a large lake, on the first leg of a two-pronged quest. The date is 29 October and in two days' time – on 1 November – a festival is celebrated here that in its rituals and imagery reflects both the ancient culture and religion of the region and the Roman Catholic beliefs introduced by the Spanish Conquistadors from the early 16th century.

The date of the festival is, perhaps, the most revealing thing about it. In Flores and the neighbouring villages the festival starts on the Christian Holy Day of All Saints and continues into the following All Souls' Day – so the whole event could be seen as a purely Christian celebration. But it's not – the festival also evokes memories of the older gods, in this region the gods of the Maya. So the festival – famed internationally as the Day of the Dead – is my first quest; the second is the Maya. To explore their history I plan to investigate the ruined 1,800-year-old city of Yaxha, which lies deep in rainforest, an hour's drive from Flores.

Flores is something of a tourist destination. The site of an ancient Mayan village, it was rebuilt by the Spaniards from the late 17th century and now comprises one- and two-storey buildings – many sporting charming classical detail and painted bright colours. It's organised on a regular grid of streets with a main plaza and church in the centre, and is the very model of a Spanish colonial town (see page 301). Flores contains many small hotels and scores of restaurants and bars, but most are generally pretty empty. The clue as to why was supplied by the gunfire that greeted me on my first night in Guatemala City and by the fact that even guards in restaurant car parks are armed with mean-looking shotguns. Guatemala is a dangerous land, with a ferocious murder rate, particularly of women. Part of the problem is that Guatemala lies on the illicit drug and emigrant route from South and Central America to the United States, and many of its people, desperately poor and in want, are drawn into the lawless underside of society. Also it's a land haunted – brutalised – by recent political and social upheavals. The terror and hatred caused by 36 years of civil war that started in 1960 simmers just below the surface, and goes a long way to explain the extreme levels of violence that characterise life and crime here.

All Saints' Day begins quietly. People are in the cemeteries visiting dead relatives and decorating graves with flowers. A few market stalls sell regalia useful for the celebrations, most of which are overtly Christian in character. I'm surprised. There are not the brightly coloured candy skulls or wooden skeletons that characterise the more flamboyant, and famous 'dia de muertos', the Day of the Dead celebrations in neighbouring Mexico. But the meaning is the same. On this day the souls of the dead return to the earth for a limited period, and can visit their villages and families. These souls, through the process of death, have acquired supernatural and prophetic powers, so their living relatives want to please, appease and, if possible, consult them about important family matters. As is central to the Catholic faith, it is assumed that the dead can intervene for the good of the living. But although the celebration takes place on a Christian feast day and reflects Christian belief, the festival is viewed very warily by the Catholic Church, which in fact does not officially recognise it as an act of Christian worship. But in one of the villages around the lake a happy compromise has been reached. The start of the festival – on the night of All Saints' – is celebrated in a Catholic church, and ancient skulls are venerated on the altar. But, to make this acceptable to Christian sensibilities, these skulls are classified as sacred Christian relics. No one knows for sure whom the skulls once belonged to – long-martyred Christian missionaries or Mayan shamans or warriors.

I board a small craft at Flores and, as the sun sets, glide across the wide and calm lake towards the village of San José, Petén. Here I will witness, in the village church, the service in honour of 'las Santas Calaveras'. After the service the skulls are, I hear, paraded through the village, from house to house, giving blessing to each home, calling and guiding the souls of the dead. Crossing the lake is like crossing the River Styx – from the land of the living to the land of the dead. Dramatically, and on cue, as I approach San José the sun finally sinks below the horizon and I arrive in glowing twilight.

The church is modern and full of light and bustle. On the altar sit three skulls, each with a cross drawn on the forehead. The service is long, but the singing, from a small female Mayan choir, is sweet. The sentiments expressed are generally conventionally Christian although one hymn refers to visitations from the souls of the dead. Then, as the time moves towards midnight and the dawn of All Souls' Day, one of the skulls is placed on a cushion and a procession forms. The skull is on its journey around the town. I join the loose collection of pilgrims as they make their way to the first house. We enter, all is ready. There is an offering table – an altar really – on which the skull is placed. It is surrounded by Christian images, portraits of Christ or the Virgin, but also bowls of food and even a bottle of beer. These are there to attract and nourish the souls of the dead – not much Christian doctrine about this. There is a cross next to the skull, but here even this image has a far from clear meaning. For Christians it is a crucifix, but for the Maya the cross was also a sacred symbol, much to the astonishment of early Christian missionaries, representing the Tree of Life connecting the three worlds – the heavens, the world of man (suggested by the horizontal cross-bar) and the underworld. It's all very ambiguous.

The occupants of the house are very kind to me, even though I'm a stranger invading a most personal ritual. They offer me food and hot chocolate. I thought the food and drink was for the dead, I say. Yes, but the dead enjoy the aroma while we enjoy the substance. Of course, the dead are nourished by the spiritual side of the food while I enjoy its more material aspect. I chat to the family after the procession has moved on, with the skull, to bless another house. This festival is to welcome and entertain dead ancestors, they admit, and they see it as a powerful connection with their Mayan ancestors and the old gods. Do they know when the dead are with them? I ask. They all smile, a silly question. The dead are always with us, but tonight they are especially welcome and able to be with the living. Yes, I understand. Here death is seen as a friend rather than the end, as part of life not the termination of life. Finally I leave and rejoin the procession. As the hours pass the procession gradually disperses. Eventually there are no more than small groups of people talking quietly in gardens, and some lying on the road, apparently asleep. I steal away as dawn breaks.

Today I want to go back to the roots of the Day of the Dead, to the Mayan civilisation that flourished in Central America from around AD 200, reached its peak – the so-called Classic Period – from around AD 600 until about 900 and then, dramatically and mysteriously, went into rapid and terminal decline. The Mayan civilisation – which was the earliest and most impressive in Central America – was composed of a number of City States. It is one of these that I am now going to see, the ruined and long-lost lakeside city of Yaxha.

The city lies beside a vast lake and was only discovered by a western explorer in 1904 when an eccentric Austrian named Teobert Maler stepped from a small boat and, to his amazement and great satisfaction, found mighty structures – step-pyramids, terraces and temples – lurking in the dense rainforest. The city was probably founded about 1,800 years ago but the major surviving structures date from the late Classic period. There are several groups dispersed over a large area but these reveal only the sacred and ceremonial part of the city – they are pyramid temples, observatories and palaces. The majority of the city has long gone, swallowed up and destroyed by voracious nature after the city was abandoned around a thousand years ago.

Mayan cities are haunted places full of mystery. Their civilisation was sophisticated yet prone to indulge in savage human blood sacrifice and their collapse and abandonment of their great cities complete and speedy. Especially tantalising is the evidence that the civilisation turned against itself, that the ordinary, long-exploited people attacked their demanding gods and rebelled violently against the elite Maya aristocracy that had so long ruled the land. Was this rebellion provoked by climate change, floods and starvation that revealed the impotence of the gods and the aristocracy? No one is now sure. All that's certain is that when the Spaniards arrived in the area during the 16th century most of the cities had long been abandoned – although Mayan civilisation, much diluted, did survive. And this civilisation was impressive – in fact, so impressive that it positively frightened the Spaniards. They had morally justified their conquest and pillage of the New World by claiming it was inhabited by savages, whose souls they were saving through forced conversion to Roman Catholicism. But the remains of the Mayan civilisation revealed this was not true. The Maya had a written language, laid out large regular cities that were marvels of civil engineering, constructed huge and beautifully wrought buildings, had mastered mathematics and astronomy, and had an incredibly accurate calendar, finely developed arts and crafts, and a theology that, eerily for the Spaniards, even seemed to embrace aspects and imagery of Christianity – such as the cross and notions about resurrection.

Now I come upon the first recognisable fragment of Mayan architecture. These are the structures that Maler discovered in 1904: a platform, step-pyramids and a large round, broken stone – an altar. I press on, for there are four groups of buildings I want to see and explore before nightfall, and these are some distance apart. There is the observatory, the twin pyramid complex, a small plaza defined by three closely set step-pyramids – surely a most visually dramatic creation – and the tallest pyramid in Yaxha. From here I will be able to survey the entire city site and the lake. I want to get to it by sunset.

Among the trees I see a huge mound, sprouting trees and undergrowth. This I recognise was once a great stone-built step-pyramid – now no more than a vast stump being rapidly reclaimed by nature. I look to its east and see a long, equally overgrown, flat-topped terrace running from north to south. I have arrived at one of the city's observatories. Theories abound about its function and the way astronomical observations were applied. But what is clear is that its design and orientation are very exact. From a position on the eastern staircase on the step-pyramid, and looking east towards the three temples that once stood spaced along the top of the terrace, an observer would, four times of the year, have had a very reassuring experience. Once, each year, the sun when travelling north would rise directly over the centre of the middle temple on 21 March – the vernal equinox. It would rise behind the northernmost corner of the north temple on 21 June, the summer solstice; behind the middle temple again on its way south on 23 September, the autumnal equinox; and, finally, behind the southernmost corner of the south temple on 21 December, the winter solstice. So this complex of structures marked the longest and shortest days of the year and the intermediate days when day and night are of equal duration. Quite how the Maya applied the information acquired from their observation of the heavens is not clear, but one thing they certainly did was to produce a phenomenally accurate calendar, and this they must have used to calculate practical things such as crop management and as a means of prophecy. It also seems to have given them the sense of creation as a great cycle with life following death as the dawn follows sunset – all part of a timeless continuum.

I press on through the rainforest looking for my next target. Suddenly the three-pyramid complex appears. These pyramids have been heavily restored so that their geometric form is clear. For the Maya number was all-important. It symbolised – perhaps even evoked – natural and supernatural powers, the world that had been, that was and that was to come. The fact that there are three pyramids placed together is revealing, for the number three was most significant – representing the world above, the world of man and the underworld. The number of steps on each pyramid must also have had meaning. The Maya believed there were 13 levels to the heavens above and nine levels of the underworld – so nine or 13 steps are usual. The Maya also saw the orientation of the world and the ordering of creation in colours. For example, yellow represented south, death and descent into the underworld, while white represented north and ascent to the heavens. So these mighty structures – made of well-cut limestone quarried, moved and faced with stone mallets without the use of pulleys or wheels – would probably have been painted in the primary symbolic colours. It would have been an astonishing sight – these geometrically refined, and brightly painted stairways to the heavens, each with a temple perched on its summit.

I press on again and reach a small plaza, dotted with trees. This is the site of the twin pyramids – an extraordinary place that represents the Mayan vision of the cosmos. The twin step-pyramids – now no more than crumbling mounds – stand on the east and west side of the plaza, so the sun would rise behind one and set behind the other. It's a journey from birth and life to death, defining a mighty arch through the heavens. At night, the Maya believed, the sun pursued a similar course through the underworld; only because of their religious rites to appease the gods would the cycle continue and the sun be reborn each morning. So this place is the Mayan universe in miniature – the sun passing through the heavens, the square plaza representing the flat world occupied with man and, on the south side, the gate to the underworld. All that survives of this is a long horizontal mound. Originally it had nine doors, symbols of the nine levels and the nine gods of the underworld. Inside are the remains of an altar and probably – at one time – the image of the ruler. This is the palace of ascent, from where the king would join his ancestors in the heavens. This complex of buildings was used to celebrate time – the completion of twenty 360-day years that were called katuns – and it also seems to have reinforced the status of the ruler as a divine being. The completion of katuns was worth celebrating because, according to Mayan calendric calculations, they are limited in number. Since, in their world view, creation moves in cycles, then there must be moments of death to allow rebirth. Translations of ancient Mayan texts reveal that their wise men worked out that the present universe was created 5,119 years ago and has nearly reached its course with the end, by means of a mighty flood, due on 12 December 2012. I await this date with interest.

As the sun begins its descent into the underworld I move to my last location. It's huge – the largest of Yaxha's step-pyramids, thrusting its tip above the surrounding foliage. I climb its staircase – there are nine steps, so this structure must have had to do with the underworld, with death. I reach the top – the view is spellbinding. I look down on the rainforest, see fragments of pyramids, and in the distance the huge lake. All is still, no branches move, there is just the occasional unearthly deep-throated moan of the howler monkeys. On the top of this pyramid are the substantial remains of a temple, with parts of its corbel vault surviving – a structural speciality of the Maya. This temple, now mostly open to the sky, would once have been dark and housed images of Mayan deities. And it was in places such as this that the most troubling rite of human sacrifice would have been enacted.

The person to be sacrificed – typically an enemy captured in battle – would be brought up the steps of the pyramid, their body painted blue, the colour of sacrifice. They would be held down over a convex-topped stone altar, then a sharp stone knife would be inserted below their ribcage, the heart ripped out and the spurting blood offered to the gods. The body of the victim was then thrown down the steps to the base of the pyramid where it would be flayed, and the ghastly, gory garment worn by the officiating priest who would dance in solemn manner around the crowd assembled to witness the ritual. Parts of the body of the victim would also have been preserved – bones or skull – and, if a brave warrior, the flesh eaten so that the prowess of the slain could be absorbed by the living. Shocking, of course, seemingly a taint on the civilisation of the Maya.

But nothing is what it seems, certainly not to modern eyes. The Maya were engaged in a battle to save the world, to ensure the sun would rise each day, and to do this they had to help, they had to feed the gods who were toiling on their behalf. And what the gods love above all, what gave them strength, was blood. For the Maya all creation shared a sacred life essence they called K'ul and in living beings this essence dwelt in precious blood. Nobles would give their own blood – and the nobler you were the better the blood. Queens would pierce their tongues with sharp thorns, and kings would thrust quills into their penises, and both would feed their blood to their gods. So human sacrifice was an act of love, not hate, not a reflection of contempt for human life but the most precious gift man could offer the gods; human blood was a vitalising liquid essential to the battle to preserve the world.

I reflect on all this as the sun goes down. I am filled with a sense of peace. I find this positive response to death – both here and in the Day of the Dead ceremonies – reassuring. Death as a means to continuing life, death seen not as an end but as an old and welcome friend, as part of the natural cycle of human existence. Here death does lose its sting. I witness the scene that the Maya would have watched, with trepidation, from this spot 1,200 years ago. The sun starts to die, sinking below the horizon. They would have wondered if the gods had been given the strength to ensure sunrise. I ponder a slightly different question. Has mankind yet inflicted enough damage on this hapless planet to ensure there will be no more sunrises? Perhaps global warming will mean that Mayan predictions about a cataclysmic flood come to pass. Full of foreboding I descend from this man-made sacred mountain. I must hurry, the forest is getting dark and I have a long journey ahead of me.

Ornate chapel housing the bones of thousands

Sedlec Ossuary, Czech Republic

The City of Kutna Hora in the Czech Republic is just a couple of hours' drive outside Prague. We arrive late in the afternoon and after passing through dreary suburbs find ourselves in an extraordinary place. Built on a medieval plan, this is a Baroque city that was once the most important in Bohemia after Prague. Its streets swirl up from the site of its now lost city walls to a cathedral dedicated to St Barbara, the patron saint of architects and miners – a reminder that the city's fortunes were based on silver won from the ground on which it stands. I'm on my way to the small town of Sedlec, a few miles outside Kutna Hora, to see a chapel which, in many ways, is the ultimate shrine of death in the Christian world. I'm told it contains the remains of 40,000 people – interred in the vicinity of the chapel since the late 13th century – arranged in a breathtakingly ornamental manner. In this chapel, apparently, death is not only triumphant but also beautiful and a wonder to behold.

The European Christian attitude to death and the disposal of the body is a most peculiar thing. It's a mix of ideas, seemingly culled from other more ancient religions, which seek to combine strange, contradictory, exotic – not to say supernatural – notions about resurrection and judgement. All three of the religions that take Abraham as their seminal prophet – Judaism, Islam and Christianity – believe in a Last Judgement, when the dead undergo resurrection; the wicked are consigned to hell and the good to heaven – a belief that makes essential the preservation of the bones of the body. Christians hold this belief in a more explicit and powerful form because Christ himself underwent resurrection. So the belief in resurrection after death is fundamental to the belief in Christ and Christian faith.

In the past the scriptures were taken more literally than they are now, and the preservation of the body after death was seen as something of prime importance. Quite simply it was feared that if the body were lost, resurrection would be impossible. With no resurrection there would be no judgement and so, for the just, no chance of paradise, no eternal life with Christ. For medieval man the death and dispersal or loss of the body meant the death and loss of the soul. The only way to ensure the safe and satisfactory preservation of the body was its interment or burial after death within a site that had been consecrated or blessed to keep evil spirits at bay, to stop the devil purloining your mortal remains. Within this consecrated site the body could be kept intact within a tomb, or it could be moved, its bones stacked or disposed in any way that was convenient. God, it was reckoned, was clever enough to reassemble a dispersed skeleton in the correct order at the time of the Last Judgement. All that mattered was that the bones remained within the protected consecrated enclosure and that they were treated with respect. And it's the architectural expression of this conviction that the chapel at Sedlec is all about.

In 1142 a Cistercian monastery was founded in Sedlec and in 1278 its abbot, while in Jerusalem, collected earth from what he believed to be the site of Christ's crucifixion. Back at Sedlec he scattered this earth on the monastic burial ground and, by so doing and by popular consensus, transformed a part of Sedlec into the Holy Land. This had great advantages for the monastery and for the local population. It was accepted by all Christians in the Middle Ages that pilgrimage could bring real spiritual advantages. Visiting a sacred site or venerating the relic of a saint secured reduction of those years in purgatory that all souls must spend, no matter how good, after death and before judgement. A pilgrimage to the Holy Land was the desire of every Christian, so to be buried at Sedlec was viewed by the population of Bohemia as the equivalent of a pilgrimage to Jerusalem and a real blessing.

For the monastery the desire for burial in its holy grounds brought fame, pilgrims and wealth. The monastery became rich, an elegant chapel was built in its famed graveyard and a huge cathedral rose nearby. Tens of thousands of people were interred in this Holy Land during the next 140 years, including victims of the Black Death, which swept through the area in the 1340s. The small graveyard – which could not be extended for liturgical reasons – could only cope with the demand by graves being constantly emptied and the bones stacked in orderly piles in the charnel house, or ossuary, beneath the chapel to await resurrection. Then, quite suddenly, this peaceful, profitable and orderly machine of Christian death and resurrection was overtaken by calamitous events.

In the 1420s, moves to reform the Roman Catholic Church in Bohemia led to fighting between the followers of an executed cleric called Jan Hus and the conservative authority of the Holy Roman Empire. The Hussite Wars, as the struggle was called, lasted more than 15 years, and led to violence and bloodshed as the Roman Catholic Church fought to impose its will on a people who wanted to free themselves of much of the ceremony and power of the Catholic Church. Crusades were launched against the Hussites, whom hysterical Catholics declared heretics, but eventually an uneasy accommodation was reached, for the Hussites proved too strong militarily for the Catholic Church to crush. But during the savage fighting such rich and powerful Catholic establishments as the monastery at Sedlec were natural targets for Hussite wrath, and in 1421 it was plundered and the cathedral gutted by fire. When the fighting eventually ended in the mid-1430s Sedlec lay abandoned. The bodies of those killed in the fighting went to swell the population of its burial ground, but the golden age of the monastery could not be regained, for the world had changed.

The cathedral remained a gutted shell for nearly 200 years but the monks stayed on, although in greatly straitened circumstances. Even if the fashion to be buried in Sedlec's Holy Land was over, the monastery retained a sacred duty to the thousands of Christian bodies – and by implication souls – in its care. What was to be done? In 1511 a monk started to salvage and arrange the bones, estimated to be the remains of 40,000 people, packed into various monastic buildings. It's the bones preserved by this conscientious cleric that form the basis of the weird world that I am now about to visit.

I arrive at Sedlec and see a small medieval chapel presiding over an equally small and neat-looking cemetery, packed with closely set and generally ugly 20th-century tombstones. Before entering I take a look at the surroundings. I'm curious to see what they can tell me about the monastery whose fortunes, I know, finally revived during the 17th century. This was the result of a traumatic event in Bohemian history – the defeat in 1620 of the Czechs, whose Hussite beliefs had led them to become part of the Protestant Reformation, by Roman Catholic forces at the Battle of the White Mountain. This led to the re-imposition of Roman Catholic authority in Bohemia and, more significantly, to the crushing of the Czech spirit of independence. As a result of this Catholic resurgence, the Cistercian monastery at Sedlec was re-established and new buildings erected from the late 17th century. But now there is not much evidence of this renaissance. Most of the buildings created at this time have gone. But the cathedral survives, its medieval outer walls enclosing an interior designed by Jan Santini – the outstanding architect of early 18th-century Bohemia – who worked in an inspired Baroque idiom fused with Gothic. His work can be weird and original, but the interior of the cathedral is not particularly gripping. It's vast and empty, and the Gothic detail is thin. The adjoining monastic buildings are extensive, in good repair, and are currently occupied by a tobacco company that until recently entertained hopes of expanding into the cathedral. Oh dear, such is the thrusting and materialistic nature of much of newly independent Eastern Europe. I'm surprised by this extraordinary attempt to turn an ancient cathedral into offices, and ask my local fixer to explain. Is not Bohemia now a devout Roman Catholic country? He smiles and explains that it was the diocese that wanted to sell the cathedral! Amazing. Yes, he says, Bohemia is, in theory, a Roman Catholic land but the people here are by nature atheists. So if most Czechs are unbelievers, the survival of this bizarre Christian shrine to death is even more odd. What can the people here now really think of it?

I walk back to the graveyard, past the remains of an 18th-century mansion that once belonged to the powerful Schwartzenberg family, who acquired the monastic property when the Cistercian monastery was finally dissolved in the 1780s. As I get nearer the chapel I see that it is indeed medieval but its lower portion, its extensive crypt, is later. There's been some massive structural manipulation here, which probably explains why the front elevation of the chapel is leaning dramatically to one side. I look at the detailing on the wall of the projecting crypt. Of course, all of this is the work of the early 18th century, of Santini. First I go to the upper world of the chapel. I walk up a flight of steps and enter a splendid Gothic space full of light streaming through tall arched windows. This is all to do with life, with resurrection. Below, in the crypt, is the world of the dead. And it's this world I'm interested in. I leave the light, descend to ground level and enter the most bizarre world. Everywhere are human bones, thousands and thousands of them, and they are arranged to delight the eye and to amuse. I pass festoons of bones, skulls stacked one upon another with long bones hanging below them. I recognise this design – they're parodies of the Baroque image of cherubs, putti, faces floating above wings. What on earth is going on here?

The answer is complex. When Santini was commissioned in about 1700 to rebuild and extend the crypt he created an astonishing Baroque theatre of death. He pushed the crypt out in all four directions from below the chapel, gave his new vaults simple Gothic details and lit them with high, oval windows, set just above ground level. And what these windows illuminate are pyramids of bones, neatly ordered – large bones at the bottom, medium-sized bones in the middle and skulls at the top. When Santini found the derelict chapel he discovered it packed with the bones stored there during the early 16th century. The solution he struck upon was to turn the bones into ornament – but ornament loaded with symbolism and meaning. He rearranged the bones to create six mighty pyramidal piles, each about ten metres high, which were intended to represent the bells that would toll at the time of the Last Judgement to raise the dead. In 1741 a later theatrically minded designer created four obelisks within the crypt, each embellished with tiers of skulls and topped by cherubs, carved in wood, which blow trumpets – reminders of the trumpets that will sound at the end of time. The meaning of these bony monuments is pretty clear. They speak of the transience of life; they are intended to remind us that one day soon we will be thus, dead and awaiting judgement; they extol us to behave well during life to avoid punishment after death. What's astonishing is that these skeletal monuments were created in the 18th century, when it had been long established that individuals favoured individual graves, places that would serve as their memorials and keep their skeletons intact until Judgement Day. The display of bones, mixed together and grouped by type and size rather than by person, is entirely medieval in feel – and was only possible to create in the early 18th century because the bones belonged to anonymous individuals whose skeletons had long been dismembered. This all adds to the uncanny nature of the place, the bones of the long dead being used to carry a message to the living, to hint at the future.

But this 18th-century manipulation of the remains of the dead is nothing in comparison with what happened in the ossuary in the late 19th century. The Schwartzenbergs decided to tidy things up and in the late 1860s employed a local woodcarver named Frantisec Rint, who seems to have been overcome with the powerful atmosphere of the place. He dismantled two of Santini's symbolical bells and used the bones, which he whitened with bleach, to create a variety of startling embellishments. He formed a vast chandelier, which incorporated an example of every bone in the human body, festoons of skulls, and a huge symbolic chalice and monstrance of bones. Perhaps most disconcerting of all is a vast coat of arms of the Schwartzenberg family which incorporates the heraldic device of a bird picking out the eye of a captive Muslim Turk.

The chapel is expensive to maintain but to judge by the coachloads of tourists, it earns a small fortune. Death, in this form, is compellingly attractive. I ask the priest why he thinks so many people flock here. Is there a spiritual power that attracts them, is it a sobering experience that reminds them of mortality? He smiles. No, most come here just to gawk. But what do I think? To me it's a reminder of a time in the Christian West when death was fully part of life, when the dead had lessons to teach the living and were a reminder to lead a moral life. And this display of bones – grim or amusing depending on your point of view – reflects an open and positive attitude to death. In Rint's creations humble bones are transformed into works of art that reveal the wonder and engineering beauty of the human body; here art was created from the dead to inspire the living. This is far healthier than the West's current relationship with mortality where, more likely than not, bodies are speedily cremated as if to hide the evidence of death. Yes, much better to become familiar with death for, like it or not, we're all going to have to deal with it one day.

Building for eternity to achieve immortality through architecture

Hatshepsut's Mortuary Temple, Luxor, Egypt

I arrive at Luxor just as the sun is setting over the west bank of the Nile. This was once known as Thebes and in front of me is what the Ancient Egyptians regarded as the land of the dead, the place where the sun sets – where it dies – each night. Just before the sun rises in the morning I will cross the Nile, to the land of the dead, to see the tomb and mortuary temple of one of the most intriguing and mysterious characters in Egyptian history – a woman who ruled Egypt nearly 3,500 years ago, but as a man, a pharaoh. This ruler's birth name was Maat-Ke-Re, but she is far better known by her throne name – Hatshepsut.

Next morning I arrive at the tomb; its entrance is really no more than a large hole in the ground at the base of the hill that masks the valley from the east. The tomb was evidently never completed – the walls are rough hewn, no sign of paint or plaster, the floor is covered with a thick layer of dust and rubble – and the descent is very steep. The burial chamber lies about 200 metres below the entrance and the passage meanders as if its builders were trying to find something. Finally I reach a low rock-cut lintel. We crawl beneath its crumbling surface. This is the first burial chamber – it looks like a natural cavern. In one corner is a narrow ramp leading to a much smaller chamber where Hatshepsut's sarcophagus was discovered in 1902, together with that of her father, Tuthmosis I.

When found the sarcophagi were empty. They have been long

removed from the tomb, as have other fragments including canopic jars (vessels in which certain organs from the body were preserved), a magical shawabati figure that was probably an image of Hatshepsut, and a stone vessel inscribed with Hatshepsut's name. So there is little to see, but I wanted to experience the last earthly resting place of this powerful and enigmatic woman. And the search for her only starts here. The tomb builders, as they wound deeper underground, had indeed been looking for something, for a spot immediately beneath a structure some hundreds of metres above my head. As I squat in the burial chamber I am below the inner portions of the mortuary temple that Hatshepsut constructed in the bright sun above. Both tomb and temple were clearly intended to work together, to ensure the survival and safe journey of Hatshepsut's soul after death, to allow her to live for eternity.

The mortuary temple is my next stop. I clamber out of the tomb and climb over the hill that rises above it. On the eastern side of this hill, indeed partly built into it, is Hatshepsut's temple. Its prime purpose was to preserve Hatshepsut's name and memory after death, to ensure her perpetual life. Egyptians believed that as long as a name lived so did the soul – the essential spirit and life-force – and if a name were destroyed or forgotten all would be lost. And to live after death the soul – the spirit – had to be sustained. This is, indeed, the architecture of eternity, for mortuary temples were designed and built to last and this particular example is one of the most dramatic and architecturally exciting structures in Egypt. The conception of the building – a series of courts and terraces moving ever higher and penetrating into the heart of the sacred hill out of which it seems to grow – is magnificent, its execution is flawless and it retains tremendous presence and power despite the fact that much is missing, and much that is now visible was reconstructed in the last 100 years or so.

The temple now consists of a large forecourt, almost square in plan, that was originally entered via a pylon – a monumental gateway – long since gone. At the west end of this first forecourt is a row of piers, of rectangular section, that shelter a gallery containing fragments of wall paintings and hieroglyphs. And set between these piers is a wide ramp that rises up to a second courtyard. This courtyard is a rectangle of Golden Section proportion with the long side set parallel with the courtyard below. Along its west side is also a row of piers, again sheltering a gallery. But at the north and south side of this gallery are two structures that, although integrated into the architecture of the courtyard, are also distinctly different. The structure to the south is a temple to Hathor and it is approached through piers set slightly forward of the main row. Hathor was the great nurturing goddess, often shown in the form of a cow or as a beautiful female with cow horns and disc set on her head. She is the mortuary goddess of Thebes, the personification of the western hill below which this temple sits. As a great emblem of female power – an honoured wife and mother of divine kings – Hathor had particular meaning for Hatshepsut. Within this shrine – now open to the sky – are columns that terminate in a massive female head, each the image of Hathor.

The structure to the north of the gallery is a shrine to Anubis – the jackal-headed god of mummification – and its architecture is quite different; instead of piers it has fluted columns of round section. I stand and stare. All this is astonishing. The bold simplicity of the architecture of this temple, the way the elemental post and lintel construction is honestly expressed, the minimalism, makes it so timeless, so modern. And these columns suggest this temple has much to do with the origin of architecture, or of classical architecture anyway, because their form and detail are clearly the ancestors of the Greek Doric Order.

From this second courtyard another ramp rises to the north, and leads to a narrow terrace. Here the square section columns were faced with giant statues of Osiris – the god of the underworld, the Lord of the Dead – but few survive intact. Portraits of Osiris are standard in mortuary temples and, although the statues here are archetypal, they were meant to represent Hatshepsut. In these statues she is both pharaoh and god, both the person whose soul is to be judged after her death and the judge who decides whether or not she is justified, is 'true of voice' or to be condemned to oblivion.

Walking through a temple is a journey – some go in quest of their soul or the gods. I'm going in quest of the soul and spirit of another. What can this place tell me about this strange woman who ruled against the odds, against tradition? She was the eldest daughter of the Pharaoh Tuthmosis I and Queen Ahmose yet claimed to be the daughter of Amun-Re. She married her half-brother Tuthmosis II and was guardian of her stepson and nephew Tuthmosis III. After the death of her husband she initially ruled as Royal Regent for Tuthmosis III, yet soon overturned this arrangement and for about 20 years ruled alone, as pharaoh. All of this is extraordinary. It challenged the Egyptian sense of divine order and harmony, of truth and justice, what they called Maat. According to this view it was the duty of the pharaoh to maintain the correct order of the universe – established by the gods – as part of the continuous battle against chaos and dark malevolent forces. So divine balance and symmetry were essential – the rule of a king and a queen was regarded as an expression of correct order, of Maat, as fundamental as the division of humanity into men and women, as the division of the seasons into summer and winter, as night and day, as darkness and light. For a woman to rule as a man, without a queen, was extraordinary, it was a challenge on Maat. How did Hatshepsut do it? Was the claim to divine parentage enough?

As I walk across the courtyard I realise that part of the answer lies in the design of the temple itself. As if to compensate for the irregularity of her position Hatshepsut ensured that the place enshrining her memory is a stupendous monument to Maat. The design proclaims serene harmony and divine symmetry dominating raw nature, the primordial chaos represented by the rough and undulating cliff face that wraps around the temple site. The temple is Maat personified. It's an instrument of balance, creating order and truth to counteract chaos. The sense of harmony rings down the centuries; it's eternal – I feel it still.

But mortuary temples were not only to do with spiritual power and rebirth, they were also places in which those who made them declared their worldly achievements and revealed their pedigree; they can be very political places and Hatshepsut's temple is no exception. Within the gallery, and set behind the piers of this second court, is a series of scenes calculated to impress the viewers with the legitimacy and worth of Hatshepsut's rule. In the northern portion are wall paintings that portray Hatshepsut's divine birth and election to the throne. The paintings are now much damaged but it's still possible to make out Ahmose – Hatshepsut's mother – being visited by the god Amun-Re. But decency is maintained because the god comes in the guise of the queen's husband, Tuthmosis I. We are told Amun-Re wanted to create a pharaoh for the throne and when he had accomplished the task he revealed to the queen the name of the 'Divine majesty' to whom she would give birth and who would 'reign benevolently over the whole earth' – none other, of course, than Hatshepsut. Finally we follow – cartoon fashion – her subsequent history until enthroned and acknowledged by Amun-Re as his true child. Powerful stuff – to challenge Hatshepsut's right to rule would have been seen as tantamount to a challenge to Amun-Re himself.

I move up to the next stage of the temple, to its most secret and holy places. I walk up the second ramp and into the upper court. I turn to the left to see the mortuary complex that includes a shrine to Hatshepsut and to her earthly father. I enter a room, partly cut into the cliff face, and see an amazing sight. The walls are covered with tiers of marching figures, each holding an offering. It was in this room that the spirit of Hatshepsut was to be sustained in the underworld by regular prayer, portions of food, and the aroma of incense. At the far end of the room are the remains of an ornamental door – but it can never have led anywhere, it's a false door, a door not to the material but to the celestial world, it's the door through which Hatshepsut's spirit would have entered and left her mortuary temple, the door through which it would have moved to and from her tomb almost immediately below.

Now nothing is left for me to explore but the inner shrine of the temple. This shrine, dedicated to Hatshepsut's 'father' Amun-Re, formed a key part in one of the great annual religious celebrations of Thebes when, during the 'Beautiful Festival of the Valley' Amun-Re's barque – his celestial boat through which as the life-giving Sun he moved across the sky – was carried in procession from his great temple at Karnak to this sanctuary. Hatshepsut's move to associate the great sun god of Thebes with her mortuary temple was, of course, a brilliant political move. But as I contemplate the entrance to this shrine Amun-Re is departing – the sun is setting. I want to enter this inner shrine as it was intended to be entered, to enter it with the first sunrays at dawn, with the energy of Amun-Re himself.

I'm in Luxor just a couple of days before the winter solstice – the moment when one solar year dies and another is born – and I'm intrigued to see how this particular arrangement of the heavens affects the temple. I return just before dawn and am not disappointed. As I walk up the ramps towards the inner shrine the sun rises behind my back – exactly behind it! As I approach Amun-Re's shrine, narrow and set deep in the cliff face, it is aglow with a golden light and its interior is illuminated in a spectacular manner. The rays of the rising sun penetrate straight and true, through the entrance into the upper court, to the centre of the shrine. I can now see clearly the site of Amun-Re's altar, and where his image and his barque would have been. The sight must have been stunning – the image and interior, strongly coloured and embellished with gold leaf, would have sparkled and pulsated with life. I reach the threshold of the temple and look back, towards the sun, along the route of the long-lost avenue leading to the Nile and to the great temple of Karnak. Of course, Hatshepsut's temple and that at Karnak are linked powerfully by the sun – in fact as I look east I realise that the sun is rising between the obelisks and the massive pylon that Hatshepsut built at Karnak. She wanted to leave her mark on this sacred landscape – to define the points where the sun rose and where it set, to link her mortuary temple and that of Karnak by a long east–west axis that represents the path of the sun and its energising rays.

I now enter the glowing shrine. In the ante-room is a damaged image of Hatshepsut and her daughter. This daughter played the role of queen to her mother's pharaoh – she was her symbolic wife. Presumably Hatshepsut embraced this subterfuge because she recognised that her behaviour challenged Maat. It was an attempt to restore order. And then there are images of food – supplies for the journey to the underworld. In here even images of Amun-Re have been damaged, attacked just over 100 years later during the reign of the pharaoh Akhenaten who attempted to replace the ancient gods of Egypt with what he argued was the one and only true God – the Aten.

Now I enter the inner portion of the shrine. On one wall is an image of Hatshepsut which has miraculously survived – in the form of a pharaoh – venerating Amun-Re. And above it is her cartouche – damaged but recognisable. It's her birth name,

Maat-Ka-Re. So all the earthly remains of Hatshepsut were not destroyed. But she has dwelt for thousands of years in the underworld without offerings or prayers. She must be famished. I burn some incense below her image to offer nourishment. Hatshepsut lives because she is remembered. This great female pharaoh – this strong-willed, powerful woman who ruled in a man's world – was not consigned to oblivion and her enemies did not triumph.

Ultimate city of death
on the banks of the Ganges
Varanasi, Uttar Pradesh, India

I arrive by road at the place that Hindus believe is the sacred centre of the earth. Varanasi is, say Hindus, where creation started. The exact site is now marked by the Lotus Pool, said to have been dug by Vishnu – one of the great Hindu trilogy of gods – as his first act of creation. Displayed here are his footprints, and they are now a major focus for pilgrims. These are the emblem of the continuing presence of the god.

I rumble through the outskirts of the town – it is congested and full of life and bustle. Looking at this scene you would not believe that Varanasi is the ultimate city of death. This is where Hindus come to die, or at least where they long to have their bodies cremated and their ashes scattered in the Ganges. Quite simply, if this happens, the soul achieves moksha – the release from the eternal and often painful cycle of birth, death and rebirth on earth. To die here means salvation; it's a joyful event that makes life worth living. In fact, even to make the pilgrimage to Varanasi and to bathe in the Ganges is a great blessing which, I'm told, not only washes away past and present sins, but is also a cure against future wrong-doings. Quite a promise – no wonder the city is packed with hopeful visitors.

I've come here to see the rituals associated with these extraordinary rites, and to experience the architecture that has evolved in this holy city. I pass through the cantonment area and see languishing buildings from the Raj, a splendid, now abandoned early 19th-century Anglican church – St Mary's I'm told – and stuccoed and arcaded bungalows. I pass Hindu temples and shrines, and cross the famed pilgrimage route – the Panchkrashi which runs for 50 kilometres and contains 108 Shiva shrines. It defines the sacred centre of Varanasi, stretching from the River Varuna to the River Asi, which both empty into the Ganges. And, at regular intervals, I pass bodies. They are shrouded in bright cloth, decked with flowers, and some are being carried in biers held high by family and mourners. Others are strapped to the top of vehicles. All are making their way to one of the cremation sites which border the river, and virtually all will soon be consumed by fire. Many did not die in Varanasi, but just to be cremated here is a blessing.

Then, close behind a trail of bodies, I reach the tighter grain of streets and alleys that run down to the river itself and serve the ghats – the stepped terraces and buildings lining the water's edge. These have many different names and their functions and clientele vary slightly. Some serve particular castes or social or religious groups, others different regions of the country, but they all offer unity with the great goddess that is the River Ganges, and include the sites on which the earthly remains of humans are turned to ashes and where their souls are liberated. According to Hindu belief the river – the 'river of heaven' – is a manifestation of the goddess Ganga, and its water represents the active energy of Shiva. Hindus believe that Ganga condescended to fall to earth from the world above and her falling form was caught in the hair of Shiva – to prevent her devastating impact on the earth – and spread elegantly as energy-charged water through the heart of India from the Himalayan mountains to the Bay of Bengal. The ghats themselves are a somewhat bizarre architectural mix. There are nearly 80 of them along the bank, between the rivers Asi and Varuna, and although Varanasi itself is ancient – some claim it as one of the oldest cities in the world – the ghats are relatively new, none more than 300 years old. They reflect different regional styles – those built by the Maharajas of Banares and of Mysore look princely, some with ornamental water gates now set high and dry but practical when the Ganges is in flood. Others pack a strong visual punch – the Panchaganga ghat is modern-looking and functional with its bold red and white livery and a simple flight of steps forming a strong abstract composition and booths for bathers set along the water's edge.

I have to move away from the river now for I have a date to keep, a date of a rather disturbing kind – it's a date with death. One of the more peculiar institutions of this city is the Dying House and I'm on my way to one now. The proposition is straightforward. Since it's highly beneficial to die and to be cremated within the sacred inner realm of Varanasi – or Kashi as the Hindus call it – as defined by the three rivers and the pilgrim route of the Panchkrashi, many come here to do just that. The sick, the seemingly terminally ill, are brought here by their families and – if from far away – all lodge in a Dying House to await the end. I'm going to one of these establishments to see how the business of securing release from this world is conducted. It will be a strange experience for a Westerner. We dread and fear death as something almost unnatural, something that is not talked about. But here death is, in many respects, a joyous occasion if it takes place in the right way. The family is here to ensure that its loved one is shown devotion, thanks and respect.

I walk through narrow, congested streets to the place of departure. Among this vibrant, noisy and boisterous humanity I can't imagine what awaits me – what bizarre contrast of emotions, of atmosphere, am I about to experience? I feel almost fear, certainly trepidation. Finally I arrive at my destination – it's called the Muktibhavan. The house – stuccoed and designed in an odd classical style peculiar to India – is quietly mouldering;

appropriate I suppose. As I get nearer I notice the date 1904 above the main door. It's an interesting piece of work, built as a pilgrims' lodging house and in the 1950s turned into a Dying House by the wealthy Delhi-based Dalmia family. It now operates as a charitable trust. As I enter I'm approached by a smiling man who asks me if he can be of assistance. I explain my mission and he tells me that he would be delighted if I came to visit his mother, currently dying in a nearby room. There is no doubting his sincerity, or the fact that he is genuinely pleased to see me; it's as if he's been expecting me. I enter the shady room and I'm greeted by a scene that is beautiful and memorable. Light falls from one side window to create an extraordinary chiaroscuro effect. In the centre lies an old lady, on a low bed, asleep or comatose, her long, thick grey hair thrown back and a puja mark on her forehead. Around her – supporting her – are her family. They smile and welcome me. I join the group, forming an outer ring around the dying woman. I am not an interloper; I have suddenly and quite unexpectedly become part of the scene. Now I'm beginning to feel as if I was expected – ordained to witness this significant event.

The son tells me what is going on. I have arrived at the most astrologically significant moment of his mother's sojourn in the Dying House. This is the auspicious moment to conduct a key ceremony, one that invokes the presence of the god Shiva who will come to grant the gift of moksha and one that ensures the soul a safe passage across the river of death. The family are sombre, solemn but not sad, nor fearful of the supernatural process, the ritual, in which they are involved – the passing on of a soul. A puja takes place, prayers are chanted, the dying woman is anointed with sacred water from the Ganges, a flame is passed over an altar and prasad – sanctified food – offered to all. A calf is brought into the room caparisoned in yellow. It is a sacred animal, of momentous importance in the ritual – but does not seem fully to realise it. It lolls its head, turns in circles and finally presents its posterior to the dying woman. The family all laughs. In fact, this is just where they want the creature, for the tail is put into the limp hand of the patient and prayers are said. The calf is to be the guide and safeguard of the woman's soul on its way to unity with God.

I talk with the son of the dying woman. He tells me how fortunate I was to arrive at such a spiritually charged moment and how lucky I am to be in Varanasi, with my mind and body intact. I must have done much good in past lives to merit this boon. I am very lucky and his family honoured by my presence. They all beam and I smile back. In a way I am now part of their family since I have, by fortune, shared in such a momentous family event. I know they all believe this was meant to be, that all our lives – past lives even – have been leading to this event, that we have all met before. It's intoxicating stuff, the thought that nothing in life is chance, but all is ordained, determined by karma – by the inexorable law of cause and effect. He may be right, but I pull myself back from this charming, tempting abyss of mysticism and ask more mundane questions. I discover that his mother has been here for nine days, that she had a brain haemorrhage and they are breaking with tradition and are not just giving her holy water from the Ganges but also giving some nourishment by means of a tube inserted into her nose. This could prolong life for some time, I suggest. He explains that if she does not die soon, or recovers slightly, they will take her home. This is not the right time. And if she dies, what then? Then we will have done, will do, our duty. My mother looked after me and now I will look after her. We will show her our love, he says. She's a lucky woman, I realise, to die in such a manner. Few in the West enjoy such honour and support from their families at this moment of crisis. I ask about the disposal of the body. This I know is a key moment because at the moment of death the deceased becomes two things – the body a rapidly decomposing and polluting vessel that has to be disposed of in a reverential manner, and the soul a potentially troubled and troublingly malevolent ghost unless guided correctly, unless farewells are properly said. The latter process has already started but what of the former? He explains that his mother's body will be washed, ornamented with her jewels, and basil placed in her mouth. She will be wrapped in a shroud, and her garlanded bier covered with sparkling fabric and carried to the cremation ghat. Little more than three hours after death she will be ashes. I must now witness this final act. I plunge back into the life and turmoil of the city streets and make my way to the Ganges. I'm going to board a craft and make my way to the main cremation ghat.

As I near the river bodies pass me thick and fast – some accompanied by musicians, some just with fabric covering, others with architectural decoration concealing the body. All are travelling fast, carried by eight or so mourners – and all are heading to the river. Death is big business in Varanasi – it's a way of life for many. As I get nearer the river I see an increasing number of shops and stalls selling the paraphernalia of death, the essential trappings for the correct disposal of the body. I stop at one to chat to the chap squatting on the counter. He shows me plain white shrouds, glittering fabrics incorporating golden threads, packets of ghee – clarified butter – used to anoint the body on the fire and a useful accelerant to get the fire blazing, a jar of sandal wood – a small piece of which is added to each pyre as an offering and to make a pleasant aroma. As we talk bodies rush past – I'm told about 80 are burnt on the main cremation ghat each day. Here fires burn daily throughout the year suggesting – when bodies burnt on other ghats are included – that around 40,000 corpses are burnt in Varanasi each year.

I leave the stall and board my boat. My plan is first to observe the main cremation area, beside the Manikarnika ghat, from the water and then to land for a closer look. The cremation ground comes into view. It consists of a central flight of steps and various terraces cascading down to the river's edge. Behind rise the towers of temples. On the lower terrace, pyres are burning, and in readiness, on an upper terrace, smoke is rising languidly from a pile of ashes – here a soul has just recently found release. On the water's edge is a tangle of old pyres, garlands and mounds of ash – still smoking. A new body is arriving, to join one already deposited on the stairs. Both are draped in glistening fabric. The new arrival is rushed down to the Ganges and almost fully immersed in the water. We row nearer still, until only a couple of metres from the bank. Now I see telling details – a dog is picking through the ashes and waste, presumably looking for the odd bone; a cow seems to be doing the same. They should find lean pickings. After the cremation, bones that might have survived the flames – ribcage or pelvis – are cast into the river, along with most of the ashes. Now one of the newly arrived bodies is being carried to its pyre – a pile of neatly laid logs – with good ventilation gaps, that reaches nearly a metre high. The shrouded body is placed on top, a few logs laid around it, and a large white-clad and shaven-headed fellow steps forward. He's under instruction – clearly the head mourner. He throws ghee onto the body, is brought a flame, ignites a bundle of straw and starts to walk clockwise around the pyre thrusting the burning brand into gaps in the log pyre and igniting fuel within. Soon all is ablaze. The head mourner retires and the family stands around. Now I land to get an even closer look, and climb to the higher terraces. Here business is brisk indeed. What a sight confronts me. It could be an image of hell – four bodies, in different states of combustion, lie among flames in front of me. One head is shrouded in scorched fabric, another is protruding from the flames with beard smouldering and skin blistering.

But, of course, this is really an image of paradise – souls being dispatched to a better existence.

I walk away from the cremation ground. I need to look at some architecture. Just to the south is the Manikarnika ghat with Vishnu's Lotus Pool. Here images of life replace images of death and fiery disposal. Cows and buffaloes loll on the steps along with pilgrims and, at the water's edge, there is a small temple, with a fine spire. The pool itself, a step tank, stands just above flood-level. It's surprisingly small and on one side are Vishnu's pair of footprints – carved out of a slab of stone – with an image of Shiva and Parvati nearby. So this, for Hindus, is where creation started – the equivalent of the Jews' foundation stone of the world, buried within the mound of Solomon's Temple in Jerusalem, just behind the Wailing Wall, where they believe God started His creation. Well, I've seen both now and both are extraordinary places, but this site has something extra going for it. It's not only the beginning and the end – the Alpha and Omega of creation – but is also, say Hindus, the only place that will survive the end of time. It's a divine realm, more of heaven than of earth.

Dusk is drawing near and I return to the river to see the sun setting behind the ghats. This has been an astonishing day, a day that challenges all Western conceptions of death and disposal of the body. Here death is not sad and secret but joyful and public. Varanasi teaches that death is only part of life, not the end of life. It's an explosion of emotion set within a thrilling architectural setting. Here I have confronted death – quite literally walked with death – and now see it differently. In Varanasi it has an almost sensual visual beauty, a powerful and positive meaning – it's a journey not to fear but to embrace.

4

Disaster

Journey to the centre of the earth to find crumbling beauty
Minaret at Jam, Afghanistan

e arrive at Kabul airport one afternoon in August 2007. I'm with BBC producer Graham Cooper and cameraman Hugh Hughes – both much practised in the art of working with the military in hostile environments. With us is David Holley, a former soldier and now a BBC security advisor. We are here in Afghanistan to see one of the most remote, inaccessible, and beautiful, structures on earth – one of Afghanistan's historically and architecturally most important buildings – the almost mythic 12th-century Minaret at Jam. Few have seen it – indeed it was only rediscovered by the outside world in the 1950s. It has never been filmed before and is one of the finest Islamic structures in the world. It is also one of the most threatened, a victim of its remote setting and the decades of conflict that have benighted Afghanistan.

The Minaret, at 60 metres the second tallest in the world, has suffered centuries of neglect. It has had its foundations undermined by the river on which it stands so that it now leans at a precarious angle, and in recent years it has been a victim of looting. UNESCO, which in 2002 declared the Minaret and its setting a World Heritage Site, has carried out some emergency repair work and constructed a protective river wall, but the deteriorating security situation in the country has kept UNESCO away for long periods. Although stabilised the Minaret remains under dire threat. I want to see this wondrous and magical construction and report on its current condition. But the journey is a tough one, for much of it has to be done by road and they are in poor condition and in parts potentially very dangerous, with travellers threatened by bandits, kidnappers and violent insurgents. My first step is to fly from Kabul to Herat, on the western border of Afghanistan with Iran, from where I plan to drive east into the remote heart of the country, to Jam. The journey, I'm told, could take up to 14 hours – if all goes well.

Our Afghan fixer Hanif Sherzad has done much preliminary work in Herat and has roughed out a draft plan of attack. He has asked various people, particularly the Afghan police, about the current dangers on the road to Jam, and about security and the number of vehicles we should take. We are obliged to tell the authorities our plans and get our government permissions to film at Jam validated by the office of the Governor of Herat – through whose province the road to Jam mostly runs – and by the Chiefs of Police of Herat and of the four provinces of the region, including Ghor province in which Jam is located. Informing these chaps is not only good manners but essential for security because, if things go horribly wrong, it will be their men who will, initially at least, come to our assistance. Once this round of visits is over we seem to have secured what we need and assume we'll be leaving around five the following morning with at least 20 armed police as escort.

Our security advisor, David Holley, goes off to gather additional information about the road to Jam from the Italian forces who are the NATO force currently responsible for security in this part of Afghanistan. You can't have too much 'intel' in places and times like this. The rest of us drive towards a site on the northern edge of the old city centre. It's the Musalla, a religious and university complex started in 1417, which in its prime was one of the most beautiful architectural creations in all Asia. It was started by a formidable woman named Queen Gawhar Shad, who was the daughter-in-law of the great Tamerlane and whose husband, Tamerlane's youngest son Shah Rukh, was Governor of Herat.

When Shah Rukh eventually came to rule his father's empire – an empire that stretched from the banks of the Tigris in the west to the border with China in the east – Herat enjoyed its Golden Age. Shah Rukh and his queen made it their capital and a city to rival and even surpass Tamerlane's earlier capital of Samarkand in Uzbekistan, and it was during this time that the Musalla was started. Like her husband, Gawhar Shad – a Mongol princess in her own right – was a beacon of civilisation and the Musalla a shining reflection of her enlightened spirit. It included a madrassa, mosque, minarets and mausoleum, all set within Paradise Gardens – indeed the whole creation, its exquisite structures sparkling with fine and brilliantly coloured tile-work, was an image of an Islamic heaven. Gawhar Shad's buildings were added to in the late 15th century by Sultan Husain-i-Baiqara – a great-great-grandson of Tamerlane and one of the last rulers of the soon to be eclipsed Timurid empire. Husain added a vast madrassa, with each of its corners marked by a tall and slender minaret clad with tiles and glazed and moulded brick. The Musalla fell into decay after the collapse of the Timurid empire although as late as the 1930s the British traveller Robert Byron wrote of the Musalla that it was 'the most beautiful example in colour in architecture ever devised by man to the glory of his God and himself.' But by then disaster had overtaken the place. In 1885 the British-supported ruler of Afghanistan – Amir Abdur Rahman – fearing a Tsarist Russian invasion of Herat, asked British soldiers to demolish the Musalla so as to deny its use as a fortress to attacking Russian forces and help create a clear field of fire around Herat to aid defensive artillery. The people of the city petitioned Rahman to spare their great architectural jewel, but he stated that his concern was not for the past but for the protection of the living. This was a tragedy. The Musalla complex was described in 1846 by a French traveller as the most elegant structure to be seen in all Asia. To many, when the Musalla was in the prime of its perfection, with its forest of minarets and domed structures intact, it was more beautiful than the Taj Mahal. But the barbarous act took place and when the demolition was complete only the queen's mausoleum and nine spindly and now free-standing minarets were left. Needless to say, no Russian troops ever turned up.

My first sight of the Musalla is of five tall, somewhat battered minarets rearing up among a sea of roaring traffic and sprawling modern buildings. From a distance they look for all the world like a clutch of decaying factory chimneys. During the last 80 years four of the minarets that survived the 1885 demolitions have been toppled or grievously damaged by earthquake, neglect and during fighting with the Soviets in the 1980s. I notice that all the surviving minarets have lost their top stages. Four of the standing minarets are all that remain of Husain's madrassa. The fifth minaret is an astonishing vision. It leans even more precariously than its companions and is in fact only kept standing because it is cradled by a stout cable-sling contrived some years ago by engineers from UNESCO. So serious is this minaret's structural condition that it is technically classed as collapsed – in theory it isn't capable of standing but here it is, a doughty old building that doesn't know how to fall down.

I walk through the stunted and rank remains of the Paradise Gardens towards the mausoleum. Even in its shattered and crudely patched state it is possible to comprehend its original beauty. I go inside – and am overwhelmed. All is faded now and decayed, but the walls, vaults and inner dome are still defined by an incredible and deft display of geometric pattern, with forms and ribs emphasised by painted colour and gilding. The muted colours and battered perfection of the composition makes it only more poignant, more haunting, in a way more beautiful. The

Musalla – in its neglect and obscurity – is emblematic of the fate that is overtaking history and beauty in Afghanistan. A similar fate, I fear, awaits the great Minaret at Jam. I feel desperate, and sad. I can't wait to get on the road. As I sit brooding Hanif receives a telephone call – it's a bombshell. The Chief of Police insists that we leave for Jam immediately. All has been arranged, and he will go with us, to inspect the dam that is being constructed half way along the route, just east of Chisht-i-Sharif. We are somewhat taken aback, if not entirely surprised. We expected a deception plan might be hatched, but didn't think we would also be its victims. Presumably the police assume that our original plan to leave tomorrow morning is all around Herat, so want to strike first and catch the enemy on the wrong foot. We see the logic but are slightly defeated by the logistics. We can't just leave. We have to pack our kit, to organise. We had enough foresight to charge batteries for cameras, so it's possible. We agree – confusion to our enemies – and within an hour we are on the road, part of a convey of 60 armed police in around 15 vehicles speeding east from Herat. One golden rule is not to drive on dangerous roads in darkness, but the day is late so we can't get far before nightfall. The plan, the police tell us, is to overnight at Chisht where secure accommodation will be provided, but they will say no more. We get the feeling the police don't quite trust us with our own security.

The metalled road surface soon gives way to a bumpy, compacted gravel and our vehicles billow clouds of dust. The police in front and behind our three sturdy four-by-fours travel in green-painted, open-backed Ford Ranger pick-ups, with four or five men squeezed onto exterior seats and another four or five inside. All are heavily armed with AK-47s and belt-fed General Purpose Machine Guns. Many also carry automatic pistols and some have grenade and rocket launchers. Sitting with my kevlar helmet and body armour positioned to protect me from incoming fire, I focus on the rapidly changing country. The swathes of desert outside Herat soon give way to rolling land, with strips of green and lush oasis clustered occasionally along the banks of the Hari Rud. And habitations abound – there are small villages set along the road and near the river. Their architecture is fantastic – single-storey domed structures, set side by side within enclosure walls. All is built from mud-brick and many of the domes are topped by wind-scoops, looking rather like chimneys, which catch the cool prevailing winds and carry the refreshing air into the interior. People stand and stare as we roar past. Most return my waves, often with open if quizzical smiles. The landscape changes, becomes more mountainous, more epic, with flocks of goat and sheep, and herds of camel seeking sustenance from the wizened scrub that bristles among the pebbly and broken topsoil. This is the land of nomads – the Bedouin-like Kushi – and at regular intervals are their small villages formed with black tents or round yurts clad with black fabric and rush matting. This is a land that history has forgotten; nothing seems to have changed for centuries. Gradually the domed houses give way to clusters of flat-roofed houses and ranges of curvaceous mountain ranges form an ever-shifting backdrop.

Hanif is anxious again – commendable since it's our safety that concerns him, but you can't be on high-alert all the time. It blunts your reactions if a real emergency should come. He points out notoriously dangerous stretches of road – 'bandit country' – where the neighbouring villages are in conflict, men are armed and highway robbery common, and from time to time he points out good ambush locations and prime places for roadside bombs. Useful to know, but I feel my nerves getting tense and my eyes bulging.

After a night at Chisht-i-Sharif we leave at first light and speed on our way, through a kaleidoscopic landscape of incredible and changing beauty. We pass through more villages and after about five hours' hard drive arrive at the village of Jam. The Minaret is, I believe, about two kilometres beyond this point. From the village the bad road becomes truly terrible – in fact there is no longer a road, just rocky tracks and much of the route lies across fords and along bubbling riverbeds. I can see the police are getting anxious – their vehicles are taking a bashing, they are overloaded for this work, and axles scrape along rocks and riverbeds. Since none of the police have been here before none of them knew what to expect. They look truly shocked – punch-drunk really. Then, through a cleft in the rocks I get a glimpse of something wonderful – it's the Minaret, and it looks utterly fantastic. It rises tall in a narrow valley flanked by steep mountains – an image of delicate man-made perfection set among, and in dramatic contrast with, rugged and sublime nature. It is an extraordinary scene – the thing looks magical, mysterious, beautiful. It's a wonder that it's here and, knowing its age and the centuries of neglect the Minaret has suffered, it's a wonder that it survives.

The nearer I get the more magnificent the Minaret becomes – its amazing and delicate surface decoration is revealed, as is the stunning nature of its riverside location, for it is placed to command views up and down the narrow and incredibly picturesque valley. I stop and stare – this is not only a magical, mysterious and beautiful structure but also a building of great architectural and historic significance. It's one of the tallest minarets in the world and second in height only to the Qawat Minar in Delhi, which was built a few years later by the same empire that built this Minaret at Jam. But unlike the Delhi minaret – unlike nearly all the tall early minarets of the 11th and 12th centuries – this one at Jam is virtually intact and original. It's the tallest minaret in the world that has not been partly rebuilt and it retains its slender and delicate top portions. Indeed, it's the only utterly authentic early minaret in existence. But there is more. The Minaret at Jam is a dramatic memorial to a long-lost and forgotten empire – it's the last major and nearly complete monument of the once mighty Ghorid Empire. The Ghorids rose to power and greatness in the mid-12th century, burnt bright for only a few decades and within 75 years all was over. At the height of their glory their empire embraced modern Afghanistan and Pakistan and stretched as far south as Delhi in India, but in the early 13th century the empire was weakened by internal strife and finally collapsed when attacked in the 1220s by the Mongol warriors of Genghis Khan. This minaret not only reveals the exquisite architectural taste and advanced engineering skills of the Ghorids but it also – some argue – marks the site of their long-lost and once famed summer capital of Firuzkuh.

But, beyond all of this, the Minaret has another meaning – it carries a message – and it's this message that I now go to see. I reach the base of the Minaret and run my hands over its surface – it's constructed of well-wrought, regular and very hard tile-like bricks of a mellow yellow colour. They are beautiful and very sound – and in themselves no mean technical achievement in this remote location over 800 years ago. And it is in these bricks that the message of the Minaret is written. Its lower and widest portion – representing just over half of its full height – is covered with ornate geometric patterns incorporating eight-pointed stars and other Islamic emblems, and woven into this all-enveloping pattern is Kufic text – in fact the entire 19th sura of the Koran. This is a very particular sura. Entitled Maryam, it tells of the Virgin Mary and Jesus Christ, figures greatly esteemed in Islam, and of those prophets, such as Abraham, Isaac, Joseph and Ishmael, who are venerated by the three religions of 'The Book' – Judaism, Christianity and Islam. There is much theology that divides these three religions: Judaism does not accept Christ as the Messiah, while Islam does not accept him as the son of God – such a claim, thunders the 19th sura, is 'a monstrous falsehood at which the very heavens may crack' – although Christ is esteemed by Muslims as a prophet second only to Mohammed. But, despite these differences, the 19th sura is essentially a reminder of what the three religions have in common, a reminder that they have a shared root, similar aspirations and ethics, and the vision of a day of judgement when all will ultimately be held responsible for their actions on earth, with paradise a promise for the righteous. So it seems to me that the placing of this text on this minaret is an appeal for tolerance, harmony and understanding that must surely reflect the aims of the Ghorid rulers and which, in these divided times, is more relevant than ever.

The Minaret also contains other texts: at low level in a foundation panel is the date of construction – 590 by the Islamic calendar – so some time between late 1193 and late 1194. The name of an architect is also mentioned – Ali-ibn Ibrahim al-Nisaburi, whose name suggests he was Persian in origin. In the centre of the Minaret, in large blue-glazed lettering, is the name of the ruler during whose reign it was constructed – Ghiyath al-Din – and at the top are more Koranic texts, including the 13th verse from the 48th sura entitled Victory. This strikes a strident note and sends a stern message down the valley, not to the followers of The Book but to all others: 'As for those who disbelieve in God....We have prepared a blazing Fire...God has sovereignty over the heavens and the earth. He pardons whom He will and punishes whom He pleases...'.

I want to enter this miraculous structure – but there is no door. Over the centuries the river has deposited a thick layer of silt around the base of the Minaret so the lower metres of its octagonal base are buried, presumably along with the door to its interior. But a couple of metres from the existing ground level there is a small window. I get a ladder and squeeze myself inside. It's like entering a tomb, dark and potentially hazardous. But once inside, with eyes accustomed to the dull light, I find myself wondering at the geometric and highly engineered architecture.

In front of me is a thick, brick-built newel or column into which the brick stair treads run from the outer wall. Of course, this is an incredibly strong honeycomb-like structure with thick outer walls anchored to the stout central column by a spiral of well-built steps. First I plunge down, into darkness, and find that the stair stops, is shattered. I look, see an earthen floor, and leap. I'm standing on top of the silt that has washed inside the Minaret. Somewhere below me the stair must continue, but how far no one knows. Whatever treasures and information lie below this surface remain an utter mystery. No one dares excavate because of the fear of weakening the foundations of the Minaret – it already leans due to centuries of floods which have gradually eroded the river bank and undermined its foundations. Then I walk up, slowly, until light starts to enter through small arrow-slit windows. Through each of these I see ancient watchtowers on the surrounding heights. Of course, the Minaret was defensible and a command or communications centre. Messages from these high watchtowers – with distant views over the surrounding terrain – could have been flashed to the Minaret standing in the centre of the community lodged in the valley. I continue and am suddenly in an open area flooded with light. The main spiral staircase, with its central column, ends and I find myself in a brick vaulted room with a door leading out on to the now lost platform which, supported on timber and brick corbels, ran around the exterior of the Minaret. I'm just over halfway up, and each side of me a pair of small brick stairs runs upwards to the very top of the Minaret, with its open lantern or observation post. I look down and see the wide spiral staircase I have just ascended – and I see another. In fact the lower portion of the Minaret contains two staircases, one spiralling inside the other. They form a double helix – incredible, like a diagram of DNA, like an image of life itself. I sit beneath the shallow vault and wonder. This must have been a room for reflection, for communion with God – it's halfway between heaven and earth.

Minarets are a fantastic and fascinating building type that evolved gradually in Islam. They are not mentioned in the Koran, and earlier mosques – modelled on Mohammed's traditional courtyard house in Medina – did not have them, although the tradition of the muezzin and the daily call to prayers dates from Mohammed's time. The minaret, when it first appeared 100 or so years after Mohammed's death, was just a conventional tower, often squat, and probably inspired by Christian bell-towers. But in the 11th century something extraordinary happened – the Islamic tower evolved into a distinct sacred architecture. It became tall, thin, of complex geometric form, comprising a series of cylinders of gradually decreasing diameter, growing out of an octagonal or polygonal base – and with all outer surfaces covered with religious texts and symbols. These minarets were highly functional – they offered high platforms from which the muezzin could summon the faithful to prayer, but they were also symbolic. They were intended to act as fingers to heaven and make a connection between man and God, and to mark the location of the mosque as a sacred site. They also, in a more esoteric way, were to act as a focal point around which all else revolves – an axis marking a place as the centre of the earth.

This structure at Jam, the greatest and best preserved of these pioneering early Islamic towers, is more than just a minaret. It's obviously also a watchtower, a defensive tower and might also have served as a Victory Tower, as the text from the Victory sura emblazoned on its upper portion implies. The Ghorids were fond of minaret-like victory towers that celebrated their military triumphs. If a mosque did not stand next to this tower, and so far the presence of one has not been firmly established, then perhaps it was a victory tower proclaiming the power of Islam and the Ghorid Empire. If so, then surely it does mark this site in central Afghanistan – anciently the centre of the known world

– as one of the sacred centres of the earth. Amazing, we now see this place as remote, but to the people who built this tower over 800 years ago it was the very centre of all creation, the axis around which all turned. If so, then Jam must surely have been the site of the Ghorids' summer capital and one of the most important places in their empire. I leave the tower to inspect the site of what was probably the great and mythic Firuzkuh, lost city of the Ghorids.

This narrow river valley, in which the Hari Rud meets the smaller Jam Rud, is an unlikely place for a capital city – the flat land around the rivers is very limited and the surrounding land is steep. But I suppose it all depends on what a capital city meant in this region over 800 years ago. The Ghorid were semi-nomadic and Firuzkuh was only a seasonal city. They would have lived in tents and yurts and only have occupied the site when the rivers were low and the flat riverside meadows were at their widest; in addition the Ghorids could quite easily have occupied the steep slopes by creating terraces and platforms for tents. The only solid and permanent structures such a city needed were watchtowers, walls and a fortified palace or fort – and the remains of all of these exist. In addition, there is another compelling and most telling piece of evidence that this was once home to a large community. In the 1960s archaeologists found the remains of something unexpected and extraordinary – a Hebrew cemetery, about a kilometre from the Minaret, with headstones dating from the early 12th to early 13th century and so from the Golden Age of Firuzkuh. There was clearly a Jewish community in this area, which not only offers additional evidence for an harmonious relationship between the religions of The Book but also suggests that there must have been a significant population around the Minaret which the Jews were serving as merchants or as financiers. More archaeological research is needed to establish whether Jam was merely the site of a fortified camp of the Ghorids or their summer capital that was eventually overtaken by disaster in 1222 when sacked by the Mongols. But it is getting dark and further investigation will have to wait until the morning.

At first light we cross the Hari Rud to look at the watchtower and castle on the high ground above – and at something more sinister on the slopes below it. This, like much of the ground around the Minaret, is pock-marked with 'robber holes' – illegal excavations undertaken by looters in search of valuable archaeological treasures. Through poverty, and the knowledge that ancient artefacts can fetch high prices, the local population is pillaging its own history. The people here tell me that these robber holes were dug during Taliban times – so about a decade ago – but many look more recent. Looting here is clearly an on-going business. I clamber into some of the excavations to discover the remains of a large arched construction made of bricks similar to those used in the Minaret. It's been covered by centuries of spoil from earth slides but there's compelling evidence of structures – or at least platforms for yurts – on these mountainsides. Yes, this could have been the site of Firuzkuh. I also find many artefacts lying around – pieces of glazed and decorated 12th-century pottery, fragments of terracotta architectural decoration. If these are the things the robbers have abandoned, I tremble to think what they have taken. Everything the looters steal is robbed of meaning for they dare not declare the provenance of their booty, and every theft also robs the site of its meaning because with every loss the history of this strange and enigmatic place becomes more difficult to establish. And who is ultimately responsible? We in the West provide the market for these antiquities. We give them value because we are prepared to pay high prices. It's a frightful irony. I've come all this way to document this place, and yet I bring with me the dark shadow of destruction. I look down on the Minaret and see its horribly precarious state. This site –

the looting, the abandoned and fragile nature of the Minaret – is emblematic of all those historic sites around the world that are now threatened by poverty, neglect, armed conflict and lawlessness. A notable example is, of course, Iraq – the cradle of civilisation – where 10,000 archaeological sites of international importance lie virtually unprotected and vulnerable to looting.

As I observe the Minaret the low morning light turns it into a mighty gnomon, casting a long shadow across the river and mountainside. It's a strange and haunting sight – the slowly moving shadow marking out the sacred terrain. The brick of the Minaret glows warm, its lettering – its message – reading clear in the morning sun: 'There is no god but Allah', proclaims the topmost band of Kufic lettering, making clear the Muslim belief in the utter unity of God. This Minaret is undoubtedly one of the most beautiful and miraculous creations of the Islamic world – it is powerful and memorable, it's one of the architectural wonders of world, and it's also in terrible peril. If this tower were allowed to fall, it would be an almost unimaginable disaster. It seems sound enough now, but another decade of neglect and the scouring action of the river could mean its end. All I can do is show it to the world, stop it slipping from memory and so, perhaps, help save it from oblivion. And as I look, I see the police loading their vehicles. They claim that to loiter here is dangerous – we have to go. Now all I have to survive is the long and arduous journey home, a journey from an earthly paradise that man's aggression and fear has turned into a strange netherworld. As I leave I look around – what do I see? The centre of the world, of course.

Haunted remains of a catastrophe that shook the ancient world

Palmyra, Syria

Palmyra is just a few hours' drive east of Damascus in Syria, yet the journey is from one world to another, from life to death, from a teeming, thriving metropolis to a strange spectre of a city. Palmyra was once one of the great trading cities of the world, a place of spectacular architectural beauty and imperial ambition. Then, just over 1,700 years ago, disaster struck and Palmyra, the 'Bride of the Desert', was laid waste and gradually consigned to utter oblivion. But Palmyra never truly died. Even when finally abandoned, its ruins gradually disappearing in the desert sands, it continued to live in the imagination – the wonder of its lost wealth and beauty, the audacity and fate of its ruler who had dared much and lost all.

Palmyra is of ancient origin, a key location on a caravan route between Babylon and Mesopotamia in the east and Damascus and the Mediterranean in the west. In AD 217 Emperor Caracalla declared Palmyra a Roman colony – a most privileged status that relieved the city's merchants from the need to pay certain taxes. Vast and ornate building works were completed, in a sophisticated classical style that made Palmyra one of the most beautiful cities in the empire. And as its status rose so did its wealth – and its pride.

But as Palmrya increased in importance and blossomed in architectural beauty, the world around it descended into chaos, and old allegiances shifted. With the death of the Emperor

Severus Alexander in AD 235 the Roman Empire disintegrated into a quagmire of intrigue, infighting and economic inflation that was to last for nearly 60 years. Palmyra had to fend for itself, and to counter moves by Sassanian Persia to shift the ancient trade route away from Palmyra. The member of a distinguished Palmyrene family – Septimius Odainet – rose to the challenge, supported Rome in its struggles with the Sassanians and became the uncrowned king of the city. In 260 he defeated the Sassanian monarch and was honoured by Rome for his endeavours. Odainet continued campaigning against the Sassanians but was murdered in 267 – along with his eldest son – in most mysterious circumstances. He was succeeded by his second son – Wahballat – but it was Odainet's wife Zenobia, acting as regent, who was soon the new power in the land. The extraordinary nature of Zenobia's rise and her raw ambition shocked many. It seemed clear that it was she who had instigated the murder of her husband. One of those taken aback by Zenobia's seizure of power was the current Roman emperor, Gallienus. He sent a Roman army against her but the Palmyrene army – seasoned by its sustained campaigns against the Sassanians – was triumphant on the battlefield.

The stage was now set for an epic struggle. Zenobia wanted not only to liberate Palmyra from Roman domination but also to establish her own empire in the Middle East, one that would challenge Rome itself. And to do this she proposed to grab parts of the disintegrating Roman Empire. First she seized the entire Roman province of Syria and then, to the astonishment of all, in 269 she invaded Egypt and wrenched it from Roman control. Egypt had long been the 'bread-basket' of Rome, and the loss of such an essential asset was intolerable. But, before Rome could react, Zenobia marched on to grab more of Asia Minor.

I arrive in Palmyra just before dawn. What now survives above ground at Palmyra is just a fragment of the original city – the part that contained the public buildings and richest and best stone-built structures. Running roughly from west to east through the centre of the city is Colonnade Street – a processional route lined with giant columns on which were placed statues of leading citizens. Behind were shops and public buildings. The colonnades created a powerful architectural setting for life in the city and now, mostly standing alone and without related structures, these long rows of desolate columns snake through the desert to form one of the most moving and visually stunning urban scenes from the ancient world.

I decide to explore Palmyra by walking the length of this street because all the major buildings to survive above ground are either on it, or near it. I start at the east end, with the mighty Sanctuary of Bel. This sanctuary, like virtually all the structures that survive, was built before Zenobia's time. Superficially, the architecture of Palmyra seems closely influenced by Rome, the cultural centre of the world at the time. All is classical, and virtually all the columns are of the ornamental Corinthian order, a style that originated in Greece and was then taken up by Rome. But there is much curious invention. Clearly Palmyra was a fusion – it was at the border of the eastern and western portions of the ancient world – Greece and Rome on one side, Persia and Mesopotamia on the other. The Sanctuary of Bel, dating from the 1st century AD, is like no Roman sacred building, and its huge scale suggests the power and wealth of Palmyra at the time. A huge perimeter wall, square in plan, defines the sacred court – the temenos – of the sanctuary. This wall is beautifully built and detailed, but much has fallen or been rebuilt at a later period. The north wall is particularly stunning, and retains its giant pilasters supporting an entablature and with small pediment-topped niches at ground level.

Still partially intact is the sacred heart of the sanctuary, the Temple of Bel. Its basic form is simple: a rectangular cella – or hall – framed by tall Corinthian columns rising from a low base to an entablature which, at each short end, rose to form a pair of terminal pediments. So, all much like a Greek temple of the 4th century BC. But unlike any Greek temple, the pediments were flanked by stepped finials inspired by Assyrian architecture from Mesopotamia, and the cella was entered from the side via a huge door set in an ornate surround incorporated within the Corinthian colonnade – a truly unusual and odd solution. I enter the temple into a large, roofless hall of 3:1 proportion. At each end are deep recesses called adytons – the holy of holies of Greek-inspired temples, windowless and mysterious places where the most sacred rites were celebrated and oracles delivered. I walk towards the one on my right and look inside. Above me is a magnificent coffered ceiling – one of the famed glories of Palmyra's vigorous and inventive classical architecture. It's a monolith – a vast single slab of stone – and at its centre is an image of Jupiter, surrounded by personifications of the planets and the 12 signs of the Zodiac. Beyond the Zodiac are four eagles spreading their wings – the emblem of Jupiter. So the Palmyrene Bel – a name that simply means 'Lord' or 'Master' – is the same as Jupiter, the Roman King of the Gods, the equivalent of the Greek Zeus. And this ceiling shows Bel/Jupiter as the god of the sky, of the heavens, presiding over celestial movements and the fates of men.

As I walk across the temenos, returning to the city, I imagine the atmosphere in this space, roughly 1,730 years ago. After annexing Roman Egypt to her nascent empire in AD 270 Zenobia must have thought the worst was over. But things were changing in the Roman Empire – and rapidly. An experienced general – Aurelian – had replaced Gallienus as emperor and he did not intend to tolerate the loss of Egypt or Syria. A Roman army quickly retook Egypt while Aurelian himself led the attack on Syria. He rapidly inflicted two severe defeats on the Palmyrene army and by the summer of AD 272 was at the gates of Palmyra. Soon after, in

August 272, Palmyra surrendered. Zenobia's ultimate fate is a mystery, a subject of myth. She was dispatched to Rome, loaded with chains of gold, to be the focus of a triumphal parade. Some accounts say she died on the journey, that she poisoned herself to escape the humiliation of a prisoner's march through Rome. An alternative story is that she was taken to Rome and made a prisoner for life in a suburban Roman villa.

I leave the sanctuary and walk west, back along Colonnade Street, to one of the two major architectural features surviving – the Monumental Arch. This incorporates one wide and high central arch, which spans the entire width of the street, and two smaller arches which span the pavement walks on each side of the road. The arch, which probably dates from the 2nd century, is beautifully and delicately detailed, but its most curious and admirably original feature is its form. Its wedge-shaped plan neatly accommodates the shift in axis of Colonnade Street. It is beautifully done, obvious and seemingly so simple. This magnificent example of civic design alone makes the point that Palmyra was not just a provincial trading city. Its architecture and ambitions were metropolitan in quality and scale. No wonder it bred a personality like Zenobia. To be a citizen of Palmyra was to be second to none.

I walk along the next magnificent stretch of Colonnade Street; the long vista of columns, their relentless rhythm and grandeur, makes a powerful impression. To my right are the sad remains of the Sanctuary of Nebo – a Babylonian god and evidence of Palmyra's deep emotional and spiritual links with the eastern world. On my left are the ruins of a public bath – a quintessential expression of western, Roman, civilisation. Then a theatre – Greek in inspiration – and beyond and behind it is the wide-open space of the Greek-style Agora. This was the business heart of Palmyra, just as the Sanctuary of Bel was the spiritual heart – the soul – of Palmyra. Here, within its columned porticoes, politicians and merchants gathered, to exchange views, do business, to negotiate.

The exact nature of Palmyra trade is revealed by a remarkable document – a stone slab, dated AD 137, that must have stood near the Agora and is now in the Hermitage Museum in St Petersburg. The stone slab – or stele – records financial laws and taxes and was evidently intended as a reference document for city merchants. It says how much tax was to be paid on the sale of slaves, on camel and donkey loads of 'dry goods' leaving the city, and on two Palmyra specialities – purple-dyed wool and perfumes. Also taxed are olive oil, salted fish, beasts of burden and cattle. All to do with commerce was meticulously organised, and this included the pleasures of the flesh. One clause on the stele deals with prostitutes, who were charged a monthly tax, the same amount as a client had to pay for one act.

Immediately north of the Agora is the second major architectural feature of Colonnade Street – the Tetrapylon. It is a curious monument – now much rebuilt – that is square in plan with four four-column compositions defining its corners. It all sounds complex but the purpose of the Tetrapylon is straightforward – to mark the rough centre of Colonnade Street in a grand manner and to accommodate, in an elegant way, another slight shift in its axis. It's a turning point, ennobling the street which snakes through the heart of the city – a street that in its carefully calculated sinuous form must commemorate the feminine power of one of Palmyra's great deities – the goddess Allat. In this city of the goddess, Zenobia's rise to power seems not so strange.

The day is drawing to a close and I continue my pilgrimage west along Colonnade Street to a powerful porticoed façade. It's called the Funerary Temple but really was a house of the dead, a grand tomb belonging to one of the city's prominent families. It's an extraordinary structure, a portico – a portal – leading to the land of the dead that lies beyond to the west. To the north of the Funerary Temple is another porticoed structure – the Temple of Baal Shamin, the 'Master of the Heavens' and one of the great Arab gods of Petra, while to the south of the Funerary Temple is the site of the temple of the great goddess Allat.

I walk, through the city wall of Palmyra, into the Valley of the Tombs, the city's land of the dead. On either side of me rise the ruins of stone-built towers, each one the property of a Palmyrene family and packed, tier upon tier, with their dead ancestors. I ponder this valley and the strange history of the city. The paradox of Palmyra is that its destruction froze Palmyra in time, cast it into the realm of myth. Ever since its ruins were rediscovered by the western world in the late 17th century they have had a powerful influence on western culture. The first detailed survey, *The Ruins of Palmyra* by Robert Wood and James Dawkins, caused a sensation when it appeared in 1753 and had a profound influence on contemporary European classical architecture. The book's powerful engravings helped to reinvigorate contemporary classicism and imbue it with a new sense of archaeological authenticity. The book became one of the key documents of the Neo-Classical movement that swept through Europe and the United States in the late 18th century, and as I walk through Palmyra I spot details made familiar by their use in Georgian architecture.

A little distance in front of me is one of the best preserved of the tower tombs. It dates from around AD 100. It belonged to the Maani, a prominent Palmyra family, and is named after one of its members – Elahbel. The tomb rises from the sand, roughly a double cube in form and set upon a stepped base. The interior is architecturally dazzling, a series of giant Corinthian pilasters frame recesses in which coffins of the dead would have been stacked. I calculate that each of these recesses would have accommodated around eight bodies – so over 70 members of the

Maani clan would have been stacked in this space – and then there are two more storeys above. On the ceiling, on the wall, in recesses are carved portraits of the people whose spirits inhabit this tomb.

The sun sinks. Standing inside this well-preserved tomb, peopled with citizens of Palmyra, I feel almost as if the city survives, that when I step across the threshold I will see it sparkling in the distance. This is an intoxicating and powerful place. I suppose if spirits do indeed dwell in this tomb, as Palmyrenes believed, then the city – their pride and joy – does for them still live. The interior of the tomb is disappearing into shadow; in the mysterious half-light I begin to fancy that the carved figures are starting to stir. It's time I left.

History reborn in a city ravaged by war

Dresden, Germany

Dresden, the capital city of Saxony in Germany, became known as the Florence on the Elbe because of the spectacular Baroque architecture constructed there during the 18th century. Dresden was the ultimate expression of a city as a work of art, in which monumental public buildings and more humble private buildings coalesced to create a place of outstanding beauty.

This great and civilised creation, one of the world's most compelling artistic and cultural jewels, remained little altered until disaster overtook it on the night of 13 February 1945. Then, after a few brief hours of aerial attack, Dresden ceased to exist as an internationally important and coherent masterpiece. Seventy-five per cent of its historic core was destroyed or seriously damaged, leaving 15 square kilometres desolate and between 25,000 and 35,000 people dead. Whether or not the brutal and bloody attack on this architectural gem was a war crime or a justified military action remains hotly argued, but while this debate about the past continues, the future also has to be addressed. Should the city attempt to recreate the lost buildings of its historic core? Would these buildings have meaning and spirit or be mere soulless façades? If lost architectural masterpieces are rebuilt, would the memories of the destruction be less painful and would the wounds the war inflicted finally start to heal?

The transformation of the fortified market town of Dresden, founded in 1206, into one of the most beautiful classical cities in the world was due largely to Augustus II – the Strong – who inherited the throne of Saxony in 1694. During the late 1680s Augustus had travelled through France and had been deeply impressed by what he saw, particularly by Versailles, the palace built for Louis XIV which, in its plan and ostentatious Baroque architecture and decoration, expressed perfectly the power of an absolute monarch. As soon as he was on the throne, Augustus started to apply the lessons he had learned – through art and architecture he would make his power manifest, give his reign substance and so confirm his legitimate right to rule. Artists and musicians were invited to Dresden to hasten the city's transformation from fortress town to cultural masterpiece. Augustus's ambition was unbounded. In 1697 he acquired the Polish throne, even though it meant abandoning his Protestant faith and converting to Roman Catholicism, and by his death in 1733 Dresden had become one of the political and cultural centres of the world.

During the first five years of World War II, Dresden, despite its large size and the allied air forces' policy of launching strategic bombing raids against major German cities, suffered no serious air raids. This gave rise to a sense of safety – almost invulnerability. Dresdeners knew their city housed a large garrison and so was a bulwark against invasion from the east. But Dresden seemed to be protected by its very beauty. The people of Dresden believed that no one would stoop so low as to bomb a city acknowledged as one of the most magnificent in the world. More important, most of the population of Dresden assumed it was an innocent city and certainly not the centre of major arms production or a legitimate military target. But, as allied forces converged on Dresden – from the west and from the east – never had a sense of security been so false. What most Dresdeners did not know is that throughout the war their city had possessed a significant arms industry making small-scale precision items such as gun-sights. The people of the city also did not know that on 1 January 1945 the German military had secretly classified Dresden a 'Defensive City'. It was not to be an 'open city' that would be evacuated by the military to spare it if the enemy advanced, but was to be defended stubbornly. One consequence of this decision was obvious – fortifications started to be created along the banks of the Elbe.

But the most important thing that the people of Dresden did not know was that the city had long been on the allies' target list. It was perceived – beautiful or not – as a military target of increasing strategic importance. The allies knew about Dresdens' arms manufacturing capability and they also recognised that it was a centre of communications crucial to the rapid dispatch of German troops to the east to oppose the Soviet advance. In addition, the allies viewed Dresden as a Nazi city; during the 1932 election that put Hitler in power, Dresden was second only to Breslau in its support for the Nazis.

The reasons for the allied attack were clearly and simply explained by Sir Arthur Harris – head of RAF Bomber Command – immediately after the raid: 'Dresden was a mass of munitions works, an intact government centre and a key transportation centre. Now it is none of those things.'

The attack, when it came on the night of 13 February, was not exceptional in its tactics or strength but was in its destructive consequences. It has been described as an attack in which everything 'went horrifyingly right'. The weather and visibility were good for the attackers; they arrived and bombed on time and as planned; and the city was undefended, since its anti-aircraft batteries had been removed to protect targets that the Germans believed more vulnerable. Seven hundred and ninety-six Lancaster heavy bombers came over in two waves, with a three-hour gap between them. The first bombs fell at 10.03 in the evening and were, in their tonnage, a roughly equal mix of high explosive and incendiary bombs. Such was the accuracy of the bombing and the intensity of the fire that the RAF destroyed more urban area in a single night during this apocalyptic raid than ever before. The ghastly tragedy is that this record was set during an attack on what was arguably Germany's most beautiful historic city. The following day the USAAF struck again, so that by 12.30 pm on 15 February, 3,900 tons of bombs had been dropped on Dresden, with an estimated 24,866 houses and apartment blocks destroyed or seriously damaged out of a total of 28,410 in the city centre.

I arrive in Dresden on a stormy day in the summer of 2007. As I drive through the suburbs towards the city centre one thing becomes clear. Dresden is now a mighty modern city – the wide straight roads are lined with slabs of housing built when this was a socialist city in East Germany and part of the Soviet-controlled German Democratic Republic. But there is also much slick-looking modern architecture, the product of the more affluent years since Germany's re-unification in 1990. And occasionally, between this post-war architecture, are the ragged remains of some of the city's 19th-century building that escaped the bombing. What's obvious is that the current debate about the reconstruction of Dresden's lost pre-war streets and buildings applies only to the relatively small historic core of the city. The modern character of the city as a whole was long ago established.

I reach the River Elbe and board a paddle-steamer. I want to see the old city centre from where it looked its best in the past – from the water. As I get nearer to the centre, an astonishing sight confronts me. The famed pre-war skyline of the Aldstadt, formed by towers, domes and spires of various public buildings, is intact. This post-war repair and reconstruction started under the GDR in the early 1950s and was completed only in 2004, when the mighty stone dome of the rebuilt, early 18th-century

Frauenkirche – the Protestant Cathedral of Our Lady – reappeared on the scene. The beautiful silhouette of Dresden's historic heart exists once more, but all here is not what it seems. The history of the rebuilding of Dresden is fascinating, and a direct reflection of the differing political ideologies and social aspirations that divided Europe for over 40 years during the period of the Cold War. Dresden presented the socialist government that came to power in East Germany in 1945 with a huge challenge. The devastation had to be cleared, people had to be housed and the city made to function again. But then there was the question of what to restore and how. And this was as much an ideological as a technical, artistic or economic issue. What meaning did the ruins of aristocratic, religious or bourgeois architectural ruins have for an atheistic socialist regime pressed with the need to reconstruct a ruined country? Incredibly, the socialists quickly decided that the ruins did have meaning, or at least some of them. They were the repositories of German culture; they may have been made for the elite of the land but now belonged to the people and, if they could be given new socially and politically acceptable uses, as museums or places of public recreation, then repair, even reconstruction, was possible.

Also repair made a powerful political point. The destruction of Dresden had been provoked by the Nazis and carried out by the forces of the capitalistic West, and the city would now be re-beautified for the delight of the population, by the socialists. So the early 18th-century ruins of the Zwinger – a pleasure ground created for Augustus the Strong as a miniature Versailles – were stabilised and their repair put in hand; the shells of the mid-19th-century opera house and of the Royal Palace were also stabilised and even the court church – the Hofkirche – was repaired (with financial support from the Roman Catholic Church) as was the mid-18th-century Protestant Kreuzkirche. During the 1950s work started on the repair of the city's major public buildings, but not on its vast number of ruined but repairable private buildings. It's been estimated that of the 25 per cent of the city centre which survived the bombing, intact or salvageable, four fifths were demolished during the decade after the war to make room for wide new socialist avenues and row upon row of slab blocks to house the people of the city. And so the second destruction of Dresden took place – but, of course, much the same was happening in Western Europe where the old was being cleared to allow the creation of a bright new world. In Dresden this new spirit led to the cutting of a wide new road – the Wilsdrufferstrasse – right through the heart of the Aldstadt to provide a location for the major and modernistic buildings of the socialist GDR regime, including a huge, flat-roofed and thoroughly modern People's Palace of Culture. But by the time this people's palace was completed in 1969 the GDR's early and relatively enlightened policy on historic ruins had changed. In the future not even the ruins of major public buildings would be safe. In 1958 the GDR announced at its party congress that official planning principles had changed in favour of new buildings rather than the repair of surviving ruins, and in 1962 this new policy manifested itself with the demolition of the entirely restorable ruins of the medieval Sophienkirche. Even the ruins of the Frauenkirche were not now safe. It had remained a ruin through the 1950s partly to serve a political end – the GDR used it as a symbol of Western aggression – but its eventual rebuilding had always been assumed. But in the later years of the GDR not even the ruins of the Frauenkirche were shown on city development plans.

I get off the paddle steamer, enter the Aldstadt and head for its heart, the rebuilt Frauenkirche and the Neumarkt. All here is intense activity. For the first time since the war it's not just monuments that are being repaired or reconstructed but entire streets. The GDR, when it rebuilt on the site of cleared ruins, applied modernist principles and often replaced ancient streets with characterless blocks of houses standing in small parks. Now these small parks, and other tracts of historic city centre that have lain barren and un-built on since 1945, are being excavated. All around me are ancient cellars marking the location of long-lost blocks of buildings and streets. This is like being among the archaeological remains of an antique city. Discoveries made during these excavations – such as the precise locations and dimensions of individual buildings – are recorded so as to inform rebuilding. It's amazing – these cellars are like tombs from which the dead will rise. I walk towards the Frauenkirche, past a block of buildings that have recently been completed with elevations made to match those of the 18th-century buildings that stood on the site until 1945. One of the buildings is a mighty mansion – the Cosel Palace, designed in the 1740s – while the others are merchant houses decorated with rich Baroque detail. Across the Neumarkt another block is rising and next to it – on Rampischestrasse – another still. It's quite extraordinary – the reconstructed monuments of central Dresden are gradually being put back in their correct setting so that, with luck, the old town will once again read as a harmonious and coherent work of art. I study the recently completed buildings in front of me – they serve as bars, restaurants and hotels. Yes, all is driven by commerce, fuelled by the city's growing tourist industry. These streets of buildings are being created by private developers working to legislation drawn up by the city planners. Corners are being cut – insides are modern and most minor streets are in traditional scale, but elevations are more economically constructed, compromises between old and new. Clearly, it's difficult to realise a vision while respecting the exigencies of market forces. The battle for the soul of Dresden is continuing – authentic recreations or approximations compatible with the demands of economy and commerce. To get it absolutely right would be expensive and demand huge state subsidies. It seems to me that the politicians and planners of Dresden ought to be braver. The suffering and wartime destruction of Dresden were exceptional and so should be its recreation. There should be no mealy-mouthed half measures here – tear down the ugly modern buildings that stand in the way and make a brave, bold and complete recreation of the historic city centre. This would be inspirational and show that it is possible to restore lost beauty and make the past live again. The people of Dresden deserve no less. The one building in the Neumarkt that really shows what can be achieved is the Frauenkirche. When completed in 1736 to the designs of George Bahr, this was one of the best Baroque buildings in northern Europe. It reflected perfectly the aspirations of the wealthy Protestant population of Dresden and, in its powerful domed design, made a significant contribution to the beauty of the city as a whole. The decision to rebuild was taken in 1992 and was to symbolise not just the rebirth of central Dresden but also of the newly united nation of Germany. It was once again to serve as a church but also act as a reminder of the horrors of war and a gesture of peace and reconciliation. I approach the church – its stone-built exterior is mottled because new sandstone is mixed with blackened old blocks. In fact 45 per cent of the stones used in the construction are original, salvaged from the site so in a sense the Frauenkirche is not so much an archaeologically correct recreation as a radical repair. Its exterior certainly has a tremendous air of authenticity. I go inside – and it's sensational. The materials and means of construction are authentic, as is the design with its tiers of galleries and painted dome. Timber and stone are gilded and painted to simulate marble; nothing in the interior is quite what it seems – it really is a fantastic piece of Baroque theatre. The altar, a huge sculptural affair, is a jigsaw of nearly 2,000 original fragments, meticulously assembled. This church is an amazing act of love and commitment – funded by donations coming from all over the world – and this gives it a soul and character of its own, makes it more than just a replica.

I leave the church to see more of the city centre. I walk past the sprawling Royal Palace, now also in the midst of a long-term restoration project, and cross the Elbe into the Neustadt, an area which was developed during the 18th century. It was also much destroyed during the raid but, around Königsstrasse some significant groups of 18th-century houses survived. Here you can still get a sense of the architectural treasures – and the civilised way of life – that were destroyed in February 1945. I walk past some of the 18th-century houses, complemented by some sympathetically designed new Baroque buildings. This is a wonderful and most moving fragment of city, full of visual surprises. I find myself in the long and wide main avenue of the Neustadt – Hauptstrasse – and virtually all here is modernistic post-war reconstruction, but suddenly I see a group of fine 18th-century houses. They are authentic survivors. Each is wide with a large arch in the centre of its ground floor. I walk through one of the arches and it leads to a passage through the house – a carriageway I suppose – then to a delightful top-lit court. Beyond is a herb garden with a pretty Baroque building and fountain at its far end, terminating the vista along the passage. I walk into the garden and marvel. What a wonderful organisation for a city building – private apartments above an intimate public passageway lined with shops and leading to beautiful secret gardens. And then the horror of the loss strikes me – there were thousands of beautiful houses like this in Dresden until February 1945 – houses that reflected and created a most civilised way of life – and now there is only a handful left. What a tragedy! It makes me reflect again on what happened here, on the morality of the raid on this city. Dresden may not have been an entirely innocent city but it was a stunningly beautiful one. Did its destruction really help bring the war to a speedier end? Did it save the lives of allied soldiers?

Was the horror inflicted here justified or a war crime – not morally equivalent to the worst crimes committed by the Nazis, but a crime nevertheless? This question can, I suppose, never be answered, not least because it is surely absurd, even hypocritical, to try to resolve issues of morality, ethics and humanity in total war which, by its nature, is immoral, unethical and inhumane.

I have a meeting with a survivor of the attack, Helga Siviers, who as a 20-year-old nurse helped refugees sheltering in the cellar of a school near the Neustadt. I ask Helga about the bombing, but she clearly doesn't want to say much. She tells me that the first school they sheltered in started to burn. In between the waves of bombers they started to make for the Elbe but instead took shelter in the basement of another school. There she worked for the remainder of the night, throwing incendiary bombs off the roof. I ask her about the morning after, the first sight of the familiar and beautiful city in ruins. She is silent, tears start to well in her eyes, and she talks of the dead – of the refugees in the cellar of the school almost dying from oxygen starvation caused by the firestorm. Then I ask her about the current rebuilding of lost historic buildings in the city centre – does it help to ease the pain of what happened? Yes, she says, 'for me the war did not end until the Frauenkirche was rebuilt.'

I ponder the rebuilding of the city. An old building's not just masonry and mortar and the attractive patina of age – it's also a memory, an idea that's embodied in its design. And even if its stones are scattered the idea – preserved in archaeological evidence, old drawings or photographs – can live on and be reborn, and sometimes it should be. What took place in Dresden must never be forgotten. If that happens all the suffering will have been in vain. But the faithful reconstruction of the lost city can help to make the memory less painful. If Dresden's historic centre is properly rebuilt the wounds of the war will finally start to heal.

Staglieno Cemetery, Genoa, Italy A detail of the enigmatic and sexually ambiguous angel dominating the Oneto tomb and carved in 1882 by Giulio Monteverde.

Yaxha, Guatemala One of the three step-pyramids at Yaxha. It would originally have been painted in bright colours, each with a symbolic and spiritual value. Its nine major steps represent the nine levels of the Mayan underworld and a temple would have stood on the top platform.

A Mayan structural innovation – the corbel vault, an inspired way to span wide spaces and carry massive weights.

Czech Republic The Sedlec Ossuary – home to the bones of around 40,000 people. The vaulting is early 18th century, the obelisks and angels date from the 1740s, while the skeletal chandelier and swags were composed in the late 1860s.

Luxor, Egypt Hatshepsut's mortuary temple, from the north at dawn. Great mortuary temples were not only places of death but also machines of rebirth – 'Mansions of the Millions of Years' – intended to keep the name and memory of their builder alive for eternity.

Varanasi, Uttar Pradesh, India A temple slowly subsides into the sacred water.

A corpse, bedecked in finery, has been carried to the water's edge by friends and family to be ritually cleansed with holy water before being committed to the flames.

Afghanistan Clockwise from top left: 12th-century ruins of high quality Ghorid architecture at Chisht-i-Sharif, both domed originally and perhaps the remains of mausoleums or of a madrassa; within the remains of the Paradise Garden in the Musalla in Herat next to the sad stub of a minaret. In the background are Queen Gawhar Shad's domed mausoleum and the late 15th-century minarets of a madrassa demolished in the 1880s; detail of the shaft of the Minaret at Jam. The lettering in blue-glazed brick spells out the name of the sultan who built the Minaret – Ghiyath al-Din; inside the Minaret – two spiral staircases entwine to form the double helix; my police guard takes tea on the road from Herat to Jam; the magnificent citadel at Herat. Its medieval brick walls were once clad with bright glazed and patterned tiles.

Germany The centre of Dresden immediately after the bombing raids. In the distance are the shattered towers of the royal palace and Roman Catholic Hofkirche.

The historic centre of Dresden is now being rebuilt. The reconstruction of the Frauenkirche, designed in the 1730s and virtually obliterated during the bombing, was completed in 2004.

USA The two faces of San Francisco seen from Alamo Square. In the foreground is a group of late 19th-century houses. In the background are the towers of the Financial District. Both stand under the shadow of disaster, for it is now nearly twice as likely as not that a major earthquake will hit the city within the next 30 years.

Yemen The central square in Shibham. The city itself is around 2,500 years old, but most of its towering, sculptural houses are less than 300 years old.

Astana, Kazakhstan Clockwise from top left: The Presidential Palace stands in splendid and autocratic isolation; the Bayterek Tower – the Kazakh Tree of Life – is the symbolic heart of the city; the image of the sun in the apex of the pyramidal Palace of Peace and Reconciliation; the pyramid at sunset. The transparent top is the eyrie from which President Nazarbayev can admire his new city; a model of the city with the pyramid in the centre; view from the top of the Bayterek Tower towards the domed Presidential Palace and the pyramid.

Living under the shadow of disaster

San Francisco, USA

San Francisco, on the west coast of the United States, is one of the most beautiful cities in the world. It wraps itself around a vast and majestic series of bays that are so large in scale and complex in form they feel like a network of lakes. The scale of the site means that San Francisco embraces a stunningly varied geography and contains an astonishing mixture of urban forms. There are the clustered commercial towers of the Financial District, the old US Navy docks and fishing quays of Fort Mason and Fisherman's Wharf, the ornate late 19th- and early 20th-century terraces of Haight-Ashbury, Mission and the Castro, the smart modern houses of the Marina, and the picturesque Bay-side towns in Marin County, like Sausalito and Tiburon. And all are linked together by ferries and a series of heroic 20th-century bridges, including the world-famous Golden Gate Bridge. Completed in 1937, this frames the entry into the bay – indeed into America – from the Pacific. All of these works of man are set among stunning natural beauty – not just the sparkling lakes but beaches and rolling and wooded hills. It's the natural beauty of the site that makes San Francisco so memorable, but it's also nature that is the city's great and perpetual enemy. There is a price to pay for living in such a sensational location. San Francisco is one of the half-dozen most threatened cities in the world and lives under the shadow of natural disaster. I've come to see what structural and architectural solutions have been found to accommodate the wrath of nature and to discover how people live in a city that is simultaneously blessed and cursed.

The problem facing San Francisco is serious and far from abstract. It's now nearly twice as likely as not that a major earthquake will hit the city and the Bay area within the next 30 years – that's an estimated 62 per cent likelihood. It could happen at any moment, dramatically and with little warning, causing massive damage to the city. I'm intrigued to see the role architecture plays for, if appropriately designed and constructed, buildings offer a solution to disaster by providing safe havens, but if inappropriate then architecture is the problem. An earthquake that strikes an open area is of little danger but when one hits a city it becomes deadly indeed. Then, with ghastly irony, architecture – designed to offer shelter and protection – becomes the greatest danger to life as buildings splinter and collapse.

The coastal area in which San Francisco stands is riven by faults in the earth's crust. It's part of the complex boundary system between the Pacific and North American plates and these plates are in slight but constant motion. As these vast masses of the globe's surface try to shift, terrific forces build up until, suddenly, they are released – often with catastrophic consequences. The last major earthquake to strike San Francisco came in 1989 and at its epicentre measured 7.1 on the Richter scale. It caused the collapse of part of the carriageway of the Bay Bridge, around 100,000 buildings were damaged, a ruptured gas pipe in the Marina district ignited and destroyed swathes of the area, and in all nearly 70 people were killed. This calamity prompted a vast programme of repair and structural upgrading of buildings and infrastructure. So far around $30 billion has been spent. The most significant 'seismic event' before 1989 came in 1968 when the Hayward Fault, the one that runs through Berkeley, shifted. Many now think that this fault line is due to move again soon, and could be the cause of the 'next big one'. But the most famous fault in the Bay area – indeed probably in the world – is the San Andreas, and that's because when it shifted in 1906 the consequence was one of the greatest natural calamities in recorded history.

The city of San Francisco was little more than 100 years old when the earthquake struck in 1906. It had been founded in the late 18th century as a Spanish colonial mission but had been annexed along with much of California by the US from Mexico in 1846, boomed during the California Gold Rush of 1849, then grew rich and expanded rapidly due to silver mining, railways, shipping and commerce. By 1906 San Francisco – the seventh largest city in the US – sprawled around the west side of the Bay, and although it contained substantial public and commercial buildings it was still essentially a boom city, built rapidly and slightly in a largely uncontrolled manner, and the bulk of its private buildings were timber-built with chimney stacks and occasionally party walls of brick. Given its location, San Francisco was a city waiting for disaster to strike – and in April 1906 it did. The first tremor lasted 40 seconds and at its epicentre measured 8.2 on the Richter scale. After three days of horror 2,800 acres of the city centre was a blackened waste, with 30,000 buildings destroyed, including 30 schools and 80 churches; 250,000 people were homeless and more than 2,000 had died. This is the spectre that haunts San Francisco.

What, I wonder, would happen to the city – and its people – if an earthquake of similar intensity to that of 1906 hit now? To get a view I meet Mary Lou Zoback, a research scientist specialising in the hazards of earthquake. What interests me most is the fate that the city's typical residential buildings would suffer. What is being done to protect them? She gives me an alarming reply: 'If the 1906 earthquake were to repeat today, something like 70 per cent of the damage would be to residential structures. Many tens of thousands of buildings would collapse.' I've met Mary Lou in the Mission, a district that largely survived destruction in 1906 and is full of charming late 19th- and early 20th-century houses. I ask if historic houses like these have been upgraded, have building codes been applied? She tells me that California has the strictest building codes for seismic safety in the country and assures me that modern constructions 'will not collapse in an earthquake', but 'the problem is that 85 per cent of the residences in San Francisco were built prior to the most modern building codes and half were built prior to any building codes at all related to earthquakes.' She explains that the codes are not enforced retroactively so homes built long before modern building codes will only be strengthened if there's any remodelling, when owners are generally required to bring the building up to modern codes. I ask what proportion of the city houses have been upgraded. Mary Lou looks forlorn: 'We have a phenomenon here called rent control. It's a great way to keep the city liveable and affordable but, because rents are capped below market rates, it also provides a tremendous disincentive for landlords to invest in their properties.' I begin to see the nature of the problem. How would the structure of unstrengthened houses fail if an earthquake struck now and how should they be upgraded? 'Our biggest concern is that many of these tall old houses have ground-floor garages cut into them. We can see that all around here. This is fine as long as the load is vertical, but as soon as you start shaking from side to side, as in an earthquake, the ground floor just pancakes and the building falls on top of it. It's relatively easy to fix this problem – for example, you can brace the structural frame with plywood sheets or put a steel frame around the garage door – it's amazing that more people haven't done it.' I ponder the strangeness of human nature. People who live in San Francisco know an earthquake could strike at any moment, and that it could be big. What on earth do they imagine will happen to them if they don't bother to protect themselves? I ask Mary Lou her opinion about the 'worst case scenario' if an earthquake of the severity of that of 1906 struck now. She's explicit. 'Up to 40 per cent of the city's buildings would be destroyed, damaged or uninhabitable. Half a million people would be homeless and up to 5,000 dead, depending on the time of day that it struck.'

Clearly it's hard to persuade the public and public officials to commit large sums of money to guard against events that may not happen. Such is human nature. But I want to see what is being done – both to safeguard old structures and to make new ones earthquake proof. To see what's known locally as 'retrofitting' I go to the seat of local government – the handsome City Hall on Civic Center Plaza. City Hall is a fine stone-built structure of classical design which, when completed in 1915, dominated the heart of the city. The building is a really fine piece of work but, although started in 1908 to replace the previous city hall that was shattered and burnt in 1906, it was far from earthquake proof. Consequently, during the last eight years the city has spent $300 million restoring and 'retrofitting' it. To find out how this has been achieved I meet Eric Elsesser, the veteran structural engineer largely responsible for the work. He takes me into the basement where, he says, he wants to show me something. I clad myself in a boiler-suit and drop through a hatch in the floor. I find myself in an appalling place. It's dusty, dark and so low we have to lie flat on wheeled carts to propel ourselves around. As my eyes adjust to the conditions I see the space is huge. Vistas disappear into the gloom, seemingly stretching into infinity, with the ceiling – in fact City Hall – just above my head and supported by ranks of squat columns. Eric explains: 'This is the isolator space and these columns are the isolators – there are 530 of them, and they are like shock absorbers and carry the weight of the entire building. In fact the building no longer touches the ground. The isolators can move 30 inches laterally in any direction.' I'm amazed. What would happen if an earthquake struck right now? I ask. 'You'd see a lot of motion above, might even bang your head if you're next to an isolator, but the building would move as one object, not collapse, because it sits on a steel frame carried by the isolators. The isolators are made of rubber and steel and are flexible, they wouldn't break. We'd be fine.' Up to what level of earthquake? 'We designed it to resist about magnitude eight on the Richter scale.' I'm puzzled. How would the building's outer walls move? 'We've excavated a wide moat around the building,' Eric explains, 'and it would move into that.' These works were prompted by the '89 earthquake, and I ask Eric what happened here. 'Well, the building had no flexible element like this and suffered a lot of damage. If there had been another five seconds of motion we figure the building would have collapsed.' This is the state-of-the-art and a most elegant solution to earthquake risk: brace a building and allow it to roll with the punches; allow it to move as a single object rather than just beef it up by filling it with extra structure. But it's expensive. This part of City Hall retrofit cost around $120 million. I ask Eric how many other public buildings in the city have received similar treatment. 'Only about four,' he says.

My last destination is a major structure only now being built and the scene of one of the major structural failures caused by the 1989 earthquake – it's the eastern portion of the Bay Bridge. The bridge, completed in 1936, is really two bridges. It takes the form of an elegant suspension bridge from the city to Yerba Buena island, located in the Bay, and from there a robust steel-truss bridge spans the remaining stretch of water to Oakland. During the 1989 earthquake a 50-foot section of carriageway of the steel-truss collapsed, killing two people. The bridge was quickly repaired but it was soon decided that while the west portion of the bridge could be strengthened, it would be cheaper to start from scratch with the east portion. For the last few years a new bridge between Oakland and the island has been under construction and is due to open in 2012. Completion has been delayed and costs continue to escalate – current estimates suggest it will cost around $8 billion – but it promises to be one of the greatest bridges in the world. It has not only to be earthquake proof but also to be an iconic design worthy of its spectacular location, and a fitting companion for the epic and neighbouring Golden Gate Bridge. So the design and construction of the new east span of the Bay Bridge is a mighty technical and artistic challenge that has to reconcile potentially conflicting requirements in a creative manner. Beauty requires a bridge that is minimal and structurally breathtaking, while safety suggests bulk and built-in redundancy. The new bridge seems an inspired solution. It incorporates a self-anchored, single-tower suspension span of heroic scale with a tower that will rise 525 feet above water level. This, clearly, is to be the eye-catching and iconic portion of the bridge. This suspension span, 130 feet off the water, will be linked to Oakland by a pair of elevated carriageways – or 'skyways' – composed of a series of long sections carried on tall and elegant reinforced concrete piers. I get on a boat and make my way to one of the piers. I've come to meet Marwan Nader, one of the senior engineers working on the bridge for the California Department of Transport. I climb to the top of a pier and meet Marwan on the skyway. This bridge, he says, is one of the city's key life-lines – it's essential to the economic wellbeing of San Francisco and can't be out of action, as happened in '89. Part of the design brief is that any damage caused by earthquake must be easy and quick to repair. To explain more Marwan takes me through a manhole in the road surface of the skyway and into a strange world. The skyway is made of hollow concrete frames each about 500 yards long and containing walkways and service ducts. The separate frames do not abut but meet at expansion joints. We arrive at one and Marwand shows me how the bridge works: 'If there's an earthquake the frames are going to shake and move in different directions. They could move about half a metre relative to each other.' Within the expansion joint, and anchored in compartments within the adjoining frames, are huge, stainless-steel tubes. 'These are the shear link beams,' explains Marwan, 'they're exactly like a fuse at home – they're designed so that if there's movement the shear beam will absorb the energy, will take the deformation. We want to concentrate all the damage in the fuse, and like an overloaded fuse, it fails first and protects the structure.' He emphasises the logic: 'The shear beam goes rather than the whole structure.' I'm impressed; as at City Hall flexibility is the key. And like fuses, the shear link beams can be quickly inspected to determine if damage has been caused and replaced and the bridge would be operational again within a few days.

I head back to the city. It looks beautiful, but so vulnerable. Much has been done to secure the city from disaster, but there is still much to do. Despite all the preparations that have been made and ingenious solutions that have been applied, the people of this city remain terrifyingly vulnerable to the powerful forces of nature. This is a city in waiting. People living here know that there is disaster to come because the forces of nature are still clearly in control, still calling the shots. They don't know when it will happen but they do know how – one day, this great city will once again be laid low by a mighty earthquake.

5

Dreams

Mirage of a mud-built Manhattan in the desert

Shibam, Yemen

My first glimpse of Shibam is extraordinary. I'm flying at about 5,000 feet approaching the airport on a flight from Sana'a, the capital of Yemen. The terrain below is tough – desert with puffs of pale green, bleached-looking trees and bush, all framed by rearing, flat-topped and rugged cliffs. Then, suddenly, the vintage Boeing airliner in which I'm flying banks, comes in low over a high peak and, almost in the long shadow of the cliff, sits the ancient city of Shibam. It is a magical vision. The city is constrained by its walls, sits hard on the edge of a dry riverbed with, stretching beyond it, an irregular patchwork of large fields. Some are green and well irrigated; others are dusty brown, now only dim memories of fertility and plenty.

Yemen is a fascinating land with a culture and traditions that single it out from its neighbours. As a nation it's a relatively new creation, but it possesses some of the oldest memories in the world. It is one of the possible locations – many would say the preferred location – for the realm of the Queen of Sheba who, around 3,000 years ago, displayed her wealth and wit during her legendary journey to King Solomon in Jerusalem. This may just be myth but what is certain is that Yemen contains some of the oldest cities in the world. While many of the people in the region were nomadic, those who lived in what is now Yemen were sedentary. The land was rich and well enough irrigated for them to grow crops and keep animals without having to roam to search for pastures, and being on the sea and astride ancient trade routes – notable for the traffic of incense – the people congregated from early times in cities. Shibam is not one of the oldest – current thinking is that it dates from around 2,500 years ago – but it is certainly now one of the most remarkable. Its buildings are made of sun-dried mud bricks and rise so high that from afar the city looks like a strange mirage rising above the dusty plain. Naturally, and not without cause, Shibam is now popularly called the Manhattan of the desert.

I've come here to see how the city was built, and how its buildings are maintained and lived in. I want to meet the people of Shibam – the families who occupy these unlikely towers, the brick-makers, the builders, the merchants that keep the city a living place.

Before going to Shibam I visit a brick-maker. The scene is incredible, timeless. Bricks have been made like this in the Middle East for at least 10,000 years. The work is carried out around a grove of palms near the dry riverbed. When the river rises for a brief spell each year rich alluvial soil is deposited on its banks, and that collected around the bases of the palms – a soil that lies in the shade and cannot easily be used for farming – is collected for the brick-making. I see this rich soil – a renewable resource thanks to the river – being scooped from the ground, mixed with straw and water and then laid flat upon the ground where gangs of workers rapidly mould it into large, square, tile-like bricks. The bricks are left to dry in the sun for three days and are then ready for use. As I observe the industry of the workers one thing is clear – speed is of the essence. They must be paid for each brick made. I ask how many his gang of ten or so men can make in a day. Three thousand, I'm told. This is back-breaking work, and to toil virtually non-stop from dawn to dusk must be exhausting.

Now I want to see exactly how this very basic material is used to construct buildings that tower as much as eight or nine storeys high. I hope I'll find the answer in the city that appears before me. Strange from the air, Shibam is even more surprising from ground level. Its buildings are so strikingly abstract, sculptural – modern – in appearance. All seems determined by functional and utilitarian demands, by a resolve to push the potential of basic mud construction to the limits. It seems a city ahead of its time – a striking vision of the future, a dream of things to come. A mud-built city wall surrounds the perimeter of the plateau on which the city was laid out and which still defines the perimeter of Shibam. The city cannot grow beyond this ancient barrier because outside the wall the lower ground is subject to flooding and too fertile and precious to build on.

I enter Shibam by the sole city gate. It's provided with a wide and tall arch for camels and merchants' caravans and a smaller arch for pedestrians. I enter and find myself in an irregular open space, once the market I presume. There are no shops, no sprawling souk as in the past, now just a few stalls. What a strange place; all is quiet; the floor of the old market and square – and all the streets and alleys that lead off it – are unpaved, just floored with beaten sand. Men stroll by and smile, townswomen clad in black and veiled flit to and fro as do Bedouin women, also veiled but wearing extraordinary tall-crowned straw hats, and bands of laughing children cavort around me.

And all around, wandering and lazing in the shade, are flocks of goats. The sun, the sand, the aroma of goats and of human beings all makes for a heady atmosphere. Here is the authentic urban smell of the past, of our ancestors – the scent of life. This is a living city, clearly no mere museum piece. But I have a date. I'm to meet a family who lives in one of these tower houses, to find out about life in Shibam. So I explore, looking for my destination. The houses are simple, beautiful, yet with intricate, crafted details – especially the finely wrought timber doors, many furnished with large wooden locks operated by a timber key, rather like a big toothbrush and fitted with 'bristles', that unlocks the mechanism.

As I look I begin to understand the nature of the place. The houses – varied slightly in scale, detail and height – are essentially individual towers, each the property of a family or clan. They are symbols of power and status, and also defensible, each potentially a mini-fortress with a well-secured door and virtually no windows on the lower floors. These contain storerooms that in the past were packed with supplies so each house could withstand a long siege. The enemy could be a rival family or a foreign invader but, well prepared and well defended, these towers would have been very difficult to take by storm.

The age of each house is almost impossible to determine because construction is traditional and, being mud-built, maintenance and rebuilding are constant. Many houses are dated above their doors, but that usually refers merely to the date of the last major overhaul. A couple of houses in Shibam have documented histories dating back 400 years or so, but most were probably substantially rebuilt during the last 200 years. But no one is really sure.

I near my destination, then I see what I've been hoping to find. A building site and – yes – outside is a stack of fragile-looking, sun-dried bricks. Like all the mud-built houses in Shibam, this one has a very characterful external appearance. Its walls taper, thicker at the bottom than the top. This is very logical. The walls of the houses are load-bearing but sun-dried bricks are not very strong; they don't have great compressive strength. So if you are to build tall you must have thick walls, and these have to be thicker at the bottom than the top because the lower walls carry more weight than the upper floors. Indeed very practical and modern – architectural form expressing the nature of the materials and construction techniques. I like it. I climb to the top of the building and there is the bricklayer with his mate. He is rapidly rebuilding the upper walls. The bricks are being hauled up by rope and in the middle of the floor is a pile of mud. This is the mortar and the same material from which the bricks are made. Extraordinarily clever this. Since the bricks and mortar are the same material they respond in the same way to changing weather conditions and so are less likely to crack.

Deeply impressed by these simple, yet strong and sensible building methods, I arrive at the house of my Shibam host. I ring the door-bell and – nothing happens. Then, high up, a latticed window opens, a face emerges and cracks a smile. I'm in. Various strings and wires are pulled and a latch released. I let myself into a yard. I'm surprised, it's a rather unusual arrangement. Then I realise what's going on. The tower houses of Shibam all conform to a traditional plan, evolved over centuries – fortified entrances with storerooms and stabling for animals on the lower couple of floors and an internal top-lit court – to get air and light into the heart of the house. Sometimes the internal court is shared by a couple of houses, but here the neighbouring house has been demolished, transforming an internal court into an external yard. On one side of it is a door and I ascend a staircase. On each floor are storerooms – doors firmly fastened – and the stairs wind around a stout wall. I get to the second floor and this is where the house proper starts, the first of the inhabited rooms. I take off my shoes and enter. I pass into a vestibule where I am greeted by my host. Then the main room, and this is magnificent. It is large, square in plan, and high, with small squat openings set above the main oblong windows. These squat windows are part of a clever system of natural ventilation. The hot air in the room rises and leaves via these openings, allowing cooler air to be sucked in from the windows below. In the centre of the room are four slender, square-section posts topped by timber capitals that look like stylised rams' horns. These columns support the floor above, allowing for an open, flexible and well-lit interior, with few load-bearing internal walls. Again all very modern – and the light is soft and sparkling with shadow and movement as it filters in through the lattice window-shutters. I sit on the carpet-covered floor next to half-shuttered windows, with their sills set at the correct low level to offer ideal views from floor level. Everything is beautifully considered.

I am offered mint tea and I fall into conversation with my host. He tells me his family has occupied the house for generations, that it is around 250 years old, and that he and his family are proud to live in Shibam – the world's first high-rise city! I ask about the problems of living in and maintaining a mud-built house. He smiles and looks rueful. Yes, it is very demanding. Water is the great enemy, maintenance must be constant. As we talk, more people join us, sit against the wall, nod and smile towards us and observe. It's now mid-afternoon and many are chewing qat – a leaf that is clearly a habit-forming pastime for I notice that once a chap starts it is apparently difficult to stop. Soon mastication becomes general, each chap popping the luscious leaf into his mouth until the cheeks swell out, hamster-like. To show some solidarity I sample a handful. It's not unpleasant – bitter-sweet.

Another thing I observe as I sit among my friends is that no women are present, or have even appeared. I ask why. Well, this is the men's room I am told. A similar room, for women and children, exists on the floor above. Sensing the futility of my question, I ask if I can ascend to meet and thank my hostess. Oh no, she and the other women have secreted themselves while we are in the house. I'm welcome to see their world – their drawing room and the kitchen – but I can't see them. I go upstairs and inspect the corresponding columned hall, which is similar in scale to the one below but less ornamented. Off it are a couple of small rooms with closed doors. This must be where the women are. Then I cross a corridor and enter the kitchen. This is a fascinating place. Yemeni food is simple but good. Lamb and rice dishes – mendi, madhby and capsah – are favourites, along with potato, tomato and beans. And there's 'big fish' – tuna from the Arabian Sea. This kitchen is where these dishes are created – on one side there's a large brick-built oven in which bread and lamb are baked – but all is eerily still and quiet. No women. I ask my host where the pots and dishes are kept. He shrugs and smiles wanly – no idea. Cooking is clearly not man's work.

The sun is setting and it's time to take tea on a roof terrace overlooking the city wall. More male guests have arrived. They are leaning against the wall, chewing qat, chatting, the mint tea is brewing. I sit among them and the tea is served. It's sweet, pungent, restorative – just what a chap needs in the evening. Shibam is a marvellous historic city but one full of vitality, authenticity, no fossil – it's a dream of the past, but a living dream. I love it here.

A bright dream that turned dark

Eastern State Penitentiary, Philadelphia, USA

I arrive in Philadelphia, the crucible and once the capital of the United States of America. Here, in many senses, the nation was born and in the late 18th and early 19th centuries the city was a place of extraordinary optimism, vision, energy and revolutionary idealism. The people of this new nation, the most radical yet to appear in the New World, were linked culturally and ethnically to the Old World, but they were determined to forge a new and very different way of living. They wanted a more equitable and just society, one that reflected the ringing phrases of the Declaration of Independence – 'all men are created equal' and endowed with 'certain unalienable rights' including 'life, liberty and the pursuit of happiness'. But the realities of this new society, its trade and economy inherited from its ousted imperial masters, made these ideals hard to realise. Equality was not achieved. Slavery, fundamental to the prosperity of many of the states in the new nation, was not outlawed and, of course, common crime did not disappear with the arrival of political independence. Liberty, like freedom, was not guaranteed to all inhabitants of this revolutionary land.

It's easy to understand why. Resolving the issue of slavery was too much of a challenge for the first generations of the new nation, a number of whose founding fathers were themselves slave-owners. It was clear that if pursued the issue of slavery could divide and destroy the nation. But a new approach to the treatment of its criminals was contemplated and investigated, and methods sought that were less barbaric than those commonly practised in the Old World, where corporal punishment, exile and execution were the common responses to crime. Could not prison, reformers in the New World argued, be a place where wrong-doers were reformed rather than brutally punished? Could not criminals be made to feel penitence, see the error of their ways, be morally and spiritually saved and reintroduced – reborn – into society? This was the dream, and the great laboratory where this experiment was to be conducted was constructed in Philadelphia, a city that in the early decades of the 19th century was still dominated by the non-violent philosophy of its 17th-century Quaker pioneers.

The Eastern State Penitentiary opened in 1829. Prison historian Norman Johnston describes it as 'not only one of the largest and most expensive structures in the country at the time but also, in both its architecture and its program, the most influential prison ever built'. My first sight of it is a tall, dark stone wall that is chilling, almost monstrous, in its massive scale and blank, forbidding presence. The place looks stern and grim. Its high walls have a psychological as well as a functional purpose. They're a reminder to passers-by – do evil and you will end up in a place like this! All seems substantially intact but – more obviously – all is derelict. I spy a weird array of rusting metal entwined with rank vegetation. There is an overpowering air of decay. This place is melancholy, haunted by the spirits of the human beings who came here in misery and terror and were surely crushed, rather than reformed, by the system. The penitentiary closed in 1970, was abandoned for 20 years and now is preserved as a 'controlled' ruin. Since 1994 it has functioned as a museum, but really it's a warning. It shows how an idealistic dream can come unhinged, for despite the original intentions of its founders, this utopian prison soon went terribly wrong.

The background to the construction of the pioneering building is fascinating, for its architecture and organisation were based on theories developed by some of the most advanced and humane thinkers in late 18th-century Europe, including the radical and generally enlightened Jeremy Bentham. Bentham, born in London in 1748, was a philosopher, lawyer, social reformer and radical who, among many things, championed women's rights and opposed slavery. Bentham was also gripped by the issue of prison reform and in 1791 published his ideas on a new type of prison design and system. The design he had in mind, called a panopticon, was a huge circular building comprising tiers of cells, reached by galleries and arranged around an open court, in the centre of which was to be located an observation tower from which each cell could be watched. Bentham's two big ideas were that prisoners were to be aware that their actions could be observed at all times while themselves being unable to observe their observers, and they were to be isolated, each in his own cell.

The awful psychological consequences for the prisoner of constant observation and isolation had probably not occurred to Bentham. Indeed, it was many years before prison authorities realised the full psychological power of these weapons and when they did many abused them. For Bentham, isolation seems merely to have been a way of saving criminals from vices they were exposed to, and corrupted by, when held in traditional prisons with their common and crowded cells. Inspired by the notion of medieval monastic cells in which monks would meditate and commune with God, individual prison cells were conceived as a means of reformation. They were to be quiet and calm places of retreat, where prisoners, as penitents, would ponder their past ill deeds, and resolve to do better in future.

By the time the Eastern State Penitentiary came to be designed Bentham's essential ideas had been long embraced by progressive prison designers, but developed to create a distinctly different architectural form. In the 1820s the optimum form of the modern gaol comprised blocks of varied design, but usually with cells placed off a central corridor or gallery, radiating from an observation tower. From this tower, guards had a good view over the entire gaol and along each of the corridors or galleries in the radiating blocks. This design was preferable to Bentham's because it produced a gaol that was easier to control and more flexible in its function, as the small, individual blocks could each be secured, controlled or put to varied uses as and when desired. What made the Eastern State Penitentiary pioneering, world important and a model for prison designers was that it united new theories about penal servitude, and then refined and realised them on a vast scale within a powerful and precisely designed architectural setting. The new architectural form and prison organisation that was the result of this fusion of influences became known as the 'Pennsylvania System'.

I walk into the now ruined ground-floor vestibule of the central observation building from where I can look into the corridors of the seven original radiating blocks, and via large mirrors, into the corridors of wings added at later dates as the prison expanded. As I walk I peer into cells, all in different states of decay. Some have rusting prison furniture still in place; all have peeling paint and crumbling plaster. The original arrangement and regime of these cell blocks was eccentric, to put it mildly – almost perverse. Isolation was to be complete. There were not even doors connecting the corridor to the cells, just a hatch through which warders, wearing thick socks to muffle the sound of their tread, would insert food. The prisoner entered the cell through a small opening, fitted with an iron grille and timber door, which led off the exercise yard. When being transported to this cell the prisoner was forced to wear a black hood so that he would know nothing – not the guards nor the prison – beyond the walls of the tiny world he was to inhabit for the duration of his sentence. He could have no visitors, no human contact beyond his 'moral instructor', who would visit him in the cell, or an occasional interview with the governor.

I enter a cell. It measures 7 feet by 12, has a stone barrel-vaulted ceiling and is furnished as it would have been when a prisoner arrived – hooded, alone, with no prospect of escape or even of normal human contact for the years ahead. There is a simple bed, a table at which a prisoner was obliged to undertake honest work, a Bible, and that was it. Here the prisoner was to be penitent, to reflect on his wrong-doing, pray for forgiveness and resolve to offend no more. I sit on the bed and brood. Even now the sense of claustrophobia in this white-painted enclosed space is almost overpowering although, it must be admitted, the physical conditions were comfortable – indeed advanced – for the 1820s. Each cell had a rudimentary flush lavatory and was centrally heated with hot water, so technically more up-to-date than virtually any rich mansion in Philadelphia, but the mental anguish must have been extreme. Among the more disorientating and disturbing aspects of the cell is the lack of daylight and prospect. There is only a small porthole set in the vault which prisoners called the 'eye of God', the orifice through which they could see the sky and measure the passing of time. What a now incomprehensible institution this was. It was created to be an improvement over crowded, disease-ridden, violent and corrupting contemporary gaols yet, ironically, was probably far crueller because the regime was essentially a profound act of violence against the minds of those in its power. Solitary confinement is now recognised as a speedy way of breaking human resolve and spirit and regarded as an extreme form of punishment, but here it was seen as a means of salvation. If a prisoner rebelled – whistled or sang – they could be denied meals for up to a week, but not beaten as in other gaols. Corporal punishment was not part of the Pennsylvania System. I walk out into the tiny yard and see the patch of sky framed by

12-foot-high walls. Into pens like this prisoners were permitted to escape twice a day, for exercise in the company of the heavens. These must have been blessed moments.

The construction was completed in 1836 and, due to the increase in size of four of the seven cell blocks was able to house around 450 prisoners rather than the projected 250. Also increased were the costs which rose from an estimated $100,000 to a staggering $800,000. Needless to say many were shocked by the rise in expenditure and, in gradually mounting numbers, observers were also increasingly concerned about the nature of the Pennsylvania System. Did solitary confinement do more harm than good? Were prisoners in fact reformed? These were very reasonable questions to ask. Many of those who came to the Eastern State Penitentiary in its first decades must have been in fragile mental states, so no matter how noble the intentions of those who operated this system might have been, the gaol must have caused immense psychological damage.

The deep problems of the Pennsylvania System were recognised, almost intuitively, by one of the prison's early visitors. In 1842 Charles Dickens visited the gaol, was horrified by the effects of solitary confinement, and damned it in no uncertain terms. Soon after Dickens visited the gaol the rigid regime of isolation started to break down, with certain prisoners starting to share cells. Between 1877 and 1894 additional cell blocks were inserted in the spaces between the original seven blocks and by 1900 the gaol contained 1,400 prisoners, in some cases with four to a cell. By this time the model of penal servitude offered by the Eastern State Penitentiary had been challenged by other large gaols – notably Auburn and Sing Sing in New York State. These embraced regimes that were very different to the Pennsylvania System. They used brutal corporal punishment to maintain discipline and permitted prisoners to work together during the day, which presented the opportunity for the growth of a pernicious criminal sub-culture, inmate victimisation, and prisoner insurrection. The Pennsylvania System may have been flawed, but at least it was based on an enlightened ideal. These other systems evidently were not.

I walk through the rotting prison. Among all this decay I spy a cell that is furnished in a most comfortable manner, with carpets, paintings, ornate furniture and a cabinet radio. It's the cell occupied by racketeer Al Capone for eight months in 1929 and has been restored to reflect the luxurious manner in which he did his time. Then I enter one of the two-storey cell blocks dating from the 1830s. This is a spectacular space. It contains iron staircases of surprisingly elegant and fashionable Greek revival form, with beautiful balusters topped with Ionic capitals, which serve galleries off which the first-floor cells are reached. The vista is remarkable; the long central corridor, the high vault-like roof, the solemn light all create an atmosphere that is familiar if unlikely – it's like looking down the nave of a noble church. Extraordinary – but I suppose this is the morally charged effect that was intended.

Despite evidence that prisoners were no more likely to be reformed here than at other gaols, the Eastern State Penitentiary and the Pennsylvania System went on to exert immense influence. It was the first building of international importance erected in the United States, the first to have wide influence abroad, and it's been calculated that at least 300 prisons around the globe were inspired by it. Clearly prison authorities throughout the world were seduced, presumably by the high level of mental and physical control over prisoners that this model offered. But it was a heartless idea, and the Quakers and other Christian philanthropists behind the design of this gaol and the system of solitary confinement around which it was organised had only to study their Bibles to see the error of their ways. Verse 18 in the second chapter of the book of Genesis contains sound and sensible advice, offered by no less an authority than God Himself: 'And the Lord God said, It is not good that the man should be alone.' Yes, indeed.

Building the best of the modern with the best of the old

Thimpu, Bhutan

The aircraft descends into a narrow valley. I've arrived at Paro in the mountain kingdom of Bhutan. This land – the only independent Tantric Buddhist nation in the world – is currently locked in a fascinating social and cultural experiment. The ruling powers are attempting the tricky feat of controlling time. They want to make a modern Utopia by building creatively and selectively on the past, by preserving the traditions that give the nation its distinct national character. The ruling powers are not democratically elected – they are the king, Jigme Singye Wangchuck, who rules by decree, and a corps of civil servants, nominated by the king, who vote ministers from their ranks. They have a mighty task – to create a model society that escapes the soulless, blandness of globalisation, and instead incorporates what is perceived to be the best of the modern world with the best of the old.

Many people dream of living in such a land but, I suppose, the real point here is – do the majority of the people who live in Bhutan share the king and government's bold vision? The intentions of the ruling elite may be admirable – they are particularly concerned to preserve the nation's visually powerful and particular vernacular architecture – but do they represent a national consensus? Is Bhutan merely a benign dictatorship, with its ruler simply imposing his will on the people? I suppose the answer to this question will start to emerge in 2008 when

Bhutan is due to become a democracy and its people start to vote for those who govern them and have a more direct say in the life they live. We will soon see if the people really support their king's dream. At the moment all is being achieved through paternalistic decrees. There is legislation to enforce the construction of traditional buildings, mostly by example rather than by draconian compulsion, and the people are very strongly encouraged to wear their national dress. This official encouragement towards the outward expression of a strong national pride and identity has, of course, chilling reminders of non-democratic regimes in the past that have made much of national or racial pride and identity. Already in Bhutan minority peoples – especially the largely Hindu Nepalese who in the past immigrated to Bhutan in great numbers – are feeling alienated and regulated against, cast beyond the pale of the emerging Utopia. Here, clearly, is a mighty problem in store, the dark side of the resolve to protect and promote Bhutan's endangered national identity and culture. And this is why I've come to Bhutan – to see the reality of this dream, to see the consequences of an attempt to preserve tradition and culture through legislation.

Bhutan was once an entirely feudal society, largely physically and emotionally isolated from the rest of the world. The population was made up mostly of subsistence farmers, isolated in their remote villages in the Himalayan valleys, their lives steeped in tradition. But then in 1950 came the Chinese invasion of neighbouring Tibet. Bhutanese culture and Buddhism have much in common with Tibet, and cultural and trade links were close. Bhutan was shocked – and terrified that it might suffer a similar fate. The newly empowered Chinese communists justified their invasion of Tibet by claiming they were liberating the people from domination by a ruling minority of monks and aristocracy, and they succeeded because Tibet was isolated from the world community and could not muster world support in its desperate hour of need. The Bhutanese looked on and learned. There was a rush to modernise, to make connections with the outer world, to find allies. If Bhutan did not put its house in order then others would. So Bhutan, with immediate protection from expansionist Communist China offered by the buffer of the Himalayas, looked to India and the West. Roads to India were constructed, and a modern educational system and a good free health service established. The then king, Jigme Dorji Wangchuck, decided that the country needed a new Western-type capital containing government buildings, law courts and national library and so Thimpu was born.

But Bhutan's only international airport is in Paro – around two hours' drive from Thimpu – so my first experience of the country is not its capital but one of its major provincial cites. Paro is no disappointment and turns out to be an extremely charming place – not a city but a large and straggling town, with its houses grouped loosely around a river and spreading out into farmland. The sky and air are immensely fresh and invigorating. I'm at around 2,750 metres, in the foothills of the Himalayas. As I drive through the town and the surrounding country several things become clear. In Paro, at least, traditional architecture dominates and it is very beautiful; much of it appears relatively new. Houses are large, well ordered, delicately and emblematically painted, set in neatly maintained gardens or fields. The kilted figures make all seem rather like the Scottish Highlands; the deep-eaved chalet-like houses give the land a distinctly Swiss feel. And all looks so affluent. These may mostly be the houses of farmers existing little above subsistence level but they are far from huts – they all look exquisite and jewel-like. This is a rare experience anywhere in the world these days. I'm driving through a magnificent natural setting, past buildings that are mostly pretty new, and they do not detract from but are a positive ornament in the landscape.

The traditional Bhutanese house is an inspired marriage of rational construction that makes the most of regional building materials. These houses are generally two to four storeys with the lower level made of earth pounded into a timber mould or shuttering. As the earth dries, the shuttering is moved up and another course is pounded on top, with the walls being tied together by internal timber beams that also carry the floor structure. The storeys above the earth-built lower structure are timber framed. These storeys – in which the box-frame is exposed, with its panels filled with woven bamboo covered with pine needle-bound mud – contain the main windows of the house. These are generally fine examples of ornamental carpentry, incorporating a cornice embellished with stout blocks of wood that help support the weight above the window opening. Below the window are curvaceous decorative corbels that are in fact the projecting ends of floor joists. Also finely detailed is the timber cornice that tops the house. These invariably consist of three tiers of square blocks – set among delicate emblematic carving – that project one above the other. Visually satisfying but again functional in origin, for the square blocks are the external expression of the joists supporting the top ceiling of the house. Soaring above this ceiling is the house's most decorative and structurally spectacular and sculptural element – the roof structure, which is almost a building in its own right. It can take several forms but essentially is built with triangular trusses strengthened by centrally placed king posts and struts, and with horizontal tie beams projecting to form a deep eave all around the house. Traditionally this low-pitched roof was clad with tile-like timber shingles held down against the wind by rows of large stones; now many are clad with corrugated steel sheets. These roof structures perch above the house they protect, sitting on posts or squat masonry piers, and are effectively transparent – of the house yet strangely not of it, almost part of the outer, public world. Whatever happens within them can be seen, although occasionally their inner parts are concealed with modesty screens formed of painted bamboo matting. Altogether extraordinary; everything in these houses that appears ornamental is in fact a consequence of the materials and means of construction or a reflection of function. And this goes for the painting too. The pounded earth is generally painted with white lime wash to protect it from the rain, while timber ornament is also given a protective coating of paint with its detail coloured and picked out to reveal or underline its meaning. In Buddhism colours can have deep spiritual significance, as revealed in the colours of prayer flags and scarves. So all the colours used on these houses have something to say – to those in the know Bhutanese houses can be read like a book. A trifle more obvious are the figurative images painted on the external walls. These are mostly to give protection from evil, to confer benefits on the occupants.

I drive on to the area of Punakha in western Bhutan, to the remote village of Shengana. It's all incredibly beautiful – and everywhere there are spectacular farmhouses. As I drive I begin to notice that the painted motifs on the houses start to take on a most exotic character – it all happens near Dochu La, a pass over a 3,000-metre-high peak that offers spectacular views of the snow-capped peaks of the Himalayas. On many houses, generally painted near the front door, is a gigantic, erect penis, ejaculating in a most florid way, attached to a pair of bulging testicles and generally with a decorative ribbon wrapped around the centre of the shaft. I am not really surprised – some forms of Tantric Buddhism honestly applaud the power of sex, seeing the moment of orgasmic ecstasy as akin to the bliss reached through meditation. So to see renderings of the tool of enlightenment emblazed on the houses seems merely logical. But I do ask my Bhutanese guide, Tshewang Rinchen, if he can throw a little more light on the memorable imagery. Yes, he says, in Vajrayana

Buddhism – as Tantric Buddhism is called here – the image is intended to keep evil from the home – not only unquiet spirits but also disease and famine. I wonder if the locals admire each other's varied and heroic renderings of this mighty male motif? He explains that Buddhists recognise that everything positive contains a seed of negative and vice versa, and the penis is intended to attract comments and admiration – and the little bit of negativity that comes with their admiration is absorbed by the image and does not enter the house or its inhabitants.

We now journey to the capital city of Thimpu. I wonder what to expect of a city that has grown from a mere village in little over 50 years. It now has a population of 65,000, small for a capital but the entire population of Bhutan is only 700,000. New buildings are rising everywhere, and if not high-rise many are large and constructed not of local and traditional materials but out of steel-reinforced concrete or concrete blocks. All have at least a sprinkling of traditional forms and decoration but sometimes no more than a rather sad veneer that just emphasises the clash of cultures. But I also notice that some relatively new buildings, houses and certain prestigious government buildings like the National Library, are entirely and lavishly traditional. Clearly here there are parallel worlds.

We drive to the epicentre of Thimpu – the Tashichoe Dzong. Dzong means fortress and there are many such buildings in the land but this is the most important. Like most dzongs it doubles as both monastery and fortification but this one also contains accommodation for the king, for his government and for Bhutan's chief abbot. This building is the seat of government and it's the powerhouse from which all secular and religious matters in the country are controlled. I approach the dzong – it looks every inch a great medieval fortress. It has high, white-painted walls with windows only at a high level, and rising within is a great tower – called the utse – that contains important shrines but also, as with the keep of a medieval castle, acts as an inner bastion. We have gained permission to enter for an hour or so – a rare privilege – and I walk past guards, through a strong gate, ascend an internal staircase and arrive in a large courtyard. It's sensational. To my right are monastic buildings – recognisable from the broad red horizontal stripes set beneath their eaves – to my left is a free-standing temple and beyond that is a second courtyard around which is arranged the accommodation of the king and government. The dzong is a wonderful place which, in its traditional form and functions, encapsulates the spirit and aspirations of Bhutan. It's amazing that a seat of government should look like this – and even more amazing when you realise that most of the building is less than 50 years old. There has been a dzong on this site since the 1770s but it was damaged by fire and earthquake, and in 1962 King Jigme Dorji decided to rebuild to create the spiritual and administrative heart of the nation. This was a bold decision, a declaration of faith in a future that would be most decidedly built on the past. The truth of the matter is that things had started to go wrong with the plan to save the nation by embracing modernity and the West. As could be predicted, almost immediately old values were under attack and traditions rapidly started to erode – and it is the regime's attempt to balance the forces of old and new that now make Bhutan so fascinating.

Walking around Thimpu it's easy to see what started to go wrong. There are a number of dreadful concrete buildings dating from the 1970s, which are characterless and owe nothing to the culture of Bhutan. Creations like these, and the growing influence of foreign ideas and the number of foreigners in the country, spurred the current King of Bhutan into action. When he inherited the throne in 1972 it was a moment of cultural crisis – something had to be done quickly or all would be lost. It was decided that Bhutan would no longer attempt to keep up with the Western world economically, but would still be firmly in its sphere of interest. The new policy was not about Gross National Product but, charmingly, about achieving Gross National Happiness. Not that Bhutan's economy was stagnating. It had developed a profitable income by selling hydroelectric power, fruit and vegetables to India.

The focus has moved dramatically from global trade to the preservation of the national culture and the pristine environment. The king initially resorted to enforcement – or at least vigorous regulation – combined with encouragement. By the early 1980s Bhutan was steered towards a new course. Satellite dishes were removed so that the Bhutanese could no longer watch television for fear that it would introduce too many pernicious foreign ideas, and the king issued royal decrees stating that the people should wear national dress and that all new buildings – be they petrol stations or office blocks – had to be in the traditional style.

Things have mellowed somewhat in recent years – for example television was reintroduced in 1999 because the king believed its presence would, on balance, increase Gross National Happiness. I walk the streets of Thimpu to pick up the atmosphere. Everyone I speak to supports the king and his aims – there is an overwhelming consensus in favour of protecting the cultural traditions of the land and the environment. Indeed, people have a lot to be pleased with. Healthcare and education are very good, selling hydroelectricity to India is the greatest national money earner and does negligible damage to the environment, and tourism is increasing. It seems like the royal experiment is working – the brutal chaos that has overtaken the Nepalese monarchy has been avoided, China is kept at bay, and the ground is set for a move towards democracy in 2008.

It seems to me that the king's intentions are honourable and admirable. There are problems of course, imposing old forms on new functions and this can create architectural oddities on which traditional ornament is merely an awkward veneer. But these are problems that can be solved, and all does indeed seem to be increasing Gross National Happiness.

A 21st-century capital city
Astana, Kazakhstan

We arrive at the airport in Astana – the new capital of Kazakhstan – at 1.25 in the morning. It's been a long, slow flight and we are all tired. As I walk towards passport control I see two tall, beautiful women, scanning the sea of arriving faces. They wear long dresses, colourful frock coats and conical fur-trimmed hats topped by plumes of feathers, and each holds a bouquet of roses. They are clearly waiting to welcome someone. Who on earth can it be at this time in the morning? Our eyes meet – they smile. It's me! Welcome to Astana, the dream of an extraordinary man and one of the strangest cities on earth.

Kazakhstan became an independent nation in December 1991, following the break-up of the Soviet Union. It had never been independent before and although as big as India – or the countries of Western Europe combined – Kazakhstan has a population of a little over 15 million people. It's one of the largest countries in the world and also one of the emptiest. This is because much of it is steppe, the vast semi-arid plain that spreads across central Asia and by tradition is home to a scattering of nomadic people of Mongolian descent. The man who gained power in 1991 as president was the man who had held power under communism, Nursultan Nazarbayev. Despite his authoritarian regime and banning of opposition groups, Nazarbayev is not deeply unpopular at home or abroad, and this is largely due to one thing – oil. Kazakhstan is one of the largest oil producers in the world. It is estimated that it will be among the world's top five oil exporters by 2015, and Nazarbayev has skilfully used the country's economic growth and rising prosperity to consolidate his rule and create a sense of social and political stability. Kazakhstan is now being energetically presented to the international business community as a good and safe place in which to invest – and one of the things calculated to attract is the president's attitude to religion. Kazakhstan is a Muslim nation, but Nazarbayev runs it as a secular state and does not tolerate expressions of fundamentalism. Needless to say this makes his regime – despite some of its worrying characteristics – most satisfactory to those Western nations who fear the growth of fundamentalist-sponsored terrorism in this region.

As we speed through the night I get my first glimpse of Astana, which is effectively the first capital city to be built in the 21st century. Until 1997 the capital of Kazakhstan was the old city of Almaty which nestles in the more habitable southern portion of the country, near the Chinese border. But as oil money started to roll in and it became clear there were foreigners willing to invest in the future of the country, Nazarbayev decided the new nation needed a new capital. He chose a minor Soviet-period city as the location and wasted no time commissioning a master plan for a major extension. This new capital, named Astana which means 'capital' in the Kazakh language, was to become the heart and soul of the nation and give it pride and identity – and the Nazarbayev regime would be irrevocably associated with its birth and architectural form. This city is very much Nazarbayev's vision. Architects and planners were appointed, but the president is on record as saying, 'this is my city, my creation'. But the thing that's most notable now is the deep snow and the cold. Its location in the steppe is very remote and exceedingly cold – indeed, almost impossibly so in the heart of winter. Astana is the second coldest capital city in the world after Ulaanbaatar in neighbouring Mongolia. When it was announced in December 1997 that the capital of Kazakhstan would move to such a bleak location the world gasped – it was dismissed as 'bizarre', 'extravagant' and 'mystifying'. Since then much has happened and around two billion dollars a year of public and private money has been pumped into the city. It's the result of these ten years of expenditure that I want to see.

Our first appointment in the morning is to meet the city architect who has a massive model of the city so I'll be able to see – and understand – the breadth and extent of Nazarbayev's vision. The model is indeed huge – and not a little shocking because all is rather predictable. As with most autocratic or imperial city designs in the past – Speer's Berlin, Lutyens's New Delhi or Ceausescu's Bucharest – Astana is organised around a vast straight central avenue that oozes power and suggests that very nature is subservient to the will of one man. This avenue, which incorporates eight lanes for traffic on each side of a wide central island, is lined with government and commercial buildings – many of them towers standing in splendid, sculptural isolation. Parallel to this central axis are smaller roads lined with somewhat smaller buildings – hotels and the like – and beyond them are grids of streets containing smaller buildings still, perhaps even some houses. At either end of this three-kilometre-long central axis are grouped the major public and ceremonial buildings of the city, including the president's brand-new palace. All this was drawn up by the eminent Japanese architect Kisho Kurokawa, who in late 1998 won the competition to find a master plan for the new city. Then Nazarbayev got his hands on the plan and made it his own, which perhaps explains why it possesses the genuine autocratic touch. I ask about the architecture, any architectural principles being applied to the design of the city which is, in the end, meant to be the 'symbol' of this new nation? Does anything go here? Who is designing these things? Anyone who pays, I'm told. Most buildings are the work of foreign investors and the designs are generally produced by development companies rather than by top-notch architects. But all designs have to be approved by a central committee, the architect adds. Oh dear. Then he smiles again – you can have one of the plots and put up a building, if you write a cheque right now. I feel that he's only half joking.

But not all the buildings of the new city are being churned out by developers. The buildings at either end of the axis are the exception. At one end is a massive tent-like structure inspired, I assume, by the traditional home of the nomadic steppe dweller – the yurt. And at the other end, beyond the domed presidential palace and huge artificial lake, there is – of all things – a mighty pyramid. Both tent and pyramid have been designed by one of the leading architectural practices in the world – the London-based Norman Foster and Partners.

We leave the model and walk from one end of the axis to the other, from west to east. In the distance I can see a globe-topped tower and, behind it, the dome of the Presidential Palace. This great avenue is orientated to the east and now I see its symbolism – each day the sun will rise behind the palace and cast its light along this avenue, bringing the slumbering city to life. I'm beginning to understand Nazarbayev a little better – and, even if most of the buildings around me are pretty dreary, it's amazing to see a new capital city rising before my very eyes. Soon we reach the tower I spied from a distance. This, we are told, is the symbolic heart of the new capital and, with its spiky top, represents the Tree of Life – what Kazakhs call the Bayterek. The golden sphere perched on top of the tower relates to the Kazakh legend of the mythic Samruck bird. It lays a golden egg each spring, obviously representing the sun that brings summer, which is devoured each year by the dragon of winter and night. So, the sun again. We climb to the top of the 97-metre tower to inspect the interior of the globe. From it we get a tinted panorama over the city – or rather the building site below – and then climb onto a central platform. On this is a pedestal supporting a solid lump of gold in which is cut the impression of a massive hand. This, I'm told, is the handprint of the president. I'm urged to fit my hand in his and as I do, there's a surge of very loud music. What is it? My charming guide – a handsome Kazakh girl – smiles in delight. It's the national anthem, of course.

We descend and continue our journey. In front, framed by a pair of towers clad with copper glass and which appear to be perfectly empty, is the Presidential Palace. Architecturally, with its bow-fronted elevation and implied classical detail, it looks like a slightly demented parody of the White House. But this building is no joke. It sits in a commanding place in this new city, as if watching – dominating – all. It's a rather depressing expression of power – large, ugly, intimidating, omnipresent. We pass it quickly, walk over the bridge and get our first close-up view of the pyramid. It looks sensational – a pyramid surrounded not by sand but by snow and ice. The pyramid – the form that Nazarbayev regards as symbolic of all religions – was started in July 2004 and is termed the Palace of Peace and Reconciliation. Within it the president intends to preside – from time to time – over conclaves of holy men from all the world's religions. A nice idea, and one that could help to put Astana on the map. As I get nearer it becomes obvious that this structure owes little to the ancient world – it's very much a pyramid for the 21st century. It's realised in modern materials – glass and steel – and is an elegant example of contemporary engineered construction. And its shape is different. Egyptian pyramids have shallow sloping sides but here the sides are steep. The pyramid is 62 metres wide and its apex is 62 metres from ground level, so its volume fits neatly inside a cube. Egyptian pyramids are things of mystery – I wonder what secrets this modern pyramid holds. I walk inside – all is black – and then into a large open space, so from light to dark and then to light again. This is impressive architectural theatre. I suppose I'm on a symbolic journey from night to day, from winter to summer. To find out more about this I descend into the bowels of the pyramid and find myself in a large, subterranean opera house. Of course, an opera house is a sign that you've arrived, culturally at least. This is a most important place for Astana. As I contemplate the auditorium – large enough to seat 1,500 people – it suddenly comes to life. To our utter amazement the entire opera company – well over 100 artists – snaps into action. Singers in full costume bound onto the stage and break into song while the orchestra accompanies them with great gusto from the pit.

As I sit and listen I notice that the ceiling of the opera house is embellished with a large disc from which burst triangular rays – the sun again, clearly the favoured motif of this freezing and snow-bound land. Once the singers have finished I climb within the pyramid – up towards its apex. A staircase rises through the space above the entrance hall and leads into a fantastic, minimally detailed, tapering volume above the opera house with, on the convex floor, the reverse side of the sun I saw on the opera house ceiling. I go to inspect and see that there are sheets of glass between the rays of the sun which allow me to peer down into the opera house. I stand on the centre of this sun and look up, towards the top of the pyramid. The upper portion is fully glazed and light floods in to illuminate a round gallery within the apex of the pyramid. In the sunlight this circular floor glows – another image of the sun. I walk higher, along a staircase and ramp that winds through an internal garden, and finally reach the round gallery, which is surrounded by huge windows decorated with images of the dove of peace. It's in this luminous space, bathed in light warmed by the tinted glass, that the president holds conferences. I walk around the space and am dazzled by the breathtaking views. Now I understand Nazarbayev's thinking behind this building, and the images of the sun which occur through Astana. From this airy pinnacle, the president – the modern-day sun god from whom emanates all power in Kazakhstan – can survey his creation, his city, his dream. As I look from the pyramid I see the sun setting, dipping below the far end of the central avenue. Yes, in Astana, even the sun in the heavens seems to revolve around this pyramid.

The visit ends with a feast – in a yurt – but before that we are given a display of ancient Kazakh sports. They are all to do with nomadic life: two teams of expert horsemen battle over the carcass of a dead sheep; boys gallop after girls to grab a kiss, then the girls chase the boys and whip them – most entertaining. This is followed by the simulation of a traditional Kazakh wedding, with all dressed in nomadic finery. Then the eating and drinking start. Kazakhstan is, I suppose, the only country in the world that boasts horseflesh as part of its national dish. It's tender and fresh – delicious, in fact. Then we quaff kumys – mare's milk, slightly fermented, sour and tasting like old leather. Finally toasts, with every speech followed by swigs of excellent vodka. This final gathering reveals all – the Kazakhs are forging a new nation but their pride and identity still lie in their nomadic past and traditions. As we sit, and talk and drink – with the modern towers rising in the distance – it's hard not to feel that something sad is happening, that an ancient, noble and nomadic Kazakh soul is being clumsily repackaged, forced into a somewhat bland, modern, international city. It's still too early to say what type of city Astana will be – just a government administrative centre or something more. What is certain is that the task set Astana is tremendous – to create an identity for a new nation when the city has yet to find an identity for itself.

6

Paradise

Temple suspended between heaven and earth

Hanging Temple, Shanxi, China

Shanxi Province is in the heart of China. The town I'm in is called Hunyuan and I'm surrounded by demolition and rebuilding. Charming traditional houses are being swept away before my eyes and even relatively modern reinforced concrete structures are being torn down. None of these structures has a place in the new vision of the city. This place may be in the throes of modernisation but it is also bizarrely, and worryingly, old-fashioned. Everything here is powered by coal. I can smell it in the air. People toil through the streets carrying panniers of coal over their shoulders, and mountains of it are deposited in courts and yards. This is coal town and it's an incredibly 19th-century scene. Coal is providing China with the cheap energy it needs to power its industrial and economic progress, but this headlong growth comes at a terrible environmental cost. In mid-2007 it was reported that two coal-fired power stations are opening every week in China, all helping to accelerate global warming and push the planet ever faster towards disaster.

Much of the coal burnt in China comes from Shanxi because the earth here is bountiful and generous. Yet it is also holy. Shanxi contains some of China's most sacred sites and here the landscape itself possesses spiritual qualities. It is the location of Mount Hengshan, one of China's holy mountains, and a place of peace and beauty which for thousands of years has attracted monks and monastery builders. It's an earthly paradise but how, I wonder, is this holy land enduring the tribulations of the modern industrial age?

Hunyuan sits on a large plain in the shadow of a mountain range that includes Mount Hengshan and a diverse collection of Buddhist and Taoist monasteries. Many of these were closed, vandalised – even destroyed – during the Cultural Revolution in the 1960s. But over the past 20 years, as China has re-embraced many of its diverse religious and regional cultures, these monasteries have been revived and monks have returned. I am heading towards one monastery in particular, one that dates back at least 1,500 years and largely survived the physical assault of the Red Guards. I drive towards it along narrow winding roads clogged with massive trucks, grinding slowly forward under their heavy loads of coal. The temple I'm on my way to see is called Xuankong Si, the temple in the air. It's called the Hanging Temple because, as if in defiance of the laws of gravity, it hangs off, or rather projects from, a high cliff face. It started life as a Buddhist temple but gradually incorporated Taoist shrines. It's a sign of the harmony that traditionally exists between these two ancient religions and it is now, once again, a revered sight in the Chinese religious landscape.

Tao is a fascinating and ancient religion that in its perceptive and sensitive understanding of nature has much to teach the modern world. Tao, or Dao, means 'the way' and the core of its belief is that mankind – a product and force of nature – must live in harmony with the way of nature, not against it, and must take nature as a model and learn from it. Taoists strive to follow the principle of wu-wei – of 'not forcing' – and observe that nature works by itself, just as we breathe and our hearts beat without us having to do anything. Tao points out that nature is full of instructive lessons and surprises. The weak can be strong and the apparently strong weak. As the pioneering Taoist sage Lao-tzu put it, 'nothing in the world is weaker than water, but it has no better in overcoming the hard.' Yes, you can plunge a knife into water but water can, slowly but remorselessly, cut deep canyons through the hardest rock and reconfigure entire continents. Tao, which offers psychological and philosophic insights rather than the structure of a traditional organised religion, started in China around 2,500 years ago, about the same time Buddhism started in north India. In many senses it is the Chinese national religion. The followers of the way strive to nurture their chi – their intrinsic energy – and to become one with nature, through meditation, rituals and exercises, and to develop Tao's 'Three Jewels' of compassion, moderation and humility. These were the aims pursued by a small community of monks for more than a thousand years in the temple I'm heading towards.

The narrow road winds up into the mountains, revered by Taoists as places of inner stillness and harmony. Mountains, especially the ones now towering above me, are the domain of the Taoist gods, the nature and cosmic forces in physical form. The mountain is the key to much Taoist philosophy and theology. The world – creation – is a duality composed of opposites that in Tao are called Yin and Yang. The image is familiar – a pair of black and white abstract and serpentine fishy-forms set within a circle and curving into each other. The black has a white eye and the white a black eye, signifying that although opposite, each contains the seed of the other. The Yin-Yang symbol represents the essence of all – night and day, negative and positive, male and female – and the mountain embodies this. No mountain has only one side. It must have a shady northern Yin side and a sunny, southern Yang side, and it makes the point that opposites go together; they define each other.

The road winds around a corner and I see the temple. It hangs in the air, 50 metres high from the cliff face, hovering beneath heaven and earth. It's above a stretch of placid water that once must have been more lively, because I see that beyond the temple a dam has been built. The place has been tampered with, but it is still easy to see why the Taoists were drawn here. The cliff face looks towards Mount Hengshan – this is sacred ground and here nature is triumphant and beautiful in its elemental power.

The first thing that strikes me as I look up at the temple is that during times of trouble this must also have served well as a place of refuge. Suspended high above the water it was safe from floods and sudden attack, and it is protected from the elements, as well as dropping stones, by the rocky overhangs above it. The other thing that's clear is that this temple was never remote, much less in the past than now, because it adjoins a mountain pass and the road running below it was once part of one of China's trade routes. I suppose Buddhism reached this place through monks who travelled this road, and the Taoist monks would have sat within it, in silent contemplation, as caravans from all Asia made their way below.

I cross the river and walk towards the temple, which now seems to float above me. I can see why the audacity of this structure has shocked visitors for centuries. It looks like a creation of the gods. It's built as one with the mountain – they fuse together in embrace. Mountain and temple are united and that, of course, is the point. This is a paradise in which the works of man and of nature are one. The temple is formed by a series of ornamental galleried pavilions, of different sizes and on different levels, linked by delicate timber walkways or by terraces fashioned out of natural crevices on the cliff face. The main buildings, which were mostly rebuilt during the Ming dynasty in the 16th century, are lightweight structures sitting on a series of horizontal beams which are cantilevered out of sockets cut into the rock face. These horizontal beams carry most of the weight of the structures, but I notice a few stout vertical posts, built off levelled natural crevices, which provide extra strength. It's a fascinating and sophisticated structure. All its elements and details are related and although ornamental, perform structural jobs. The screens and windows that perforate most of the wall areas of the pavilions minimise wind loading, while the delicate walkways help to brace the temple structures and give lateral stability.

Suddenly I understand – the whole structure is a demonstration of Taoist principles. All is working with, not against, nature and using nature to tame nature. Here strength is achieved through apparent weakness, weight is not opposed by weight, the structures are not sustained by massive vertical supports but by a cantilever system that in a most elegant and minimal manner utilises the structural principles of nature. The cantilever system, found in the skeletons of mammals and other natural forms, employs opposing forces. The more the horizontal beams supporting the temple pavilions are forced down, the greater the load they carry and the more firmly they are bedded in their sockets.

I reach the door to the temple. It is small and stout, set in a strong stone gate, and has fixed upon its two leaves the brazen heads of protective demons. Clearly this is a gate fortified against man and spirits. It's a portal to a magic world – a place where monks communed with Taoist 'Immortals', the gods who roamed the stars. I enter a narrow court and look around. From here, the peculiar organisation of this cliff-hanging temple makes sense. It's inspired by conventional Chinese temple plans, but reorganised in a compact manner in response to the peculiar nature of the site. The space I'm standing in is the temple courtyard. On the right are monks' prayer rooms; above is the main prayer hall; over the entrance is the drum tower and opposite is the bell tower. Higher up are various diminutive halls, monks' cells and shrines. Incredibly, this is a temple – a monastery – in miniature, with all the standard components, but slithering up a cliff face and ascending ever higher to heaven. This is like no other temple I've ever been in; its small volumes and details, the way its pavilions and bridges seem to float in the air, makes me feel like a giant as I wander through it. It's like flying in the sacred energising air of the valley.

I enter a monk's bedroom. It's small with a high, raised dais at one end. This is where monks would have slept and sat during different times of the day and night, meditating and contemplating the holy mountain opposite. Beneath the dais is a small stove, so all here would have been very snug. Next to the dais is a small shrine containing an image of one of the Immortals. These are strange-looking beings with ice-smooth flesh, snow-white skin and most peculiar features, such as square pupils and long ears. The image I stare at would have acted as guide to the monks who lived in the cell. He would have helped them in their struggle to develop their souls and so escape the cycle of birth, death and rebirth in this world and to realise mankind's natural potential to achieve immortality. The spiritual journey, undertaken in this very room, involved meditation, breathing exercises, a strict diet – and alchemy. These monks, as they sought to bring about the transformation of matter, of the soul, from coarse and material to fine and spiritual, consumed strange substances, notably cinnabar, a mix of mercury and sulphur, gold and lead. All this was to build within the earthly body an 'embryo of immortality' from which a spiritual and immortal body would be born. It hardly mattered if you poisoned yourself in the process for that was 'corpse release' – the release of the soul to immortality through the death of the body!

I leave the cell and walk along a gallery and examine one of the long, thin vertical posts that seem to give added support to the temple structures. I push it and it wobbles. As I thought, these vertical posts add nothing structural, they are purely ornamental, giving reassurance to those in doubt. I enter a hall and see images of three Tao deities that represent water, heaven and earth. I suppose these reflect the essence of this sacred site

– the monastery floats in heaven, the earth is the cliff face off which it hangs and water is the river over which it presides. But, this hall, like the other shrines, is strangely quiet, and I find there is an abiding sadness about this temple. It survives physically, but it no longer functions. There are devotees here occasionally, but no monks. Its life as a working and living monastery ended with the Cultural Revolution. Then the temple was vandalised and the monks were ordered to leave, were exiled from paradise. It seemed that the Taoist religion, after nearly 2,500 years, was dead in China.

The time has now come to ascend the sacred mountain. As I do, I notice many other monasteries and shrines, nestling in mountain crevices or standing on high plateaus. Most of these have evidently been rebuilt or restored in recent years and are inhabited by monks. The dramatic reversal of fortunes represented by these reborn monasteries seems a concise Taoist homily. The Cultural Revolution attempted to go against the forces of human nature, to go against the flow. It seemed strong but was weak. Taoism seemed weak but was strong. The Cultural Revolution has disappeared into history while Taoism has returned. I must try to speak to one of the Taoist monks, to find out more about the recent history of these monasteries and about the mountain's sacred power. I make for a monastery near the top. Its outer walls carry huge Yin-Yang symbols and the bell and drum are in place in the towers that flank the central court. I see a shrine in front of me and within it a monk sits in meditation. This monastery is clearly a working proposition. When the monk – a diminutive, elderly man – leaves the shrine he agrees, with great warmth and goodwill, to talk to me. His name, he tells me, is Guo Zhidan and the temple, recently built after being demolished during the Cultural Revolution, is called the Ninth Paradise after the goddess who is worshipped in it. I ask him about the ultimate goal of Taoism. He explains it is to get rid of vice and greed, with a rather too understanding look on his face. He adds that it is important to cultivate the heart, the mind, the chi – it adds to life expectancy and, in the end, you will live in perfect harmony with the earth, sky, sun and moon. I ask about living high on the sacred mountain – does he feel closer to the Immortals? The monk looks intently, smiles again and shares a secret. Yes, he confides, they are even closer than you can imagine.

I leave the monastery and contemplate the spectacular view. This does feel like the domain of the gods. I can see why so many monasteries were built high in these sacred mountains. It's easier up here to feel close to the elemental forces of nature. And all still feels pristine. Despite creeping industry and pollution in the world below, the forces of nature prevail in these mountains. This paradise has not been lost; it endures – but for how long?

A Christian paradise
in a land of snow and ice
Church of the Transfiguration, Kizhi, Russia

I arrive at the new train station on the edge of St Petersburg. It's late at night and I'm catching a sleeper to Petrozovodsk, about 500 kilometres to the north in Karelia. At every door stands a guard, dressed in a long, tight-waisted, brass-buttoned coat and wearing a tall fur hat. Very Tsarist. These guards are unusual – they are all female, mostly young, glamorous and sporting high-heeled boots. Clearly rail transport in Russia is looking up. I scramble aboard and, precisely on schedule, the train moves off and the strange waxworks on the platform and in the corridors momentarily come to life. They shout and gesticulate, then like spectres all disappear in the dark, mist and falling snow.

Train journeys in Russia are strangely solemn affairs, almost religious acts of departure. Tonight this sacred atmosphere is most appropriate because we are on a pilgrimage of sorts. We're on our way to a place regarded by Russians as the spiritual heart of their nation, as the tangible expression of time-honoured Russian values and spirit; it is the repository of the national soul, a very personal evocation of paradise. We're going to an island that lies in Lake Onega – a vast expanse of water, and the second largest lake in Europe – to see a collection of ancient timber-built churches. I'm told they are buildings of exceptional beauty, masterpieces of traditional engineering. The island is called Kizhi and at this time of year, the heart of winter, it's locked in a world of snow and ice.

Petrozovodsk was founded in the early 18th century by Peter the Great as an industrial city, but it now has the look of a typical Stalinist-era Socialist Realist new town, its long straight streets with hulking blocks bedecked in most incongruous manner with delicate neo-classical frills. We drive through these unprepossessing boulevards and arrive by the side of the lake. It's an amazing sight: frozen solid, white and vast. We climb aboard a small hovercraft and glide away. The journey will take about two hours, we're told, depending on the weather. We scoot along on our cushion of air and we are soon lost in a world of white. We can see no shore, no sky – just icy white. It's disconcerting, I can tell you.

Finally a tree-lined shore comes into view, then groups of small houses almost buried in snowdrifts, and suddenly a mighty form like a huge fir tree appears. It's the Church of the Transfiguration of the Saviour, and the strange shape of the church is compelling. Its silhouette, almost black against the leaden sky and white snow, is formed by a cascade of cross-topped, timber-clad onion domes. I'm drawn towards its towering form – around 37 metres high, it's a sign of God in a landscape which may be idyllic in summer but is bleak and unforgiving in winter. I crunch through the snow and approach the church from the frozen lake. I'm overwhelmed by the power and beauty of the place. Here, all man's creations appear in harmony with this elemental landscape. The man-made structures I see are wrought from the trees that grow on the island, and all are designed and built to flow with the forces of nature. I observe that roofs are pitched to shed snow in the most efficient manner and windows are small to keep heat in and cold out. This is true, traditional, organic architecture.

The Church of the Transfiguration forms part of a group of sacred buildings surrounded by a low wall, a log-built stockade, which includes corner towers. All within is blessed and consecrated – a spiritual refuge built in a land where the old gods were not yet dead. Christianity only came to this area around 800 years ago and soon appropriated the ancient holy sites of Kizhi – an island long sacred to the sun goddess. The towering church in front of me dates from 1714, but there was a church here before that, securing this site for Christians. No wonder this was a fortified space, walled to keep out the prowling gods of the old faith.

I enter the gate, crossing from the profane into the sacred. This consecrated ground is called a pogost – it's spiritually charged. So this is what paradise looks like in a Russian winter; banks of snow and sparkling ice. Yes, there is a pure and pristine beauty to this vision. I can see why Kizhi is perceived as inspirational, a place of earthy honesty. On one side is the towering Church of the Transfiguration and on the other the smaller Church of the Intercession of the Blessed Virgin; between them is a tall bell-tower. The smaller, cosier Church of the Intercession, built in 1764, was for use in the winter, while the more voluminous Church of the Transfiguration was for summer use.

I climb the bell-tower to get a different perspective on the scene. At the top, beneath its timber spire, is a platform from which the rows of bells are rung. Beyond the bells rises the Transfiguration. It is a truly astonishing construction – not only in its scale, but also because of its complex design and materials and methods of construction. These domed churches of the Russian Orthodox religion are inspired by the Byzantine churches of early Christianity – in their turn inspired by the classical domed structures of Imperial Rome. So this weird and wonderful construction is derived from the Pantheon in Rome, via the Hagia Sophia in Istanbul. But as I unravel its form this ancestry does not seem so unlikely. Its plan is formed by two squares of equal size, one turned at 90 degrees over the other to form an eight-pointed star – a favourite symbol in early Christian churches as well as in mosques. The inner space defined by this turning of one square over another is a regular octagon and it's this form that is the key motif of the design. On alternate faces of the octagonal plan are placed square extensions to create a cross with four arms of equal length – a Greek cross. The church rises four floor levels above ground, but each level is smaller in area than the level below it – and this gives the church its tiered, pyramid-like profile.

But the most dramatic visual device is the placing of an onion dome above the arms of each of the crosses – and since these diminish in area with each floor level, there are opportunities for lots of domes. In fact, including a large dome on the top of the church, another above the sanctuary at the east end, and four at high level between each of the arms of the Greek cross plan, the church has no fewer than 22 domes. These domes – each an image of the vault of heaven – are loaded with symbolism. The large dome at the top and the four around and slightly below it are a standard design in Russian Orthodox churches and represent Christ and the four Evangelists – Matthew, Mark, Luke and John, the authors of the Gospels. But why 22 domes? As we ponder, the bell-ringer appears. He chimes away, and then we talk about numbers and meaning. It seems no one can quite agree about what the original designer of the Church of the Transfiguration was trying to say. The best bet is that it's a reference to the Book of Revelation – a most important apocalyptic text for the Orthodox Church – which is composed in 22 chapters. And the bell-ringer points out that within the pogost there are 33 domes in all – Christ's age at the time of his death. I suppose this all makes sense. This pogost – this graveyard and icy piece of paradise at the edge of the world – is to do with death, judgement and the life to come.

To see the manner of the church's timber construction I descend from the bell-tower and wade towards it through the snowdrifts. I can see that it is indeed an incredible work of art.

The carpenters who made this church knew their job well. The pine logs were carefully chosen, shaped by axe and adze with incredible accuracy, and laid with joints so tight that no filling was required to keep the interior windproof. What's amazing is that these softwood logs have survived so well in this wet atmosphere, and the main reason for this is the technique of cutting and shaping. A saw, cutting across the grain, weakens the log by allowing water to penetrate. An axe and an adze, cutting with the grain, create a surface that keeps water out. Traditional construction can be as simple and significant as that. The logs are beautifully jointed. At some corners they neatly overlap, as in a log cabin, while at others the ends of the abutting logs form mortise joints which are cut flush. Then there are the colours – the colours of nature. No paint is used, there is just the deep red/grey of the pine and the silver aspen of the timber slats or shingles with which the domes are clad. Construction here is moral, honest, ethical – something for a carpenter and Christian to be proud of.

I stand back and look at the church towering above me. It's sculptural and beautiful as it basks in an amazing soft and crisp light reflecting off the snow. Light is all-important in this northern land, where darkness dominates for much of the year. But light is not just essential for practical purposes – it's also holy, and the name of this church reveals that. The transfiguration of Christ is a story all about light as described by the Evangelists. Christ climbs a mountain with three of his disciples and he 'is transfigured before them, and his face did shine like the Sun and his raiment was white as the light' (Matthew 17:1–6; Mark 9:1–8; Luke 9:28–36). This miracle proclaimed Christ's holiness, confirmed Him as the Son of God. To the men who made this church light is the holy gift of God, the sign of the sacred that signifies life itself – 'and the light shineth in darkness…which lighteth every man that cometh into the world' (John 1:5–9).

But here, it seems, the light has been turned off! I enter the church and all is darkness. The interior is now full of steel and timber, a massive structure which is holding the church up while a full restoration is organised. This is meant to be completed in 2014 – the 300th birthday of the church. This is possible – let's wait and see.

To get some idea of the interior of this summer church I have to go to the more modest winter church, but first I must eat. Our guide has arranged for us to dine in a house nearby with a woman – now in her eighties – who has lived most of her life on the island. We arrive at her large log cabin, which has delightful classical details around the windows. I climb the external stairs to the main door on the first floor – the ground floor is reserved for the use of beasts. The old lady greets me. She has a strong face and huge smile. I'm seated and pressed to eat and drink. There is a mighty multi-layered pancake on the table and the samovar is steaming. I cut a slice of pancake – it's been baked in oil so the bottom is dark and sticky. It's memorable – rich and filling and clearly the right material to keep the body warm and energised in this freezing land. I ask her about the island, its isolation, its spiritual role in Russia. Yes, she tells me, almost guiltily, I have always believed in God and I love the island. God is near, that is why I'm here, and because my husband and son are buried here. Sacred land indeed.

I now make my way to the Church of the Intercession. Although more modest than the Transfiguration it is still a fine affair, beautifully built of squared pine logs and furnished with an octagonal and dome-studded tower at its east end. Russian Orthodox churches are organised in a particular way, inspired by the plan of early Byzantine churches which in turn are modelled on interpretations of Solomon's Temple in Jerusalem, described in the Old Testament. First there is an external porch and an inner room, called the trapeznaya or narthex. This is a secular space, used for village gatherings, and as a law court. This building was the scene not just of baptism, marriage, funeral rites and holy festivals but also of all the important events in the life of the community.

I pass across the trapeznaya and enter the nave. I enter the sacred world, an open hall where the congregation meet to worship – and service is about to start. I pass through another door and enter the chancel. In front of me is a screen covered with paintings – Christ, the Virgin, Evangelists and Saints. These are holy icons and the screen, rising from floor to ceiling, is called the iconostasis. It contains three doors and within it is the altar. But this space is the sanctuary, the Holy of Holies, the realm of God, and only ordained priests dare enter here. I study the icons. Many are aged and of great beauty. In the centre of the iconostasis is Christ in judgement, set within a circular Vesica Pisces – a sacred image and symbol of the passage through which the saviour entered the world. This is a scene straight from the Book of Revelation, which tells of Christ sitting in judgement upon a rainbow, surrounded by 24 elders. I count the number of people in the room…not quite enough. Near this scene of judgement is a splendid icon of the Virgin, and then I notice a startling image – Christ standing in the centre of a star-shaped explosion of light. It's the Transfiguration and floating approvingly each side of the transformed Christ are prophets from the Old Testament – Moses and Elijah.

I leave the Church of the Intercession. I'm leaving Kizhi for the return journey across the ice and swirling snow. As I trudge through the drifts I look back at the churches rearing stark and dark from the white snow into the off-white sky. I'm taken aback, as with a vision. This is ancient architecture which still retains the power to shock that it must have possessed when new. The churches still dominate this bleak and elemental landscape as they would have 250 years ago. They are wrought from the wood of the land that they dominate, utterly at one with nature, yet also somehow outside it, the creatures of man's invention and faith. This, I suppose, is how all churches should be – of the material world but portals into the spiritual, the markers of the possibility of paradise on earth. My last sight of Kizhi is the faint and distant profile of the Church of the Transfiguration – the church of God's light – disappearing into the glowing darkness as day fades in this land of white.

An Islamic vision of paradise on earth

Suleymaniye Mosque, Istanbul, Turkey

I arrive at Istanbul in the best of all possible ways – by water. I sail along the Bosphorus, the water that traditionally divides Europe from Asia, and enter the wide and majestic inlet known as the Golden Horn. In front of me rises the heart of the old city, once a Greek colony, then the Roman city of Constantinople and capital of the Christian Byzantine Empire. But in 1453 it fell to besieging Muslim Turks of the great emerging power in the world – the Ottoman Empire. Istanbul, as the Ottomans renamed their prize, contains some of the greatest buildings on earth and I'm here to see one of them – the Suleymaniye Mosque which, in its design and details, is an Islamic vision of paradise.

The mosque was named after the man who created it, the greatest Ottoman ruler of all – Suleyman the Lawmaker or, as he was known in Christian Europe, Suleyman the Magnificent. The very name of Suleyman, who came to the throne in 1520 and ruled for 46 years, struck terror into the hearts of Christians, particularly those in Europe. Suleyman was the driving force behind a successful Muslim counter-crusade and by the mid-16th century Ottoman Turks, having dominated most of their region and north Africa, were marching ever westwards towards central Europe.

Now, as I sail slowly along the Golden Horn, I see the building that was the great symbol of Suleyman and his breathtakingly successful rule. The Suleymaniye sits on one of the seven hills which rise within and around the old city. It's an amazing sight – a stone building topped by a majestic central dome surrounded by a cascade of smaller domes and, to one side, four needle-sharp minarets. The power and symbolism of the building is clear. The astonishing dome, which appears to defy the laws of nature, is Suleyman, the divine ruler chosen by Allah, presiding over his empire. It is the prophet Mohammed, the Dome of Islam – and it is God, the one and only at the centre of His creation. The dome proclaims that there is no God but Allah, Mohammed is his prophet and Suleyman is his power on earth.

I walk up the hill towards the Suleymaniye and arrive next to a hummum – a bathhouse – bearing a plaque stating 'Suleymaniye 1550–1557'. This is part of the mosque and bears its construction date. In front of me is a gate and a wide stone staircase leading upwards through a dark vault. I find myself on a well-planted terrace with the mosque rising in front of me. Along the streets all around me are buildings that form part of Suleyman's creation. He wanted not just a mosque but a whole quarter of sacred city. I enter this stupendous complex, containing religious, educational and charitable buildings, including kitchens from which destitute pilgrims could be fed. All are overseen by the mighty domed mosque framed by a pair of large, walled courts. Although the buildings forming this complex have many different scales and functions, they possess an architectural unity and are beautifully designed and constructed. This is not surprising, since all are the work of the great Ottoman architectural genius – Sinan. Nothing but the best in terms of materials or design was good enough for Suleyman. And that makes perfect sense for a monument that was to represent the triumph of Islam, reveal Suleyman in his worldly and spiritual greatness and be the earthly creation, based on sacred texts, of paradise – an image of the Garden of Eden.

I walk past the sides of the mosque and of the entrance court that stands to its west. The stonework is beautiful and I stop to admire one of the side doors to the court. Above the tall opening is a plaque bearing ornamental Arabic lettering. It's a text from the 73rd verse of the 39th sura of the Koran and proclaims, 'Peace be to you; you have led good lives. Enter paradise and dwell in it forever.' So the meaning of the mosque is pretty explicit, it's written on its walls. It's paradise. I move on and arrive at the main gate into the entrance court and gingerly push at the doors. They open. So, as promised, the gates of paradise part for the good – even the not so good! I enter the court – an austere and architectural vision of paradise. I like it! The central paved space is framed by elegant colonnades, each column slightly different and antique. No doubt reused from Roman and Byzantine buildings, the columns give the court a fine pedigree, a pleasing sense of the ancient, of eternity. All is so simple; there's a quality of purity and perfection about this place. There is much lettering on the walls – again texts from the Koran. One from the 70th sura states that only those who are attentive to their worship will dwell here, in paradise, and be honoured.

The Koran makes it clear, on innumerable occasions, that paradise is a garden well watered by rivers and fountains, and in the centre of this court is an enclosed and roofed fountain. Some say it was intended for the ritual ablutions that Muslims are obliged to perform before prayer, but this fountain cannot be for that purpose because access to the water is prevented by grilles. No, this fountain is surely a recreation on earth of al-Kawthar – the fountain of abundance that stands in paradise. The celestial rivers empty into al-Kawthar and all true believers who drink from it on Judgement Day will never hunger or thirst again, so it's a source of immortality.

I enter the great prayer hall of the mosque. It's a marvellous space and like the court possesses a bold simplicity. Its internal volumes are a celebration of the mystic power of the cube and the sphere. The high, wide central dome rises over a square area defined by four stone-built piers, which help support the dome, and by two screens formed by giant red granite columns. This square lower area symbolises the world of man, while the dome above is an image of the celestial – the vault of the heavens. Originally the interior of the dome was hung with lamps incorporating glass balls and was clearly intended, in the gloom of the evening, to look like the starry sky. This celestial imagery is confirmed by lettering in the roundels embellishing the four triangular pendentives that help to hold the dome in place above the cubical volume that it covers. These roundels contain an extract from the 35th sura of the Koran entitled The Creator and state that 'it is God who keeps the earth and sky from falling. Should they fall none could hold them back but Him.' This sura also reveals that all who undertake the 'supreme virtue' of charitable works – like Suleyman's nearby kitchen for poor pilgrims – 'shall enter the gardens of Eden' and be admitted to the 'Eternal Mansion' in which they shall 'endure no toil, no weariness'. Suleyman has created his own 'Eternal Mansion' on earth, perhaps a slightly premature reward for his religious, wise and charitable acts. I survey the interior from this central space – all is visible and united. Another symbol – it represents the unity of Suleyman's empire and the oneness of God.

This central space beneath the dome is the most spiritually charged area of the mosque and has yet more to say about Suleyman. Its cubical volume, defined by the massive piers and red granite columns, invites comparison with the Ka'ba in Mecca, the cubical shrine that holds the holy black stone of Islam. It seems that Suleyman – the caliph or spiritual leader of the Sunni Muslim faith – is saying that his mosque is not only paradise but also the new Mecca, the centre of the Islamic faith. It's incredible and audacious. I head towards one of the screens of red granite columns. These in themselves tell a fascinating and revealing story. As with the columns in the entrance court, these columns are ancient and one of them, it's said, was taken on Suleyman's orders from the Temple of Jupiter in Baalbek in Lebanon. In the 16th century in the Ottoman Empire it was believed this temple had been built by King Solomon as a palace for the Queen of Sheba. So by incorporating this column in his 'Eternal Mansion' Suleyman was declaring that he wanted his mosque to be emblematic of all great and sacred buildings and that it should include details associated with men such as the prophet Solomon, venerated by Islam.

Although the dome dominates the building's interior and suggests that its spiritual focus is its very centre, the mosque also has an orientation – a qibla – towards Mecca. The qibla is marked by a recess in the wall – a mihrab – that reveals the direction in which the congregation should pray. On each side of the mihrab are windows filled with stained glass. They are beautiful, and they filter and manipulate light to create a tranquil interior that helps prayer and reflection. Unlike Christian stained glass windows, these do not contain images of living or sentient beings. Muslims believe such things are idolatrous. They simply show plants, images of the garden in paradise. Light is important in Islam – it leads to, and is the sign of, spiritual enlightenment. The Koran contains a sura entitled Light, in which it states that 'God is the light of the heavens and the earth' and that He 'guides to his light whom He will'. This sura is mentioned in the windows – this is the message they carry. I climb a winding staircase next to the main door and come upon a small chamber. It's a remarkable space and seems to have fulfilled several functions. It was part of the mosque's system of natural ventilation: as air inside the mosque was heated by the bodies of worshippers and the hundreds of lamps and candles that were burning, it would rise and exit through various high-level apertures, including those in the floor of this chamber. Within this particular space the hot air gathered and deposited the soot it was carrying upon the vaulted ceiling before cooling and exiting through a row of low windows. As hot air exited cooler air would be sucked in through open windows below. All very clever, but there's more. The soot was scraped off the walls and mixed with water to make ink.

I continue to climb upwards, clamber through a low door, and find myself on a narrow gallery that runs around the interior of the mosque. I've come here to get a good view of the dome, to see the brilliance of its engineering. It's an incredible thing – its weight, as it's transferred to the ground, is cleverly dispersed through the structure of the building. Part is carried downwards by four massive arches that spring from, and transfer their load to, the four huge stone-built piers. Each of these piers carries the name of one of the Sunni Caliphs – the early supporters of Mohammed – who are known as the 'pillars of Islam'. So another of the symbolic meanings of the dome and its supports is pretty obvious. Part of the horizontal thrust of the dome is countered by the pair of half-domes – each approximately the same diameter as the main dome – which exert an opposite and roughly equal counter-thrust, and carry weight down to the walls below. Also, some of the weight of the dome is carried via flying buttresses, cunningly integrated into the structure, which transfer weight to the outer wall of the mosque. This careful directing and dispersing of loads means that large areas of upper level wall are relieved of any major structural responsibility and so can be pierced with tiers of windows to allow God's light to flood inside.

I want an even higher view of the mosque and the complex in which it sits and so climb one of the minarets. I look down on the mighty dome, surrounded by its satellites of minor domes. I see in the distance the inspiration for the Suleymaniye. It's the Hagia Sophia that was built as a church in the 530s – the greatest in Christendom – and converted to a mosque in 1453 when the city fell to the Muslims. Its huge scale and domed construction had been the wonder of the age and, with the construction of his mosque, Suleyman wanted to challenge it, to surpass it, to create a work of Muslim architecture in Istanbul that would at last outshine the Hagia Sophia.

As I stand on the balcony the call to prayer starts. This is Friday, the most sacred day in the week for Islam, and I want to attend Friday prayers. When Suleyman came to Friday prayers at this mosque he paraded through the city with a huge retinue of more than 7,000 soldiers and courtiers in a tremendous display of power and prestige. His journey ended in his Royal Box, located near the mihrab. I descend, mix with the crowds streaming into the mosque and climb into Suleyman's box. I imagine Suleyman sitting here, contemplating his mighty creation which he must have believed would guarantee him entry into paradise. The service starts; there is a sermon, chanting and finally congregational prayers. And now a new, functional, purpose of the dome is revealed – it's to catch, reflect and amplify the sound. It's designed to do that not only by its shape but also by its construction. The dome contains a row of hollow clay pots so it's partly hollow. It's like a sounding board, the body of a stringed instrument – it increases reverberation, increases the volume, makes few people sound like many. The hollow pots carry the sound into the very fabric of the building.

After the service I leave the mosque and enter the court to its east. This is a place of burial and contains Suleyman's tomb. I enter to see where he lies. In front of me is a large chest, draped in rich fabric and topped by a huge white turban. Below this chest is the sultan's body. Suleyman's tomb, designed before his death, says much about his aspirations during his lifetime. It's inspired by an important early Islamic building, the Dome of the Rock, which was built on the site of Solomon's Temple in Jerusalem and also covers the rock from which Mohammed is said to have made his Night Journey to heaven. So with this building Suleyman was proclaiming himself a religious leader of great importance, with affinities to Mohammed himself – and the Solomon of his age.

It's dusk, and I take one last look at this powerful religious complex. I'm overwhelmed by the mathematical precision and clarity of this image of paradise created by Suleyman. There is no god but Allah, and only the faithful and those who worship and pray correctly and who follow the strictures of the Koran will enter paradise. That's it. This machine-like building is a perfect evocation of the paradise of such an uncompromising and rational religion.

A Biblical building
set in a sacred wilderness
St Catherine's Monastery, Sinai, Egypt

This journey is strange indeed. I'm driving into a desert wilderness, in the heart of a predominantly Muslim land, to find the oldest continuously inhabited Christian monastery in the world. It's a place where, for more than 1,700 years, people have gone for seclusion, to find God. The land I'm driving through is the Sinai Desert between Egypt and the Red Sea and the modern state of Israel. It's the region through which, according to the Biblical Book of Exodus, Moses led the Children of Israel in their escape across the Red Sea from bondage in Egypt to the 'Promised Land' – to the land 'flowing with milk and honey' – the earthly paradise of the Jews. And it was here – on Mount Sinai – that God handed Moses the Tablets of the Law, the Ten Commandments, and issued lengthy instructions about correct behaviour and beneficial rituals.

My destination is the most sacred patch of this Biblical wilderness. It's the monastery of St Catherine, which stands below a mighty peak long ago identified as the Biblical Mount Sinai and on the site where, it is said, Moses had his first – and awe-inspiring – confrontation with God. After fleeing Egypt, where he had murdered an Egyptian who had been mistreating Israelite workers, Moses took refuge in the Sinai. Here he married a young shepherdess – a Bedouin – and while looking after the flock of her father – Jethro – Moses had a shattering experience that ultimately led him to liberate the Israelites in Egypt. He saw a bush that burned with fire but was not consumed and, as explained in Exodus 3, '…God called unto him out of the midst of the bush, and said, Moses, Moses. And he said, Here am I.' Moses moved towards the flames and the voice but was stopped. God said, 'Draw not nigh hither; put off thy shoes from thy feet, for the place whereon thou standest is holy ground.' It is this holy ground, the place where God walked on earth, that I'm heading to, because it has been claimed, for the last 1,800 years at least, that the site on which St Catherine's Monastery stands is the location of the Burning Bush.

I drive through the wilderness, between blasted granite peaks strewn with massive boulders, along desert roads. It's powerful, desolate – yes, here man can feel dwarfed and humbled by raw, elemental nature, by God; feel alone, exposed, stripped of futile worldly ambitions and pretensions. Here you have to confront reality, confront who you are.

Finally I reach a vehicle checkpoint. This is it. Just up ahead I see, in this bleak and raw desert landscape, the tops of tall cypress trees and then clumps of olive trees and vines – extraordinary – an oasis in the desert, a paradise in the wilderness. The monastery sits in a valley – I suppose the bed of an ancient river – with tall peaks rising each side. One of these leads to the nearby Mount Sinai. I climb some distance up the granite mount that rises to the north of the monastery and look down. There has been a Christian monastery on this site since the late 3rd century, but in its existing form the monastery dates from the early 6th century. At that time this was a largely Christian land – it was a hundred years before the rise of Islam – and the Sinai stood on the edge of the mighty Byzantine Empire – then the greatest Christian power in the world – centred on Constantinople, modern Istanbul. In 527 the Emperor Justinian decided that the collection of humble buildings gathered around the site of the Burning Bush should be rebuilt in grand style and protected from marauding pagan

Arabs by being placed within a stout wall. It seems the emperor – to honour his wife Theodora – wanted to show his respect for this sacred site and leave his mark in this holy land.

So St Catherine's was born in its present form – an architecturally admirable monastery that would serve also as a frontier fortress. I head for a small door in the west wall – a stout and ancient affair bound in iron. It's opened by a tall, gaunt monk with long greying hair and beard. He is dressed in long black robes and wears a smart black pill-box cap. The monastery is run by the Greek Orthodox Church, but the monk who greets me isn't Greek – he's a Texan. His name is Father Justin and he will show me round the monastery and explain the manner of life within it. But first, I have to meet Father Justin's superior. The head of the monastery is an archbishop, but he is away so I'm to see the second in command, Father Paulos. He is Greek, probably in his late 60s, and very warm and welcoming.

I tell Father Justin what I would like to see and then place myself in his hands. First we go to the garden just outside the wall. This is a truly impressive creation. Over the centuries monks have dug wells, collected soil and nurtured a wide variety of most useful plants. As well as vine and olive there are apricot and apple trees, date palm and extensive vegetable and strawberry beds. I see a monk pruning the olive trees – it turns out to be the delightful Father Paulos. I offer to help carry the cuttings and we take them to a pen in which a small herd of goats prance. Father Paulos steps over the wire to feed them the olive leaves. These well-groomed and loved goats are clearly not intended for the table. How do they contribute to monastic life? I ask. They give milk. Of course. We walk on to another remarkable scene. It's the fearless Father Mikail tending his beehives. He is wearing no protective gear yet, surrounded by a swarm of bees, is extracting the honeycombs to harvest the honey. What an idyllic scene to come upon in this wilderness – truly a place of milk and honey!

Father Justin leads me back inside the monastery and we head towards his particular realm. He looks after the library – and this is no ordinary collection. St Catherine's houses around 4,500 codices (manuscripts bound into volumes) along with individual manuscripts and printed books dating from the 15th century onwards. It contains the largest collection of early Christian manuscripts outside the Vatican and so is one of the most important libraries in the world. In addition it has a superlative collection of over 2,000 painted religious icons – in fact it possesses half of all the Byzantine icons still in existence.

We move on. I walk through the monastery's narrow streets and courts, look at the 12th-century dining hall, along with the graffiti carved into its door and internal stone arches by crusaders who visited after the Christian Kingdom of Jerusalem was established in 1099 and by Christian pilgrims who continued to make their way to St Catherine's long after the eclipse of Christian power in the Holy Land. These pilgrims came not just to venerate the holy site of the Burning Bush and Mount Sinai, but to see a precious relic that came into the monastery's possession in most mysterious circumstances. Originally the monastery was dedicated to the Virgin Mary, because early Christians believed that the Immaculate Conception was analogous to the way in which the bush burnt without being consumed. But the dedication was changed when the monastery came into the possession of the healing, and holy oil-oozing bones of St Catherine of Alexandria. She had been martyred in the 4th century but by 700 or so the Christian world accepted that her bones had been miraculously deposited in the Sinai and then acquired by St Catherine's. At this time saints' bones were big money earners – and thanks to a later Papal Bull, it was soon accepted that anyone who made a pilgrimage to St Catherine's would receive one year's indulgence, which is to say they would have a one-year remission of time spent in purgatory after death.

And with the pilgrims came money – the 12th and 13th centuries were an affluent time for St Catherine's.

It's time to see the church. It's a long, low structure, built around 550. I pass down a flight of steps, through the west door and enter a narrow antechamber called the narthex. There is another set of doors, dating from the mid-6th century, and I'm in the church proper.

As I walk in I notice that the doors are loaded with delicate carvings of creatures cavorting among flowers and plants. The 6th-century ceiling beams, high above, show similar scenes – images of paradise. The beams also bear the name of the Emperor Justinian, of his wife, and of the master-builder, Stephanos. This was, when new, clearly a very important place, and its meaning lies in the architecture – in its details and form. The church is a basilica in plan. There is a tall central nave flanked by narrower and lower aisles. This arrangement was derived from Roman public buildings and eventually became the common form for Christian churches in the West.

The nave is separated from the aisles by mighty monolithic granite columns, and the size and immense weight of each column (now unfortunately clad with plaster) reveal what a serious construction project this was. There are 12 of these columns – six on each side. So here's the number 12 again – 12 months of the year, 12 apostles, 12 signs of the zodiac. What can this all mean? And each column is topped by a fantastically carved granite capital. Some are arranged in matching pairs, others are individual. They sport crosses, images of the Lamb of God, and stylised leaves that make some of them look a little like Roman Corinthian capitals. One is festooned with crescent moons – the emblem of Islam nearly a century before the rise of Islam. Here it probably symbolises the Virgin Mary and relates to the ancient tradition of the Moon, the determiner of the female cycle, as an emblem of the goddess. Another capital shows a cross from which are suspended the Greek letters Alpha and Omega. This is clearly a direct reference to the Book of Revelation for in it St John has Christ make the memorable statement: 'I am Alpha and Omega, the beginning and the ending...which is, and which was, and which is to come...'. This is a clue to the meaning of the monastery's design. The Book of Revelation must have been used as a design guide. Chapter 23 talks of the holy city, 'the New Jerusalem' coming down from heaven with 'the length and the breadth and the height of it equal' and outer walls each measuring 144 cubits. So the New Jerusalem was a mighty cube, its dimensions being the product of 12 multiplied by 12. In modern terms 144 cubits is around 79 metres. I do a quick calculation of the size of St Catherine's – roughly square in plan and a place in which 12 seems such a significant number – and discover that the average measurement of its four walls is 80 metres. Good Lord. This monastery was built as the New Jerusalem – it was intended as a prophecy, the word of God in stone.

I walk along the nave. In front of me looms a massive screen festooned with icons. Behind it is the altar and above it is an incredibly fine mosaic showing the Transfiguration of Christ, probably dating from soon after the church's construction. In its top left- and right-hand corners the mosaic includes images of Moses taking off his shoes before approaching the Burning Bush, and receiving the Tablets of the Law on Mount Sinai. These images remind me of what this church is about, why it's here. I walk behind the main altar to a chapel at the east end of the church. Like Moses, I take off my shoes and enter. This is one of the most extraordinary sites in the Christian world – a site also sacred to Jews and Muslims – for since the 2nd or 3rd century it's been claimed as the site of the Burning Bush. The bush is not here, an altar stands above the site on which it grew, but the atmosphere is spellbinding. As God told Moses, this is 'holy ground'.

The day is drawing to a close and there is one last place I want to see. Set within the garden is the graveyard. I arrive as dusk starts to fall. What's surprising here is that the monastic cemetery is so small – it has room for only six graves. But that's because the bodies of the monks are regularly removed to make way for new arrivals, and their bones stacked in the adjoining Charnel House. I enter. On each side are piles of bones. I look around – these are the accumulated bodies of 14,000 years.

The monastery holds one more surprise. I slip back inside the wall and make my way towards the church. Just to the east of the chapel marking the site of the Burning Bush is – the Burning Bush! The monks here believe that the roots of the Burning Bush are still alive, below the altar in the chapel, and that it now flourishes outside – in God's light. It's an astonishing story. I look at the towering bush – it's a type of rose called *Rubus sanctus*. I finger its foliage. The Book of Revelation mentions a tree – the Tree of Life – in the New Jerusalem and states that the tree offers hope for the future because its leaves are, says the text, 'for the healing of the nations'. A beautiful thought. If St Catherine's monastery was created 1,450 years ago as the New Jerusalem and inspired by Biblical texts, then it is indeed an attempt to create paradise on earth – and this tree, and its leaves, are strangely significant. The Bible was surely the inspiration for the design of this monastery, and if so, then the Bible must hold the secret to its meaning. I look at Psalm 118, its verse emblazoned above the door of the church, and scan its 12th verse, a number that appears locked in the fabric of the monastery. It's quite a surprise. It refers to 'nations' of evil intent that '…compassed me about like bees' but 'are quenched as the fire of thorns'. I stand beneath this thorny rose bush, with its leaves for healing the nations, think of Father Mikail patiently taming his ferocious bees and, as the sun sets, feel that, this day, I've been living a parable.

Journey through the seven levels of Hindu heaven

Sri Ranganatha Temple, Srirangam, India

It's nearly five in the morning and I'm about to enter the magnificent temple town of Sri Ranganatha swami, located on the sacred island of Srirangam in south India. This huge temple, which dates from the 13th century, is dedicated to an incarnation of Vishnu – one of the three most powerful Hindu gods – and is one of the most powerful evocations of a Hindu vision of paradise. I look towards the gopuras of the temple – the tall pyramidal gates – which rise a couple of miles away, high above a dense growth of trees. The hours just before daylight are considered auspicious by the Hindus, and all around me people are hurrying to complete their rituals, praying for gods and ancestors, before the sun rises. And, just before the sun is up, I cross a branch of the Cauvery River, held by south Indians to be as holy as the Ganges in the north, and I'm on the magical island.

I head first not to the temple itself but to a ghat, here no more than a stretch of flat river bank. A group of Brahmin priests trot into sight. They are carrying a huge copper pot, slung on poles and carried by four men. I'm told they've come to collect sacred water for the god, residing in his apartment in the temple. The Brahmins rapidly fill the pot and return to the temple where the god will be woken, bathed in the sacred water, dressed, offered prasad – sanctified food – and delighted by the sight of his favoured auspicious creatures, a cow and an elephant, and by the music of the vina, a south Indian stringed instrument.

I turn away from the ghat and the bathers and follow the Brahmins to the temple. I'm dazzled by what I see. The Ranganatha temple is a truly extraordinary place – it's conceived as a giant mandala, a geometric and symbolic diagram of the universe formed by concentric enclosures that represent the various stages of a journey of the soul. At Ranganatha this journey starts at the worldly outer limits of the temple – where I'm now standing – with the route through it leading gradually to the sacred centre or nucleus – to the source, the seed, of all spiritual power and knowledge. So I have – to Hindu perceptions – entered a magic realm created by enlightened human beings to guide others to unity with god, to moksha – release from the painful and endless cycle of life, death and rebirth on earth. This temple is intended to be the whole universe in miniature, a diagram of creation, a route of escape from the pain of this world. It's the home of the gods.

I make my way to the next enclosure. The Ranganatha temple consists, in fact, of seven enclosures that cover 156 acres of ground, and within this area are not only markets but shops, workshops and houses as well as shrines and prayer halls. This temple is a world within a world, a true temple town. Each enclosure is of rectangular shape with, roughly in the centre of each of its four sides, a pyramidal entrance tower, a gopura. The alignment of the gopuras – marking the routes through the temple that all converge at the central sanctuary or vimana – has a most dramatic visual effect. As I walk through the gopura from the worldly outer enclosure – the one that contains markets and shops – I can see through the enclosures in front of me a long way towards the sacred heart of the temple, or at least get glimpses of it through gaps in the crowd of people now pouring into the place. The gopuras themselves are architecturally striking, each loaded with tiers of brightly coloured sculpture showing gods and goddesses, worldly rulers, ferocious demons and protective spirits. I notice another thing. As the gopuras march towards the centre they get gradually smaller in scale – I suppose here bigness is not best; largeness reflects the material world where the visible rules, while the smaller gopuras, nearer the holy heart of the temple, proclaim the necessity for those on a spiritual journey to embrace the non-visible spiritual world and to relinquish expressions of worldly power. Great temples like the one I am now penetrating were not just places of worship created by man – they were in themselves objects of adoration, the living body of the god to whom they are dedicated, a sacred image of the cosmos in which the gods are invoked through ritual, a paradise on earth. So to Hindus this temple is a living being, animated by divine power.

I'm now in the second enclosure – or as Hindus would say, the sixth from the sacred inner first enclosure containing the sanctuary. This second enclosure is more tranquil but still worldly, its streets lined with houses of Brahmin families that, by tradition, serve the temple. I'm on my way to meet a woman whose family has lived here for centuries, perpetual servants of the temple, familiars of the god. Morning light is now transforming the temple. Outside these Brahmin houses groups of women are just completing a ritual that started in the hours of darkness. They are putting the finishing touches to kollams placed on the ground in front of their houses. These kollams are created each morning as acts of veneration and cleansing, as prayers to the deities and ancestors, and are destroyed, by the passage of life, before the sun sets. They are made of brightly coloured rice-powder – Ranganatha is, after all, known as the Lord of Colours – and have complex geometric patterns. I stop and study one, the women making it also stop and smile at me. I ask them about the design. This is what our family have always done, they say, it's for god. Yes, each family has its own vocabulary of designs but the purpose of this one, at least, is clear. Like the temple itself, it's a mandala, the design has a six-petalled central motif reached by 12 different routes – it's an object on which to focus during meditation, a magic and protective emblem.

I walk on to the house and enter. Dr Prema Nandakumar, whose husband's family has lived in this house for 200 years, tells me about her family, their beliefs and their relationship with the temple. We meet in the large and spotless kitchen where, she tells me, food is not only prepared for the family but also for the lord. The lord? I ask. Yes, he lives next door. We walk from the kitchen into the adjoining puja room – the family chapel – and here I see an ornate shrine. Within it is an image of Vishnu in the form of Ranganatha. He is venerated, a Brahmin priest chants before him and food offerings are made. Dr Prema contemplates the image of the god fondly – devoutly. To me he is, she says, a living being, one of the family; we hate to leave him alone when we go away. She tells me of her husband's hereditary duties to the temple in which they live. This may seem complicated, she adds, at the end, but we are only human. These rituals, all the gods of Hinduism, are the only way we humans can approach the power of the one great creator.

I leave this charming house and pursue my journey to the heart of the temple. I walk across the narrow third enclosure and then enter the fourth enclosure – the fourth level of this heaven. This is, in a sense, where the temple proper starts; in the past low caste Hindus – the 'untouchables' – were prevented by the Brahmins from penetrating beyond this point. Now the profane buildings and uses decrease – no houses and only a few stalls and dining rooms for pilgrims – while the sacred structures related directly to the function of the temple and to the lives of its gods increase in number, scale and quality. I walk the circuit around this enclosure and, as is customary in most sacred buildings, I walk clockwise. Almost immediately I'm confronted by one of the temple's best architectural essays. It's the Temple of Venugopala, dedicated to Krishna – the most powerful avatar or incarnation of Vishnu – whose life, like his name, has an uncanny resemblance to that of Christ. Krishna, like Christ, is said to be a saviour who came from heaven in human form, underwent resurrection and preached mercy and love. But, unlike Christ, Krishna expressed his love in many forms and is said to have had over 16,000 wives. This is, perhaps, why the exterior of the building – said to date from the 14th century but could be as late as the 16th – is embellished with exquisite carvings of curvaceous and beautiful young women. They really are a pleasure to behold. One plays upon a vina, while another stares narcissistically into a looking glass, and one – called the 'shy girl'– lurks naked in a corner trying, not very successfully, to conceal her private parts beneath her hands.

I climb to a roof-top nearby for an overview of the temple. All around me an astonishing architectural scene unfolds. I can see the gopuras, brightly coloured and alive with carved detail, converging in regimented lines from all four points of the compass towards the golden and barrel-roofed shrine that forms the sacred heart of the temple. And because the gopuras decrease in size the nearer they get to the sacred central shrine, the scene before me seems to be a strange reversal of the laws of perspective. Here the gopuras, as they recede into the distance, get larger rather than smaller. It's quite disconcerting.

I walk around the roof, observing this architectural ballet, composing and recomposing the perspective of aligned towers. But always my eye is led back to the modestly scaled but golden and sparkling central shrine – the sanctuary. This is where Vishnu – in the form of Ranganatha – resides. By tradition he, indeed the entire temple, was being transported to Sri Lanka – where Vishnu in the incarnation of Rama battled a demon king – when all was set down here. When the time came to continue the journey Vishnu refused saying he was well satisfied with this location. The only concession Vishnu made was to shift his posture. Usually in his temples he reclines looking towards the east – to the rising sun, the same orientation preferred for ancient Egyptian temples – but here Vishnu reclines looking south towards Sri Lanka. But this central golden shrine is not just the home of the deity, it's also the heart and soul of the temple; it's what makes it, for Hindus, a living thing. When the sanctuary is constructed a vital ritual takes place – it's called the garba-nyasa – the womb installation. The ground beneath is 'impregnated' with a copper pot, the emblem of mother nature, containing nine kinds of precious things, including stones and herbs. On top of this buried pot is placed the stone slab on which the image of the god will repose. The sanctum – the womb-house of the temple – is the place of birth, and from the copper womb emerges the soul of the god that will inhabit the image. The sanctuary building itself symbolises the universe – the seven realms of the visible cosmos – consisting of the five primary elements: the copper pot is the earth, the walls are water, the vault of the sanctuary is fire, the finial pots on the roof – the four kalasas set along the top of the vault that I can just make out in the distance – represent air, while the pointed finials on top of the pots symbolise the mysterious fifth element of formless ether called akasa.

I leave the roof and continue my journey around the fourth enclosure. I walk through the Thousand Column Hall, then pass through a small sandy court, beneath a towering white-painted gopura – and enter the Sesharaya mandapa. This was constructed during the triumphant Vijayanagra period in the 16th century and, in keeping with the mood of the age, the mandapa's entrance columns take the form of huge rearing and excited horses, locked in heroic battle with roaring tigers, elephants and savage mythic creatures. Riders on the horses sabre the beasts, while hunters on foot push wobbly-bladed knives into the bellies of their unsuspecting adversaries. These hunters include some curious figures that are said to represent Portuguese – new and exotic arrivals in the region. It's all very bloodthirsty while, inside the mandapa, there are carvings of dancers.

I now pass into the fifth enclosure, a more densely packed space containing the kitchen where food is prepared for pilgrims and as offerings for the gods, a communal dining hall, an enclosure for sacred cattle, grain stores, and a 17th-century shrine to Garuda – the mythic bird that is Vishnu's sacred mount. And this is the end of my journey. The final two enclosures and the inner sanctuary are open only to Hindus, and so all I can do is stand outside and stare into this forbidden world. As in ancient Egyptian temples, the enclosures and structures within this temple get smaller, darker and more intimate as they get nearer to the sacred heart. The world beyond, which I now strain to glimpse, appears to be set in mystic gloom, with the courts mostly roofed rather than open to the sky.

But my visit to this great temple town is not yet over. This is the day of the Bhupati festival, one of the rare occasions on which the smaller processional images of Ranganatha and his consort, the goddess Lakshmi, are carried from the sanctuary and shown to the people by being taken for a tour round the town. The gorgeous images are placed on the top of a massive four-wheeled cart that is dragged around the perimeter of the large, wide and generally open third enclosure. The cart is as tall as a three-storey building, and the gods are already installed in their mobile shrine. Attached to the cart is a pair of thick ropes and on these the Brahmins, the townspeople, men and women mixed, Indians of all castes, visitors – and me – pull to get the gods on their way. This is a wonderfully inclusive and democratic festival. Gradually the cart lurches forward, stops and then, after a few moments of rest, the crowd pulls at the ropes and again the cart moves forward a short distance. And so it goes on through the day. It's exhilarating to see the people meeting, adoring – transporting – their god. I understand that the architecture and plan of the temple – although ornate and symbolic – is also highly functional because it forms a perfect theatre for the ritual being enacted around me. The temple does indeed feel like a living paradise, the body of the god animated by the love of his devotees flowing through its courts, shrines and enclosures.

7

Pleasure

City of pleasure
built on rubber

Opera House, Manaus, Brazil

Manaus lies nearly 1,500 kilometres inland from the Brazilian coast, and the most appropriate way to reach it is by travelling up the mighty River Amazon and Rio Negro. The largest, most important port on these rivers, Manaus was built on the vast wealth created during Brazil's rubber boom in the late 19th and early 20th centuries. But for the rubber merchants based here in the late 19th century money was not enough. They wanted culture and pleasure, and they wanted them in the European manner. So, in the 1890s they started to build an opera house inspired by the fashions and tastes of Paris and by 1896 they had succeeded in creating an opera house worthy of a European capital.

It is this strange creation I have come to see – a piece of allegorical architecture built almost in defiance of nature. I hear that the opera house, now called the Teatro Amazonas, is not simply a curiosity but a fine piece of late 19th-century design. Many of its key components were made in Europe and brought here, at great trouble and expense, to be assembled into an ornate confection calculated to delight the rubber barons.

I travel in a small boat, chartered for our use. As we ply upstream, we pass settlements and rainforest on distant shores. The Amazon is wide, really an inland sea. It is the greatest river in the world and accounts for 15 per cent of the fresh water emptied into the world's oceans. Before Manaus we have a stop to make. I want to find out more about the industry that transformed the region in the late 19th century. I'm going to meet a rubber-tapper.

The story of rubber is one of the strangest ever told. Suddenly the curious sap from trees in a remote region of the world became an essential material for all industrialised nations. The early European explorers of the region had seen the locals using the material to make objects such as shoes and balls. But the visitors could not think quite what to do with it, largely because it responded so dramatically to changing temperatures. In the heat it turned into sticky glue and in the cold became brittle. In the 1830s Charles Goodyear became convinced that rubber could save him from his financial plight. In collaboration with others, he tried mixing a solution of sulphur in oil of turpentine with the rubber. To his amazement this made the rubber stable when heated, and in 1839 he took out a patent on the technique. A few years more of development and the technique of vulcanisation had been discovered. The potential for a worldwide industry was created, but the huge demand didn't come until the bicycle craze of the 1890s and the motorcar from 1900. Then rubber tyres were needed and Brazil was the one great supplier. Sadly for Brazil the boom was short-lived. In a piece of extraordinary industrial espionage, rubber tree seeds were taken from Brazil by the British in the 1870s and planted in parts of the Empire. The first experiments failed but a Burma consignment thrived and the British-controlled rubber industry began. But for 30 years, until these plantations came of age, Brazil dominated the market.

I land on the banks of the Amazon. Waiting to meet me is a diminutive man in late middle age. He appears to be a native of the land – not of Portuguese stock. He is the descendant not of rubber planters or merchants but of the men who did the hard work of gathering and processing the sap of the rubber tree. His name is Mauricio Candido de Aranjo. We make our way along a narrow timber walkway raised several feet above the ground towards a small village formed by simple timber-built houses, each perched on a cluster of tall posts. Why this bizarre arrangement? I ask Mauricio. He explains that for three months of the year – from late May – the level of the Amazon rises by up to 13 metres and his little riverside village of San José is transformed into a lake. Water laps at the thresholds of the houses and travel is only possible by boat. But now it is quite different as the annual inundation receded three months before my arrival and the little earth square is dusty and baked by the heat.

Mauricio leads me into the forest, towards a young specimen of *Hevea brasiliensis* – a rubber tree. He produces a blade and quickly scores a 60-centimetre-long V-shape through the bark to reveal the white inner fabric of the tree. Immediately the milky sap appears and starts to run down towards the point of the V, where Mauricio has stuck a can to catch the precious liquid. He then takes me to gather the milky liquid, the latex, that has collected from cuts he made a couple of hours earlier. As we walk, I examine the liquid and rub some on my hand. It's like watery milk, but as I rub something strange happens. The friction and the heat created by rubbing dries the latex and it starts to congeal. It turns into a film and then, as I go on rubbing, the film rolls into a pliable, resilient, bouncy ball.

I ask Mauricio about his family, their involvement in the rubber industry and whether he has ever been to the opera house in Manaus. Mauricio's response is startling. He smiles, starts to answer politely, then becomes agitated and tears roll from his eyes. I have made him remember past shame, persecution and injustice. He tells me that his family were poor, made to work hard as tappers by the rubber merchants. They were virtual slaves. His children have achieved an education; they are free to go to the opera house, but he never would. For him it is a symbol of a time of ruthless greed and injustice, of which he is a victim.

We lunch on an array of local dishes at one of the village houses, then I board my boat and continue my journey up the Amazon. As I glide between the distant shores I ponder what has happened. My perception of the opera house is changing. Rather than a charming expression of late 19th-century eccentricity and extravagance, it's becoming a symbol of selfish indulgence and savage greed, of oppression. Soon, on my right, are the familiar outriders of a great city – industrial buildings, power station, scattered riverside housing increasing gradually in density. We land, thank our captain and crew for our safe delivery, climb the stairs from the beach and are confronted by a most elegant array of ironwork. This is the market that was designed by Gustave Eiffel, fabricated in France, and assembled in Manaus in the early 1880s. Its cast-iron detail is ornate and of the finest quality. And the place is full of life. One of the halls houses a fish market, another the meat market, and in between are stalls selling herbs and vegetables. I go on into the heart of the city. The physical evidence of the rubber boom years stands all around. Vast amounts of public and private money were used to beautify the city and the man most closely involved with the realisation of this Paris in miniature was the state governor Eduardo Goncalves Ribeiro. His name is emblazoned on the opera house, along with the date 1896, the year it was completed.

And here it is – the goal of my journey, a pink-painted architectural confection. But now, since speaking to Mauricio, I approach this monument to wealth and hunger for culture with trepidation. The architectural language is a languid classicism, late Renaissance in manner. I walk up a curving flight of steps onto a terrace on which sits the opera house. The front is dressed with a Corinthian colonnade, sitting on an arcaded ground floor and supporting a semi-circular pediment. Within the colonnade are busts of Brazilian heroes – this building is clearly all about national pride and identity. I enter a columned and curving vestibule and pass an ornamental cast-iron staircase with its structure exposed. Then I climb some steps and enter the horseshoe-plan auditorium with its ornate cast-iron gallery that was made in Glasgow. The impression is overwhelming – superb. The outside of the opera house is painted in light and simple colours, but the auditorium is dark, rich and complex. The more I look, the more I am impressed. The colours and ornament are not just mellow and well-judged but authentic. This seems to be that rare thing – an ambitious, 19th-century theatre interior that has not been sweepingly modernised or over-restored. Everything speaks of national pride, a pride in Manaus and the Amazonas region, but nowhere is there a direct reference to the source of the wealth that created this opera house, to rubber, or to those who toiled to harvest this valuable natural resource.

On the ceiling is a series of allegorical paintings that show dance, tragedy, music and the epitome of the arts, opera. But the most extraordinary thing about this painted ceiling is the frame that divides each of the four images; it is painted in imitation of ironwork, and unites into one cruciform composition. The intended illusion is that the spectator is standing below the Eiffel Tower in Paris and looking directly up!

The opera house contains one other major public interior – the ballroom set on the first floor above the main entrance. Again I encounter Baroque splendour worthy of a European palace. There are marble columns, luscious chandeliers of French-made bronze dripping sparkling Venetian glass ornament, and a complex parquet floor composed of a variety of Amazonian woods but all cut in France for assembly here. Wall paintings show the natural wonders of the region in a most romantic manner – the rainforest, its creatures, the Amazon. The ceiling is the culmination of the scheme. It shows the glorification of the Fine Arts in the Amazon and incorporates an array of naked muses. The creator of this interior was Domenico de Angelis, but the odd thing is that few can agree on the designer of the opera house itself. Some say it was Ribeiro – he had been trained as a military engineer – who took the Paris opera house as his inspiration. Others argue, less romantically, that the city authorities obtained designs from the royal office of architecture in Lisbon.

My final task is to road-test the opera house. There is a performance tonight – of the Amazon Philharmonic Orchestra playing a selection of classical music including Wagner and Mozart. But first there is someone I want to meet – a local girl who grew up in poverty and whose life has, I'm told, been transformed through classical music and the Teatro Amazonas. Her name is Elaine Martorano and she now works as a mezzo-soprano. Her story could be the antidote to Mauricio's hostility to the place. Elaine turns out to be big and beautiful. She shows me where she used to sleep in the street, after late-night work, so she could arrive on time for her singing lessons, and tells me of the power of classical music to inspire and her love for the Teatro Amazonas.

In the evening I return to the theatre. The audience, casually dressed, appears to represent a reasonable cross-section of Manaus society. The auditorium holds only 700 people; with tiers of boxes it feels full, intimate, the atmosphere is good. Yes, this is a place of beauty, the beauty of the music sustained and enhanced by the beauty of the building. It's extraordinary to sit in this theatre, to imagine the scene 100 years ago. Outside was raw, dangerous elemental nature, the teeming port and markets, the exploited and persecuted rubber-tapper. Inside were the wealthy rubber barons and their ladies, sampling the highlights of European culture. But all was doomed. In 1901–02 14,966 tons of rubber had been exported through Manaus, reaching a peak of 17,208 tons in 1909–10. Then Burmese and Malayan plantation rubber – more efficiently grown and so cheaper – started to come onto the market and by 1912 the Brazilian rubber boom was over and wealth started to ebb away.

So the Teatro Amazonas survives not only as a memorial to the rubber boom in Brazil but also to its dramatic eclipse, to the fleeting nature of all human vanity and ambition. The opera house, for me at least, serves as a sombre memorial to those who suffered, through physical toil, to create the wealth that built it.

Luxurious grandeur in a pioneering structure

Taj Mahal Hotel, Mumbai, India

It's very early in the morning and I'm in a small craft, plying through the calm waters of the Arabian Sea into Mumbai harbour. This is the way to arrive; it shows the city as it was meant to be seen and puts buildings in their proper setting. Mumbai, or Bombay as it was known, grew rapidly from its humble mercantile origins and by the late 19th century it was one of the world's great cities and ports. From my boat I can see the architectural remains of this grandeur and, as I draw near the quay of Apollo Bunder, two structures dominate the scene. One is a mighty triumphal arch – the Gateway of India, completed in 1927 to serve as the ceremonial entry point to the British-ruled sub-continent of India. The gate is of very distinct appearance – a marriage of European Imperial Classicism with Indian Mughal architecture – and was clearly designed to symbolise the unity of these two traditions within British India. Next to the gate stands a structure that is quite as symbolic as the gateway and even more architecturally impressive. It's the Taj Mahal Hotel, one of the world's great grand hotels. When the Taj opened in 1903 it was the pioneer in India of innovative building technology and truly luxurious living – the paradigm of modern pleasures. The luxury hotel, with lifts, suites of rooms, palatial restaurants and all modern conveniences, was really an American idea dating from the 1850s, and the Taj was the first of this breed to be built in India. I'm going to spend a night there to see what survives of its history and, I hope, discover what pleasures a grand hotel can give.

The hotel is still owned by the family who built it and gave it particular character and meaning. During the 1890s Jamsetji Tata, a wealthy industrialist and member of Bombay's Parsee community, hatched the dream to create and run a grand hotel. The reason why is now lost in myth, but probably has to do with Tata's pride in Bombay and his vision of the way in which the people of a great and cosmopolitan city should live together. Until the Taj opened, the great hotels of Bombay were run by Europeans and many of them operated policies of discrimination against Indians. Even the rich and powerful Jamsetji Tata could not dine at Watson's, which opened in 1869 and was among the finest of the city's hotels. Tata dealt with this intolerable situation in the most creative way possible. Rather than trying to get into the European-owned hotels, he decided to build his own. It would be the best in the world and, more important, it would be open to all, no matter what race or religion. There was only one reservation – guests had to be rich. From the start, the Taj was to be expensive and exclusive. But, as events were to prove, the fact that the Taj was open to all races made it a very important place in one of India's most important cities during the turbulent 1930s and early 1940s, when independence was very much on the political agenda. All could meet here with ease and in a relaxed way – British and Indian, Hindu and Muslim, left- and right-wing politicians. The Taj was an exclusive place for guests but its public rooms and its open policy made it a crucible for the birth of modern India.

I land beside the gateway and survey the scene. The roads are busy and noisy, and next to the Taj now stands a high tower, built by the hotel in 1973 to provide extra accommodation. This was no doubt a commercially wise move but artistically little short of disastrous, for the tower now forms a lumpen and unwelcome companion to its illustrious neighbours. I walk towards the 1903 building and as I get nearer I realise more clearly the immense importance of the hotel's architecture and of its materials and means of construction – all carry a message, and in Bombay in the late 19th century the message carried by architecture was many layered and complex. It had to do with national identity and pride, with artistic beliefs, and with the fusion of historic precedent with modern building technology. But the overriding concern was with morality and that concern has its roots in European architectural debates of the late 18th and early 19th centuries. During this period the idea emerged that there were morally right and wrong ways to build – that the honest expression of techniques of construction and of the nature of building materials is truthful and, if truth and beauty are synonymous, a morally just building must also be a more beautiful building. This theory was given an edge during the first half of the 19th century by the writings in Britain of A.W.N. Pugin and John Ruskin, who both argued the moral superiority of medieval Gothic architecture over classical. The advantages they proclaimed included the engineering sophistication of Gothic structure, the fact that it does not conceal its methods of construction but expresses them – indeed makes them its main ornament – and that Gothic architecture tends to realise the structural and artistic potential of the materials from which it is built. For this reason Ruskin particularly recommended Venetian Gothic because it made powerful decorative use of different coloured bricks and stones to enliven elevations, a technique that became known as structural polychromy. Pugin, a fervent convert to Roman Catholicism, was particularly passionate in support of the Gothic and penned many a powerful polemic pointing out that Gothic, which he believed Christian in origin, was not only constructionally more honest but spiritually superior to 'pagan' classicism. By the mid-19th century these arguments had become embroiled in the great British Battle of the Styles, in which those architects who favoured Christian Gothic architecture of varied kinds locked in heated debate with classicists over the creation of a national architectural style appropriate for the unprecedented might and power of the British Empire. Crucial to this debate was the role played by innovative structural materials such as wrought iron and glass. Should they be honestly expressed or veiled by a veneer of culturally acceptable historic detail? So, when the design of the Taj was hammered out in the 1890s the issue of architectural style was far from neutral. It had a moral charge and was the vehicle for the expression of many different desires and beliefs.

Now I'm right below the hotel's cliff-like elevation. It's clad with stone and the detail is spare. All is strictly symmetrical and the tiers of similarly sized windows have a functional and modern feel, honestly expressing the repetitious nature of the stacks of hotel suites that they serve. At ground level is an open arcade, a pleasant and shady place open to the public and so something of a contribution to life in the city and a reminder of elegant streets in Renaissance European cities. The corners of the hotel are marked by towers which terminate in domes, and in the centre of the façade is an ornamental screen rising the full height of the building. The towers and screen are richly detailed and evoke varied styles of Indian architecture. As with the Gateway of India, the Taj is attempting a kind of cultural fusion with the aim of forging a distinctly Indian urban architecture that is rich in historic references, yet modern in construction and planning.

I enter the staircase hall. It is a spectacular space, rising into the huge and mighty dome which crowns the centre of the hotel. This large, ornamental staircase well is square in plan but set below an octagonal drum and does many things. Most obvious is its role in bringing grandeur and architectural excitement to the interior of the hotel and providing the main route of circulation between floors. Not so obvious, but equally important, is the contribution it makes to the quality of life within the building. In effect it's a massive chimney which, when the hotel was new, did much to ventilate the building and keep it cool during the hot months of the year. Much of the hot air in the hotel would be drawn into the staircase well, rise naturally and leave the hotel through the openings in the drum below the dome. As this hot air left the hotel, fresh air, cooled by passing over ice manufactured and exposed in the basement, was sucked into the building at low level. The Taj scored lots of firsts in Indian architecture and this was one of them – a rudimentary but apparently effective, air-conditioning system. It was also the first building in Bombay to be lit by electricity, to have electric fans and lifts, and a Turkish Bath. I look up the staircase. It really is the great glory of the hotel, a truly magnificent affair with its tiers of galleries serving each floor and its fascinating mix of architectural detail and forms. The idea of a mighty domed space containing a cantilevered staircase and galleries is derived from Renaissance architecture, while most of the details are European Medieval Gothic in inspiration, but there are also blank arches which are distinctly Mughal in character. The designer of this splendid affair is somewhat uncertain but its mixed detailing could, perhaps, reflect its mixed origins. The plans for the hotel, which started construction in 1898 with a daunting waterside foundation 12 metres deep, are signed by the Hindu architect Sitaram Khanderao Vaidya and so the initial designs for the staircase must be his. But Vaidya died in 1900 and Tata put the completion of the hotel into the hands of British architect W. A. Chambers.

The basic plan of the hotel is simple. A circulation corridor runs towards the rear of the building and parallel to the front arcade, and off this corridor at ground level are shops, bars and restaurants. The hotel is shallow in plan, to allow cooling sea

Kizhi, Russia The walled sacred precinct – or pogost – at Kizhi. The Church of the Intercession of the Blessed Virgin is on the right, the pyramidal form of the Church of the Transfiguration in the centre, and the 19th-century bell-tower on the left. Within the wall is consecrated ground used for Christian burials.

St Catherine's Monastery, Sinai, Egypt Outside the east end of the church with Father Nilus, left, and Father Justin. We are in front of a *Rubus sanctus* thorn bush which, the monks say, grows from the roots of the original Burning Bush that once stood nearby.

Sri Ranganatha Temple, Srirangam, India This temple town, started in the 13th century but with most existing buildings dating from the 16th and 17th centuries, is organised around seven concentric enclosures that evoke the seven heavens of the Hindu cosmos.

Villa Barbaro, Maser, Italy The glorious entrance front of the villa – a place of pleasure and a working farm.

Bavaria, Germany Neuschwanstein, on its commanding mountain peak. The castle, started in 1869 for King Ludwig II of Bavaria and never completed, is the great creation of the 'Dream King'. He derived intense pleasure from turning his fantasies into romantic architecture, in which he could escape the harsh realities of the world.

Pompeii, Italy View from the Tower of Mercury, part of Pompeii's city wall, down Via Mercurios, towards the Forum. In the centre are ruins of houses. The catastrophe that overtook Pompeii nearly 2,000 years ago has preserved the evidence of daily life, allowing us to see how people lived and how they took their pleasure.

Santo Domingo, Dominican Republic
A city gate – called the Gate of
Mercy – through which Francis
Drake's men stormed when they
captured and sacked Santa Domingo
in 1586. This was one of the events
that provoked the vengeful King of
Spain to launch his ill-fated Armada
against England in 1588; the entrance
front of the cathedral of Santa Maria
was completed in 1541 in a classical
design; a straight street running the
entire length of the old city reveals
the gridiron plan of the city; the nave
of the cathedral, started in 1591,
is still in the Gothic style.

Bucharest, Romania The Boulevard of the Victory of Socialism was cut through the heart of Bucharest during the 1980s and at one end stands Nicolae Ceausescu's gigantic People's Palace. These and related projects, calculated to express and consolidate Ceausescu's hold on power, destroyed much of the city's historic character.

Qalaat Marqab, Syria The main entrance to the castle of Marqab, set below the mighty square-towered gatehouse. The castle was greatly strengthened from 1186 by the military order of the Knights Hospitaller to make it one of the most powerful Christian strongholds in the Holy Land. For more than 100 years the castle stood defiantly at the meeting point of the Christian and Muslim worlds – and in the end Marqab alone kept alive hopes of a Christian state in the Holy Land.

New Orleans, USA The entrance front of the Evergreen Plantation House – the epitome of southern commercial power and breeding. The opulent style of this splendid classical mansion is in stark contrast to the rows of utilitarian slave cabins standing close by, which reveal the ruthless and heartless nature of the place.

FACING PAGE *Istanbul, Turkey*

TOP LEFT The rooftops of the Topkapi Harem – the private world of the sultan. The complexity of the harem's form reflects the complex relationships between the communities which lived there and was calculated to confuse intruders. It may look picturesque but the harem was, essentially, a world in which men exercised power over women.

LEFT Clockwise from top left: The domed ceiling in the Throne Room; the walls of the harem are covered with sensationally beautiful 16th-century Turkish tiles. Allah is implied by the tulip, shown in many tiles, for in Arabic its name is written in a similar way to that of Allah; beautiful lettering mentioning Allah in the centre and left; a central meeting place in the harem.

Clockwise from above: One of
the sweeping staircases which
were restored during the 1940s;
a few moments' walk from the
mansion lies another world.
Here are rows of slave cabins,
organised to allow surveillance;
a cabin's veranda and a simple
chair. These evocative memorials
to the evil of slavery are among
the very few slave quarters
surviving in the United States;
inside a slave cabin. Originally
a slender partition, running
from chimney stack to door,
divided the small cabin into
two habitations.

breezes and cooled air to flow through it more easily, but has deep wings projecting to the rear which now frame a garden and swimming pool. Despite its exotic detail the hotel really is conceived as a functional machine – most modern. I walk into the garden. Originally this was the main entrance court but an early change of mind seems to have been for the better and so what was a public space, full of carriages and cars, is now a delightful and sheltered enclave.

In 2003 the Taj was thoroughly overhauled, to celebrate its centenary I'm told, but some of its curious character seems to have been lost in the process. In 1939 prohibition in the Bombay Presidency forced the hotel to the brink of bankruptcy and during the 1960s, after decades of neglect, the hotel was only just saved from demolition. But things are brighter now, for the hotel is sleek and fashionable again and has found itself a role in modern Mumbai life – it's the most desired location for grand wedding receptions, with as many as five a day being held in the ballroom and banquet suites on auspicious religious days. Ah, the ballroom – the most sumptuous and luxurious in India when the hotel opened. I ascend the staircase to see it, enter and find myself in a cavernous space that is being prepared for a wedding. But oh dear, it has been sadly transformed and now lacks character. It's hard to imagine the former glamour and glory of this room. This was the place particularly favoured by grand Indians; in here princesses and maharanis could let their hair down, dress in a fashionable Western manner and relax in ways they wouldn't dare in their own palaces, under the watchful and disapproving eyes of servants. For many, the Taj must have seemed an almost impossibly magical place. In this room princesses who'd been in strict purdah in their rural principalities could mingle freely with other guests, could even dance. But I fear these exalted ladies wouldn't now recognise their former haunt.

In the morning I rise early to see my last destination in the hotel – the roof. I climb a steep staircase and emerge into a terrain of ducts, pipes and roof lights. The roof is flat and, like the floors below, supported on huge steel girders that also allow the creation of flexible and open floor areas. Again very advanced for the 1890s but then Tata was, among other things, a manufacturer of steel. At the corners of the roof are the smaller domes, vaguely Mughal in form. The drums on which they stand look rather stunted now because an extra floor was added to the hotel. I walk to one of these domes. It is made of sheets of iron and inside is a gigantic water tank. The other domes also contain water tanks and this is the secret of one of the Taj's early boasts, that all its baths had hot water all the time – a thing virtually unknown in Victoria's India. It's brilliant – I love the ingenious and witty way modern services are cunningly integrated with the architecture. Tata and his architects knew how to use modern technology in a most creative manner, and managed to make the hotel as comfortable, functional and solid as possible. Despite all the changes, the Taj still succeeds in its primary aim – the primary aim of all grand hotels – to evoke and satisfy a fantasy, to give physical pleasure and mental satisfaction. It's a theatre of dreams created through well-judged architecture; a place in which guests can play at being princes and princesses. Here we're all treated like royalty, cosseted and fussed over.

From the roof I have a splendid view over the city centre. To my left is Back Bay with its apartment blocks and towers built on land reclaimed from the sea. On my right is the core of the old city and the docks of Bombay Harbour. In the centre is, among a host of 20th-century buildings, the glorious heart of 19th-century Bombay. Here are the University, the Secretariat and the High Court – all magnificent buildings of the 1870s which, in their different and dazzling splendour, reflect the quest for a national architectural style for India. Medieval European Gothic appears to dominate – reflecting British architectural taste at the time – but this is combined with much inventive detail inspired by Indian traditions. I make my way to the Maidan, marked by the Venetian Gothic mass of the Secretariat and the University clock tower, which is based on Giotto's campanile in Florence and furnished with a clock that chimes 'Home Sweet Home' and 'God Save the Queen'. But before I reach my destination I come upon the charming Gothic Sassoon Library of 1870 and next to it an astonishing edifice – a vast and rotting affair with tiers of galleries supported on rusting iron piers. This is the gaunt hulk of the once famed and exclusive Watson's, the most prestigious hotel in Bombay and, perhaps, the catalyst for the construction of the Taj.

Watson's was one of the first prefabricated buildings made from standardised iron components to be erected in India and was inspired ultimately by London's Crystal Palace, the centrepiece of the 1851 Great Exhibition. Started in 1867, Watson's is now the oldest iron framed building in India and of international architectural importance. The hotel's ruthlessly functional and exposed iron frame shocked the city when completed in 1869, but now shocks because of its appearance of utter abandonment. It looks impossibly and tragically derelict. I go inside and to my amazement find the place buzzing with life. Watson's now houses chambers for lawyers and other professionals. It's astonishing and wonderful – life thriving among the physical decay. People dart up and down the solid cast-iron stairs and smile and wave at me as they pass. I penetrate deeper. In the gloom I find the glass-roofed atrium court, once the restaurant and ballroom but now with mounds of rubbish rising where the band once played. Around the atrium are the collapsing remains of galleries that once served the bedrooms. This place seems a parable – a reminder that all worldly grandeur is an illusion and all quests for physical pleasure are doomed to end like this.

Golly, this wreck of a building is a sad and salutary sight in which the pursuit of pleasure has long been abandoned. But it's also magnificent in its melancholy. Here the imagination runs riot and the spectres of the past still walk. It's the very epitome of picturesque decay. In the atrium I push the noisome rubbish to one side and beneath I find delicate and long forgotten cast-iron Gothic detailing. Breathtaking. The Taj was luxurious indeed, but for me Watson's is real pleasure.

The ultimate in visual beauty and harmonious proportions

Villa Barbaro, Maser, Italy

Andrea Palladio was born 500 years ago in northern Italy, but his architecture continues to astonish, delight and inspire. Palladio was the leading architect of the Italian late Renaissance period and possessed what he believed to be the key to beauty. He used it to create buildings that offer ultimate visual pleasure. I'm on my way to visit one of his most exquisite works and to discover its secrets.

I drive into the countryside around the city of Vicenza where many Venetian grandees had their second homes in a lush and fertile landscape. I arrive at the village of Maser and see a domed and porticoed church, inspired by the ancient Pantheon in Rome. Two Venetian brothers, Daniele and Marcantonio Barbaro, commissioned Palladio in 1549 to design the church and the adjoining Villa Barbaro. These brothers, both rich, cultured and deeply involved in the political, religious and artistic life of the Venetian state, wanted Palladio to build them an ideal home – a place that offered escape from their palazzo in the city and represented a demonstration of perfect beauty. They wanted a villa that was a pleasure to occupy and a pleasure to behold, where they could live for large portions of the year when the heat and summer stench made Venice unbearable and unhealthy.

The villa, set back on rising ground and approached via a gate flanked by tall piers supporting flamboyant sculpted figures, has immense presence. The most striking thing is its rigid symmetry, which implies order, balance and harmony. The centre section of the villa is faced with giant engaged columns supporting a triangular pediment. This is one of the earliest revivals in Renaissance villa design of the Roman temple front and was intended to imbue this building with the gravity and dignity of the Golden Age of Rome. It's clear that the Barbaro brothers were seeking to give their residence and their family the gloss of antiquity and of ancient pedigree. This central section of the villa is flanked by arcaded wings, terminating in pavilions topped by huge quadrant scrolls and ornamental pediments. It's all very theatrical and makes the villa look rather urban, like part of a piazza, and a trifle startling in its rural setting. But more important is the shape of the centre section. It is square in plan and virtually as deep and wide as it's high, so the centre section of the villa reads as a mighty cube. This is a form close to Palladio's heart and the basis of his system of beauty, which is based on a harmonically related set of proportions.

Palladio believed that design should be rational, that details should reflect techniques of construction, and that interior plan and elevations should relate; nothing should be superfluous. The pediment is a direct reflection of the villa's pitched roof, while the biggest windows light the largest, most important rooms. But, as I approach the villa, I discover that here Palladio breaks some of his own basic rules. Perhaps he was overruled by the Barbaro brothers or perhaps the design was compromised because he had to incorporate the remains of a medieval house that stood on the site. The pediment should mark the position of the main entry to the villa and there is indeed an imposing door located beneath it. It's an odd affair, topped by a keystone embellished with a grotesque horned demon – a nature spirit, I presume, like the Green Man. The Barbaro brothers were part of the Humanist circle of Venice. They believed in the essential dignity and value of all people and in humanity's ability to liberate itself from mysticism and superstition and, through education and rational thinking, hammer out an ethical way of life, be able to determine right from wrong, good from evil. So what's this fantastic image doing perched above their front door? Just a bit of architectural whimsy?

I enter and discover that this really is no front door at all. Perhaps that's what this demon is saying – don't come in here. This door leads merely to a simple, utilitarian space with no clear route to the floor above. Most strange. In his villa designs, Palladio often made the ground floor utilitarian while the first floor was the piano nobile, containing the major interiors. But when this was the case he made the route to the first floor grand, usually via flights of steps, so there could be no confusion. But here it's not obvious how to get into the first floor. I follow the route that carriages would have taken in the past and arrive at one of the end pavilions. From there, I get a magnificent view down the arcaded wing. The scale is large; the architecture simple and bold. It's a noble promenade, like the approach to a public building rather than to a villa, leading from the outer world to the inner, from the rural atmosphere of the vineyard and the farm to what promises to be a most sophisticated interior, a realm of erudite beauty.

At the end of this promenade is a staircase leading to the first floor. I ascend and enter the main floor of the villa. I look around – all is not as it should be. Entering a classical building from the side is strange enough but can be made to work. Here it most definitely does not work, for the initial vista through the building seems unbalanced. On my left I have a diagonal view into a large cruciform hall with a barrel-vaulted ceiling, and the perspective is not really satisfying. Palladio experimented once or twice with halls of cruciform plan – usually they are square or rectangular in plan and cubical in volume – and now I rather wish he hadn't. On my right is a more conventional

Palladio room, one that is virtually a cube in volume. But my discomfort at the plan and entry point into the piano nobile is soothed by the surface decoration. All the walls, and some of the vaulted ceilings, are covered by stunning frescoes executed in the mid-16th century by Paolo Veronese. As I enter the room and look at these paintings, I understand what was going on, what Palladio and the Barbaro brothers were up to. It's most curious indeed. This was no conventional villa and this was not intended to be read as one space. Here two worlds met: the Barbaro brothers' formal world – the world they inhabited as great Venetian public figures – and their more intimate family world. The large cruciform hall and the smaller cubical salon are now barely divided by a large opening. I look at this opening and see that it contains evidence of hinges for a pair of large double doors. Of course, these two rooms were originally divided by double doors, virtually a wall, which more clearly defined their respective volumes and made each discrete. The cruciform hall, which the visitor enters first, is reminiscent of a church. It is the great public room and here the brothers would have received grand guests, who might never have penetrated beyond this lofty space. The cubical room is the heart of their private world and would usually, I suspect, have been entered by progressing down the rooms set within the wings. The Veronese paintings seem to confirm this division. The frescoes in the hall include large images of beguiling female musicians, suggesting this was a place of reception and entertainment, and in the centres of its longer walls are painted rural scenes, some showing ruined Roman buildings, an imaginary and ideal landscape. This is interesting, Veronese is extending the sense of space ordained by Palladio's precisely proportioned architecture. The painter has even added trompe-l'oeil pilasters and columns, and additional doors complete with painted life-size figures. From one a page emerges, just about to enter the room, and from another a child totters forward. I stand in the centre of the hall. From here all of Veronese's complicated vanishing points and false perspectives work perfectly. This clearly is the centre of the Barbaro brothers' illusionary universe, the place from where fiction looks most like fact. Amazing.

The rooms which adjoin the cruciform hall and overlook the entrance court are also richly·decorated, and their subject matter reveals their function. One has trellis and vines on its vaulted ceiling and an image of Bacchus squeezing juice from grapes, so this must have been the formal dining room of the villa. The other shows gods in debate, so is obviously the formal drawing room where guests would converse. All painted allusions are to the classical world, the world in which Renaissance Humanists believed civilisation, with its ethics and morality, had its roots. But as well as being philosophising Humanists and political figures the brothers were also part of the established Roman Catholic Church – they had to be to function within Italian society. So the symbolism of Veronese's emblematic scheme had to be most carefully orchestrated, relating stories of the classical world and its pagan gods, but only those that reflected Christian values.

I walk from the cruciform hall into the cubical salon. The walls are painted with dramatic views of Arcadian landscapes and on the ceiling is an image of Olympus, with Divine Wisdom at the centre. All around are figures representing the seven planets, the four elements and the four seasons, reclining in lofty and distant postures. This is an image of cosmological harmony as defined in the writings of Daniele Barbaro – a harmony comparable to that created by Palladio through his architecture. This fresco – and this room – must be the expression of the divine harmony that Barbaro sought and which he believed should govern the world and bring about a Humanist enlightenment to confirm, not challenge, Christian ethics. And this villa, with its frescoes and landscape, is a move towards the creation of this ideal world. It's meant to carry a message of hope to those able to read it. But this high-minded allegorical scheme – somewhat surprisingly – also includes portraits of the Barbaro family, in mid-16th-century attire, looking down onto the world of man from, as it were, the realm of heaven. Chief among the observers is Marcantonio's wife, keeping an eye on family life below. From this cubical room there is a vista along the rooms in each of the flanking wings which, with all doors aligned, are arranged en enfilade so that it is possible to see from one end of the villa to the other – a most impressive architectural effect. The rooms in the wings are also frescoed, but the most dramatic are the images of the life-size figures that terminate each view. One shows a man dressed as a hunter that, by tradition, is a self-portrait of Veronese.

This beautiful room – in which wisdom sits in majesty, and family fraternise with ancient gods – is the heart of the home, the focus of the Barbaro world. The fact that it is cubical in form, echoing harmoniously the cubical form of the villa's centre section, is most significant, and the reason why is explained by Palladio himself. In 1570 he published an architectural book – 'I quattro libri dell'architettura' – that contains fascinating insights into his architectural thinking. In this book Palladio reconstructed major antique buildings, published often idealised versions of his own designs, and discussed construction techniques and proportional systems. This discussion included a description of the seven proportions that Palladio declared would produce the 'most beautiful' rooms. These are a circle, a square, a square and a third, the diagonal of a square, a square and a half, square and two thirds, a double square. The key is that all these proportions are simple extensions, or closely related to, the same basic unit – the square, or its three-dimensional equivalent the cube. Even the diagonal of a square proportion – otherwise known as root two – if extended to root four becomes a double square. So this proportional system, organised around the square, creates a series of harmonious shapes, all of which relate to one another.

For Palladio this integration, the fact that proportions used were 'commensurate', was vitally important. It was the key to getting all elements of a buildings to relate in a pleasing manner. If this harmony were not achieved, beauty would be absent. The relation between the cubical salon and the rooms on each side of it illustrate, in a simple and direct manner, how Palladio united the different elements of a building. The flanking rooms are both the same size and proportion and make a symmetrical composition with the cubical room. But instead of being square in plan, these flanking rooms are each a double square – that is twice as long as wide, with their longest dimension being equal to the length and width of the cube room. The double square was, of course, one of Palladio's ideal proportions, and all details within these three rooms relate. For example, window openings are square in shape, door openings double-square. So this set of rooms – the entire building – is proportionately connected and starts to resonate like a piece of carefully composed music.

In 15th- and 16th-century Italy beauty was more than a means of sensual pleasure. For Palladio and the artists of the Renaissance, the beauty produced by harmonious proportions was evidence of the hand of God. They believed these proportions were the reflection of immutable and sacred laws and the means through which beauty was created in the natural world. All man had to do was to see, understand and emulate nature to create beauty in his own works. For Humanists such as the Barbaro brothers beauty was an act of faith – the rational demonstration of the will of God and of divine wisdom; the pleasure that beauty gives was seen as evidence of the existence of a beneficent god. Daniele Barbaro, as well as being a politician and a cleric, was also an architectural theorist who in 1556 published a translation of the writings of the Roman architect Vitruvius. Daniele worked closely with Palladio and some of his observations appear to explain the design of the villa and Palladio's intentions. Between them, Palladio and the Barbaros strived in the villa to create a work of architecture which evoked the cultural values of classical antiquity, while demonstrating the power of symmetry and a system of harmonious proportion to create visual pleasure.

I leave the cubical salon and walk out into the rear court, which is possible because the villa sits on rising ground; its first floor is at the same level as the court. The rear elevation of the villa is simple and at each end are wings that originally contained farm offices, a winery and dovecots in which lived a population of edible birds. Villas like this were not just architecturally beautiful places of pleasure but also – on the model of Roman villas – intended to serve as functioning farms. In the centre of the court is a pond that is the epitome of the fusion of the practical with the ornamental and symbolic. The pond was stocked with fish – most practical – but it is also the centrepiece of a crescent-shaped temple, called a nymphaeum, which celebrated the sacred power of water and was common in Roman villas. This nymphaeum is embellished with gods, goddesses and mythic beings, including two vast images of river gods and atlantes who carry the weight of the world on their shoulders. The design of this nymphaeum is thought to be too rich, too purely ornamental, to be the work of Palladio and is assumed to have been the work of one of the Barbaro brothers. I don't know. It's certainly essential to the experience of the villa because it terminates the view through the villa – from the hall and across the salon. Perhaps the use of the water – ornamental and practical – was Palladio's idea, while the exotic detailing of the nymphaeum came from the Barbaros.

I return to the villa and sit in the salon. So the secret of Palladio's architecture, his key to beauty and visual pleasure, is a set of harmonically related proportions that he believed were divine in origin, the very building blocks of God's creation. Was he right?

Was his system of proportion subjective or does it have absolute and objective power? Well that's for each individual to decide. What is certain is that the proportions employed by Palladio – the cube, the sphere, the root two proportion – have been used by different cultures for millennia, by ancient Egyptians, Greeks, Hindus, Muslims and the designers of Gothic cathedrals. So there might well be something in the argument that these proportions reflect the harmony of nature, of creation.

Also certain is that for nearly 500 years Palladio's buildings have inspired and given pleasure to generations of people from all over the world. It must be admitted that the proportions he used seem to work. I walk around the hall and salon, and enjoy the way the forms compose and recompose themselves, yet always come back to the basic ideal proportions. Yes, this is architecture that gives pleasure, and as I raise my eyes to the vault of heaven, occupied by the gods, I find Marcantonio's wife smiling down at me. She approves.

The pleasure of building castles in the sky
Neuschwanstein, Bavaria, Germany

I arrive at Schwangau, Bavaria to see a fairy-tale vision, created by a man who derived intense pleasure from turning his fantasies into architecture. This is the realm of Ludwig II – the Dream King – who built to escape the harsh realities of the world, to escape himself. Neuschwanstein, the castle which rises on a mountain above me, was started in 1869 and is the greatest architectural achievement of Ludwig's reign. In its form and decoration, the castle is a mix of Gothic fantasy, Bavarian folk myth, legends from the court of King Arthur and theatrical Roman Catholic imagery. And it was within this extraordinary work of architecture – set within a sublime landscape which had inspired his imagination since childhood – that Ludwig, at last, enjoyed perfect isolation and spiritual liberation. But this was a pleasure that could not last. It was in Neuschwanstein that Ludwig was overtaken by tragedy, and from this castle – almost mocking in its seemingly light-hearted forms – he went to his tragic and unexpected death.

Ludwig was born in 1845, the eldest son of King Maximilian II. Ludwig's father had taken the throne after Ludwig I – Ludwig's grandfather – was obliged to abdicate following a scandalous affair with a 'Spanish' dancer named Lola Montez, who turned out to be a British housewife. Ludwig's childhood was fairly miserable. Neglected by his indifferent mother and father and brutally treated at school, he escaped into an inner world of romantic fantasy and medieval myth.

At the age of 18 Ludwig became king, and soon discovered that the real world for Bavaria – and for himself – was a very difficult place indeed. In 1866 Bavaria became subservient to Prussia and in 1871 was incorporated into the Prussian-dominated German Empire. Only a few years after coming to the throne Ludwig ceased to be an independent monarch and became little more than a puppet king within the Prussian Empire. But Ludwig saw himself as the champion of the romantic medieval ideal of the just, divinely appointed and absolute monarch. He fantasised about being a great and all-powerful Christian king – and he fantasised about other things. It was clear to Ludwig – and to most other people – that he was homosexual. And Ludwig, it seems, found it virtually impossible to reconcile his passion for the physical pleasure of his own sex with his passion to be a great Christian monarch. Love, it seemed to him, was a divine force, but one which, in his sad case, could only lead to sin if indulged. One escape from misery open to Ludwig was to channel all his energies and passion into building – the only thing that could offer him creative pleasure.

I climb the hill leading to the castle, turn a corner in the road and see its almost impossibly romantic towers rising high above my head. This is a castle of dreams, of the imagination – with little grip on reality – and so, I suppose, it's an almost uncannily accurate portrait of Ludwig. It stands on a low peak, with the Tyrolean Alps rising on one side and a wide, flat plain on the other. The castle seems to be perched on the roof of the world, a place of ultimate escape. The romantic design was provided by a theatrical scene painter called Julius Jank, although the plans were drawn up and executed by architects Eduard Riedel and Georg Dollman. But the real creative force behind Neuschwanstein was Ludwig himself, and the primary inspiration was the composer Richard Wagner.

Ludwig first encountered the artistically momentous force

of Wagner in 1858 when his governess told him about the forthcoming production of Wagner's opera *Lohengrin*, about the heroic and pure 'swan-knight'. Ludwig was intrigued. The walls of the royal lodge at Schwangau – meaning swan's town – were decorated with frescoes showing Lohengrin, and the tale had become a key part of Ludwig's escapist fantasy. He acquired a copy of Wagner's libretto and was hooked. Prince and composer seemed soulmates. Ludwig's passion for Wagner found an outlet in 1863 when, reading the preface to the published libretto of *The Ring Cycle*, he noted Wagner's observations about the miserable state of the German theatre. In order for *The Ring* to be produced, moaned Wagner, an artistically enlightened and generous German prince would have to be found. To Ludwig this was a challenge from the hero he worshipped but had never met, and he resolved that he would be the prince Wagner needed. His chance came the following year when his father died and Ludwig became king. Within days of ascending to the throne, Ludwig invited Wagner to Munich, and a friendship that had existed only in Ludwig's imagination became real. The infatuation seems to have been mutual. Ludwig believed he had found a man who gave substance to his passion for the past and who, through his operas, was reviving German culture, indeed forging a modern Germanic identity inspired by ancient chivalric virtues. Wagner, flattered by Ludwig's attention and no doubt impressed by his genuine feeling for medieval myths, wrote, 'Ludwig knows and understands everything about me – understands me like my own soul.' Wagner must also have been deeply thankful that Ludwig's support took a most tangible form. The king paid off Wagner's debts, installed him in a villa in Munich and funded the completion of *The Ring*. Indeed, such was the intensity of Ludwig's support for Wagner that the composer was, in late 1865, obliged to quit Munich to allay growing suspicions. But there was no breach. Wagner knew what it was to be persecuted for your art and passions, and the king and composer remained staunch friends.

It was perhaps this severing with Wagner, and to escape the drab atmosphere of the repressive Munich court, that made Ludwig decide to build Neuschwanstein on the site of an authentic but ruined medieval castle. This castle was to be not only a place of escape but a monument to Wagner and the mythic knights and princes of his operas. As a starting point for its design, Ludwig took Wartburg Castle in Thuringia, where Wagner had set key scenes in his opera *Tannhauser*. Neuschwanstein was to be Ludwig's own castle of the Holy Grail where, as in the tale of Parsifal, redemption and forgiveness could be found.

I approach via the main gate and enter an outer court with the castle rising above me. The forms and Gothic details are as if from a fairy tale. Ludwig created the most extraordinary setting to live out the theatre of his life. This is more than just architecture – it's like entering the soul and the mind of a man in torment. I pass through a door and find myself at the foot of a richly decorated, stone-built spiral staircase. This leads up to the various worlds created within the castle. In fact, despite its seemingly rambling appearance, the castle is logically planned. At the top are the staterooms, neatly separated from Ludwig's private apartment. Below this level were to be guest rooms and below these were more utilitarian spaces. I ascend to the most symbolically important of all the spaces in the castle – the throne room. The most strikingly obvious thing about this room is that its design is based on that of a domed and columned Byzantine church, stressing Ludwig's belief in the divine nature of kingship and of anointed kings. On the floor is an image of the earth, rich in animal and vegetable life, locked in a wheel representing the cycle of earthly existence; all very Buddhist-like. Above this, on the ceiling, hovers an image of the sun and starry heavens, and, set in an apse where the altar should be, was to be the throne. It was to have been made in ivory, symbolising purity, but was never installed. Perhaps it was never meant to be for, in Ludwig's fantastical imagination, this room was not for him but for an ideal king – perhaps for a king such as he might become. Inspired by legends of Parsifal and his son Lohengrin, this room was for 'the unknown king of the Holy Grail', for a ruler who, purified and transfigured, would one day emerge to take his rightful place. Above the location reserved for the throne are images of six perfected Christian kings – all of whom by their actions vindicated kingship. Above them is Christ in Judgement, seated on a rainbow as described in the Biblical Book of Revelation. Elsewhere on the walls are images of Moses receiving the laws revealed by God – the moral code for Christian kingship – and the 12 apostles as the champions of the divine commandments.

This is a powerful and perplexing place. Here Ludwig created a temple to kingship, a sacred universe, from which he seems to have exiled himself. His sense of guilt – about his homosexuality, about his failure to live up to what he believed to be the ideals of kingship – is almost overwhelming. I stand where the throne should be to survey this world ordained by Ludwig. My eye is caught by the large mural opposite. It shows St George locked in combat with the dragon, and I notice that the battle is taking place below a rendering of Neuschwanstein perched on its rocky crag, and on St George's helmet is an heraldic swan. Of course, this is an image of Ludwig himself as the Swan Knight, a reminder that salvation could only be found if he fought and conquered the forces of physical evil, including his own desires.

I return to the staircase to reach the top floor of the castle and its largest room – the Singers' Hall. It's a magnificent room, with an open timber roof structure and a dais and minstrels' gallery at one end, and is a spectacular celebration of knightly myth and the work of Wagner. The walls here tell more of Parsifal and his quest for the Holy Grail – all inspired by Wagner's opera.

I return to the staircase to descend to explore Ludwig's private apartment located below the Singers' Hall. Here he lived utterly alone in this fantastic castle. There's a small dining room where Ludwig would feast – in the small hours of the morning – talking with imaginary guests, great figures from the past invited to be his companions for the night. Beyond is the king's bedroom. The bed itself is in the High Gothic style, holy and exalted like the shrine of a saint, and above the king's pillow a portrait of the Virgin Mary, a stern reminder to the king to keep his love pure. Indeed the whole of the bedroom is dedicated to the battle against sensuality. On the walls is painted, in splendid style, the story of Tristan and Isolde, a tragic romance set in the court of King Arthur – a tale of forbidden love in which salvation is achieved through death. Off the bedroom is a small oratory where, I imagine, Ludwig spent a lot of time on his knees, praying for forgiveness. Beyond the bedroom is an odder room still – a cave-like grotto inspired by the cave of Venus that features in Wagner's *Tannhäuser*. It is a room that's positively perverse in its utter denial of nature. Rather than being buried deep underground where it belongs, this grotto is perched high up on a mountain peak and nothing here is what it seems. The rocks are artificial, the eerie lighting comes from electric lamps. Here, Ludwig would listen via a conduit to the voices of singers in the hall above – the very image of an outcast, a human adrift in a world of fantasy and delusion.

I leave the king's apartment and go to the floor below. This is also a shock – but in a very different way. This level was for guests, but never completed because it was never needed. Ludwig had no guests. Wagner, the inspiration behind the creation of Neuschwanstein, never came here. In November 1880 he conducted a private performance for Ludwig of the prelude to his *Parsifal* and the two never met again. Ludwig, it seems, disliked the liberties Wagner had taken with what he regarded as the sacred text of the Parsifal myth. I wander around this empty floor. Neuschwanstein is in many ways the epitome of the 19th-century dream of the romantic perfection of the Middle Ages. With its thrusting towers, the castle is the ultimate expression of the Gothic Revival – the belief that artistically at least the way forward was to return to the past. But Ludwig was not obsessed by an archaeologically correct recreation of the past, as this incomplete floor makes very clear. Ludwig believed in a very modern Gothic – one that combined the look of the past with the technology of the present. As I walk through these raw rooms I can see that no attempt has been made to simulate authentic medieval-style construction. The walls are made of hard brick, clad with a veneer of stone, and metal has been used to make the structure robust and fire-proof. The whole building was heated with a hot-air system, was lit by electricity and fitted with excellent modern plumbing.

Before the castle was completed Ludwig's world fell apart. The king had no private fortune. All his building projects had to be paid from official funds which, combined with his almost complete retreat into fantasy and away from his formal duties, made Ludwig's reign increasingly intolerable to a growing number of his influential subjects. In June 1886 Ludwig was dragged from his bed and placed under arrest. He had been declared insane and his uncle was made regent. Ludwig was bundled off to nearby Berg Palace where, two days later, he was found drowned in Lake Starnberg, with the doctor who had certified him as insane. Their bodies were found by the water's edge, at a spot now marked by a simple cross. Was this suicide, with Ludwig, in the manner of Tristan, seeking salvation through death? Or was it murder? Did the doctor perish trying to save Ludwig or was he killed because he had witnessed the king's murder? It remains a mystery. What is certain is that there were many who had much to gain by the removal of such a strange and maverick monarch.

I stand by the mournful cross at sunset and ponder Ludwig's strange tale. At the time of his death he was seen as an insane wastrel and his castles as ruinously expensive follies. But now Ludwig is a hero in Bavaria, a man who preferred art and beauty to war, while his castles define the special character of Bavarian architecture. He lives on through his architecture, his greatest pleasure, which has granted him immortality.

Pleasures of daily life
preserved through catastrophe
Pompeii, Italy

I reach Pompeii on a Saturday evening in the spring and find myself in the centre of a modern city, really a suburb of nearby Naples. The main piazza is thronged with people. All is full of life and there's a sense of joy in the air; all seems focused on the pleasures of the moment, on things to come. The Roman city of Pompeii was renowned as a place of delight and a centre for the production of wine, perfume and delicately made jewellery. Visitors from Rome would flock to Pompeii and the area around the Bay of Naples to enjoy the relaxed, cultured and luxurious way of life that had evolved centuries before, when this region of Campania had been a Greek colony.

But, as I sit in the piazza, enjoying the sights, I'm aware of a spectral, haunting, presence. In the gloom, just beyond this arena of sparkling life, is the abandoned city, the realm of the dead where, in just a few hours, thousands of people died in a horrifying manner, the victims, it seemed, of the sudden and violent wrath of nature. Within moments a paradise on earth was turned into hell, a verdant plain into a bleak and lunar landscape. The story of Pompeii's sudden demise is familiar but still retains the power to shock.

The city had been badly damaged by a major earthquake in AD 62. Recovery was slow but by AD 79 reconstruction was nearly complete, the population had stabilised, and the economy largely recovered. Then, around 20 August, the Bay of Naples area suffered a series of minor earth tremors. Structural damage to buildings was minimal but what would the people of Pompeii have thought? Could lightning really strike twice? Shocks and minor earthquakes continued and by the 22nd it gradually became obvious that whatever was brewing beneath the surface of the earth was most likely going to get worse. During the morning of the 24th the first evidence of the coming disaster broke surface. Vesuvius suddenly turned murderous. There was an explosion, and sulphurous fumes and fine ash filled the air while white-hot magma started to flow towards the plain. Those who remained near Vesuvius – in villas and farms – now finally understood the ghastly truth. This was not going to be another earthquake, but something much worse.

Sometime between 10am and noon on 24 August there was a second, and far more powerful explosion as Vesuvius quite literally blew its top. A continuous, roaring fountain of ash and small pumice pebbles rose over 20 kilometres into the air. Carried by the wind and gravity, it started to descend on the sides of the volcano, on the land around its base, on isolated villas and farms, and on Pompeii and neighbouring Herculaneum. The sight was witnessed and meticulously recorded by Pliny the younger, who was staying on the Naples side of the bay. His account captures the horror and utter strangeness of the moment. It seemed the world was ending. Pliny observed that the mass of ash and debris above the volcano took the form of a gigantic umbrella pine tree, or what we would now call a mushroom cloud. It has been estimated that the explosive force unleashed by Vesuvius during the following 24 hours was equal to 100,000 times that of the atomic bomb dropped on Hiroshima. This 'frightening dark cloud' was, writes Pliny, 'rent by lightning twisted and hurled, opening to reveal huge figures of flame' and soon 'stretched down to the cloud and covered the sea'. This vast and billowing dark cloud was followed by a gush of dust. All around, in the dust and darkness, were the sounds of terror and panic: 'you could hear women lamenting, children crying, men shouting… many raised their hands to the gods, and even more believed that there were no gods any longer and that this was one last unending night for the world.'

The thick cloud of ash and pebble-like pumice that followed the first major eruption quickly started to bury Pompeii. Within minutes streets were covered with thick layers of debris and darkness descended, along with noxious fumes and the occasional larger missile. People would have been injured, terrified, disorientated and suffocating. Those out in the open, trying to flee, stood little chance. Slowed down by the layer of ash and pebbles on the ground and choking because of the hot dust and fumes, most people collapsed after only a few hundred metres and died, their bodies quickly buried by debris.

At about seven in the evening Vesuvius roared again – louder than ever – and more ash mixed with far larger stones started to fall on the city. By around 11 at night the upward force of the exploding volcano could no longer support the huge weight of the matter hanging high in the sky above it. Instead the gases issuing from the volcano were being contained. This strange balance of violent forces led to a few moments of relative calm. It seems that this was the time when survivors attempted to escape the city only to die within minutes, on top of the thick layer of ash deposits, when the volcano entered a new and truly appalling phase. The hot gases issuing up were not halted for long by those returning to earth; in fact, they were not really halted at all. The gases rising up – superheated by the core of the earth – rapidly mixed with the gases and debris that were descending and together they stormed down the side of the volcano. And as the gases escaped the eruption restarted in all its fury. This storm was the first of six pyroclastic flows to hit Pompeii and Herculaneum. They reached temperatures of 400 to 600 degrees Celsius, travelled at well over 160 kilometres per hour and the swirling wind – low in oxygen but rich in poisons – was packed with shrapnel-like debris. Buildings were instantly demolished, burnt or carbonised; human bodies were sliced and instantly baked rather than burnt. The only merciful thing about the hottest of the pyroclastic flows was that they caused death instantly.

I enter Pompeii early in the morning, a couple of hours before the crowds of tourists start to arrive. In the low morning sunlight, where some damage is concealed in shadow, and as the empty streets echo to my footsteps, this city is one of the most eerie and evocative places on earth. It had been buried under ash and debris and, after a certain amount of salvage of possessions and building materials, it was gradually forgotten. The extent of the destruction and desolation were so great that repair, even rebuilding, were out of the question. For the Roman world this once beautiful and much-loved city of pleasure was no more; it was beyond recovery – a shocking and sobering demonstration of the power of nature. It was not until the mid-18th century that Pompeii once again entered the world of the living when the coherent excavation of the city started in earnest. But the ruins give up their secrets slowly and even now nearly a third of the city remains buried by ash.

The irony of Pompeii is that the rapid and speedy destruction of all life within it also preserved it for posterity. In a matter of hours Pompeii was turned from a living and evolving city into an historical document, embodying a moment frozen in time. Its ruins offer a snapshot of a 2,000-year-old city and, although recorded at a most traumatic moment, the information enshrined in Pompeii speaks not only about the drama that overwhelmed the city but also about Roman daily life. By walking among these ruins, by looking at preserved frescoes, artefacts and the miraculously preserved ephemera of city life, I want to get to know these long-dead people, to learn about their concerns, interests, aspirations. I want to find out how their passions were roused and how they took their pleasures.

When disaster struck, Pompeii was a relatively old city. It seems to have been founded in the 6th century BC by an Italic people called the Osci. In the 5th century it came under Greek and Samnite control, and the city was not conquered by Rome until 89 BC. This long life under different peoples gave Pompeii a distinct character. It has the attributes one expects in any Roman city – gates and a city wall, a large forum flanked by public buildings, the Basilica and Temple to Jupiter, lavish public baths, theatres and amphitheatre – and much of the city is organised in a regular manner round a right-angular grid of streets. But there is also much irregularity, especially the maze of streets behind the forum, which reflects the location of the Osci settlement. Walking through Pompeii now, the thing that strikes me almost immediately is the luxury of the place. The main commercial streets are lined with the remains of shops and bars, while the higher-class residential streets contain the ruins of houses of spectacular size, generally incorporating large, open-colonnaded courts and gardens known as peristyles. I'm walking to visit one of these houses and on my way pass a large walled garden, now filled with vines. Here I can meet the people who lived – and died – in Pompeii. Lying in a row are casts of the bodies of people who failed to escape the fury of the volcano; there are men, women and children, all recorded in their death agonies. To judge by their postures, heads buried in arms or bodies tightly curled, these people were victims of a pyroclastic surge. Their bodies were buried in ash then decayed to leave nothing but a few bones and a void in the ash that hardened to form a mould. Excavators were puzzled by the voids they discovered in the ash until the grisly truth suddenly dawned, and during the 1870s a number of casts were made.

I move on, from the remains of the dead to the remains of the lives they led. I arrive in a narrow street. It is paved with large and irregular stone blocks and the high pavements are occasionally connected by raised stone slabs that were to act as stepping stones for pedestrians who wanted to escape the mire of the roadway. The street is now framed by single-storey stone-built structures, some containing small cubicles which were once shops or bars, and here and there are the remains of the plaster and bright paint that would originally have enlivened these stone walls. This is a street of houses in the better part of town and must once – with the off-white, yellow ochre and deep red walls and ornate upper storeys – have been a glorious sight. I arrive at the house I plan to visit. The first thing that confronts me as I step over the threshold is the large, painted image of a man with a gigantic penis. This is the god Priapus and he's the guardian of the garden and protector from the evil eye of jealousy. He's telling anyone entering this house not to begrudge the owners their wealth and not to steal the fruit from the trees. This really is a most extraordinary image for the modern eye – but not for the Roman. The size of the penis symbolised health and happiness and a charm for fertility. It was a reminder that mankind enjoyed a gift of the gods – the power to procreate through sexual union. In this particular instance the massive erection is being weighed against a purse of gold – proclaiming that health is worth its weight in gold. It may all now seem humorous – and was perhaps intended to amuse because the Romans believed laughter was a potent spell against evil. But for most visitors to this house Priapus was a reality and although this image raised a chuckle it would also have been somewhat intimidating. There is another detail about this image of Priapus that is revealing – he wears the red felt Phrygian cap of the Roman freedman. This is a reference to the family who occupied this house at the time of the eruption – the Vettii, who were freedmen and so members of a social group that played a very distinct role in Roman life. Italy in the 1st century AD contained a vast number of slaves – in Pompeii, about a third of the population was in bondage. Slavery could be extremely tough and brutal, especially for slaves consigned to toil on farms or in mines or the galleys. But household slaves could have a far more pleasant life and for them freedom was a distinct possibility. They could earn it, win it, be granted it when a master or mistress died and, since slaves came from a wide range of races, cultures and social groups from around the empire, there was not a deep-rooted racial contempt for them. Once a slave was made a freedman they were at liberty to mix openly in society and to prosper on virtually equal terms with citizens who had been born free. Given the numbers of slaves in Italy, and the tradition of granting freedom, in the 1st century freedmen formed a large and important group in society and were famed for their business acumen and thrusting ambition. Clearly and predictably freedmen were driven by a powerful desire to establish and prove themselves, to catch up and make their mark in the world.

Agog to see the world of a well-off family of freedmen – headed at the time of the eruption by Aulus Vettius Convivia and Aulus Vettius Restitutus – I enter the first main room of the house. This is the atrium, the typical main room of the Roman house. It's lofty, top-lit and with a pool of water in the centre – the implivium. All this was calculated to keep the room cool in summer. Around the atrium are cubicles which would have served as bedrooms. I see an opening leading to the staircase to a now missing upper level and opposite an opening that leads to a small court around which was arranged the kitchen. The atrium is a marvellous room – in many ways it would have been the heart of the house in which daily life was lived. Usually at one end of the atrium was a tablinum, a space in which the master of the house would greet guests, and where the badges of pedigree – masks and busts of honoured ancestors and family archives – were stored or put on display. But in the House of the Vettii the tablinum is conspicuous by its absence. I suppose this nouveau riche family of former slaves had little ancestry to boast about. But, perhaps by way of compensation, in the atrium were two huge treasure chests containing a sumptuous display of the family's disposable wealth. That, I suppose, was their pedigree, as the householders' names blazoned on the wall – Restitutus and Convivia – seem to suggest.

Visible from the atrium is the special glory of the house – the peristyle. It is pleasantly planted now, as it was in the time of the Vettii when the rose bushes and fruit trees stood next to fountains and marble basins cascading water. The large aqueduct serving the city made such lavish and ornamental use of water possible. The peristyle must have been a glorious retreat in summer, with cool air flowing over the bubbling water, beautifully coloured frescoes on the walls behind the fluted columns – and set among the plants is another image of a extraordinarily well-endowed Priapus promising violation to any who transgressed in his realm.

Placed off the peristyle is one of the main rooms of the house, possibly a triclinium, or dining room. If a triclinium it would have contained three couches, arranged in a U-shape around a central table, on which diners would have reclined when taking their food. What is striking about this room is the quality and subject matter of the frescoes. They are of the highest quality – it seems the house was redecorated in the most elegant and fashionable manner immediately after the earthquake of AD 62. The painted scheme is highly architectural in its composition. On the lower portion of the walls, classical columns and pilasters painted in black frame deep red panels, while above is a striking perspective view of pavilions peopled with spectators placed to stare at, or cavort before, the diners down below. But the most interesting details are nearer the floor, at the head level of diners reclining on couches. Here are panels showing beautifully painted and frolicking cherubs and what they are doing is celebrating the means by which Pompeii – and the Vettii family – made its money. There are cherubs gathering garlands of flowers, making perfume, working as goldsmiths and fullers, racing chariots and making wine – a most important image since this activity was the major source of the family's wealth.

An image of the Vettii is beginning to emerge. They were rich and displayed their wealth rather than family pedigrees. The abundant images of hermaphrodites – traditionally charms against evil – and of Priapus suggest the Vettii were superstitious but with an earthy sense of humour, while the quality of the work suggests that, at the very least, they knew artistic taste when they saw it. I now move into another room, open to the peristyle and adjoining the atrium. It was probably a smaller triclinium and is well preserved with a large fresco set in the centre of each of its three walls. The subject matter of the most striking is bizarre. It shows a scene from Greek mythology with Pasiphae – the 'wide-shining' moon goddess – contemplating the white bull that was soon to be her lover and by whom she would give birth to the Minotaur. This scene, commemorating – arguably celebrating – bestiality seems a trifle strange for a dining room. Perhaps it was intended as a witty gesture, something for the guests to laugh about as they chewed on their beef.

There is one last room in this house that I want to see. It lies in the portion of the house which would have been the realm of the slaves. I walk through the small open court next to the atrium and arrive at a door that is usually kept locked. This is, and perhaps always has been, a secret room, located in the private part of the house and hidden from the prying eyes of guests. I open the door and enter a small and very dark room, a cell really. On three of the walls are the faded remain of frescoes. The two that are reasonably well preserved each show a naked couple – a man and a women – lying on a couch and involved in sexual embrace. The frescoes are delicately drawn and the activities depicted entirely conventional. But what is a room embellished with such frescoes doing in this house? What did the Vettii use it for and what does it tell us about them? No one can agree. I ponder these scenes. We feel we know the Romans so well, but sometimes it's clear we don't really know them at all. They were technologically advanced, pioneers of many aspects of the modern world and seemingly civilised, yet they were gripped by superstition and by the dark hand of inhuman, almost soulless, cruelty. I don't know what to think – all seems so sexually charged. At best I suppose this little room was a shrine. Nearby is an altar to the Lares – the Vettii household gods and guardians of the hearth – and maybe this little cell was sacred to Priapus, to the sexual rites that lead to the creation of life, to fertility, to childbirth.

I leave the House of the Vettii and make my way to the baths. In fact, Pompeii contained several large bath complexes, but I'm going to one that lies just outside the city wall and is now known as the Suburban Baths. I pass through the Porta Marina and there are the baths below me. This bath complex was not owned by the city but was a private enterprise and the latest in luxury at the time of the eruption – it even had a large heated swimming pool. I enter – the place is very damaged but the details are exquisite, and the surviving mosaics and frescoes of the highest quality. I walk beneath a large barrel vault, its surface decorated with delicate coffering. To my right is the tepidarium and in front of me the frigidarium, its walls retaining beautiful frescoes showing marine creatures, including a huge and magnificent octopus. I turn to my right and enter the changing room – also barrel-vaulted and with its original structure exposed. It's made from pozzolana – a volcanic ash from the slopes of Vesuvius – mixed with sand and lime to form concrete. The special qualities of pozzolana – not the least of which is that it sets under water – were discovered by the Romans in the 2nd century BC and revolutionised their building world. It made possible the quick construction of Rome's harbour at Ostia, the Colosseum and vaults – like this one – in bath houses. But the vault is not the only thing of interest in the changing room. The walls retain much of their fresco decoration including a series of 16 panels. These apparently marked the location of cupboards for clothes, but each panel was also topped by a painting – eight survive – that truly eclipse the Vettii works for erotic invention. They show men and women on couches engaged in all imaginable sexual activity. In one case a man molests a man from the rear while the molested fellow has his way with a crouching female. In another a naked woman sits astride a man while clutching a long spiralling horn. What on earth can this imagery mean – is this the origin of the term horny? The purpose of these images in a bath house open to the public seems obvious – especially one, like this, that did not have separate quarters for male and female customers. These images would at the very least stimulate and encourage imitation and were probably advertising the services offered by prostitutes employed by the management. Extraordinary. In the early days of Rome, baths were seen as places where men would exercise, purify the body and soothe the mind. Things had clearly changed by the 1st century AD – at least in Pompeii.

I re-enter the city and look for a bar. The city is full of them – small ones called popina and larger specimens, more like inns, called caupona. I pass through the forum and head down one of the two main east–west streets of the town lined with shops and bars. On my route I tread over a large irregular paving stone on which stands proud a large penis and testicles – a phallus, but whether pointing towards the red-light district or merely wishing the passer-by good luck and health is hard to say. I enter a small open-fronted bar. There is the counter, containing a row of sunken clay pots in which food and drink would have been kept. Here, 2,000 years ago, I could have had a glass of the Romans' favourite tipple, Falernian wine made from grapes grown near Pompeii in the Campania, some food and lively company. It would have been noisy, smoky from its oil lamps; there would have been people gambling with dice – and prostitutes plying for trade.

The city's popinae and cauponae are rich in graffiti which offer an astonishing glimpse into the soul of a city on the eve of oblivion. The walls of Pompeii can be read like a book, its story is written on its walls, and here you discover the opinions, beliefs and passions of the population. In the House of Ceii I see graffiti about a subject close to the people's heart – gladiators and the bloody thrills of the arena. Four are named: Aracenta, Janus, Severus and Albanus, and it seems that the victories of some are listed. As far as I can make out Janus had won 13 times and Albanus 19. The names are accompanied by crude images of the different men, indicating the types of fighting gear they wore. The majority of gladiators were slaves, condemned criminals or prisoners of war, but around a third were freedmen who fought in the arena for money or for glory, both of which for a successful gladiator were in plentiful supply. One victory could win a gladiator as much money as a Roman soldier earned in an entire year, while their seeming courage, fighting skill and contempt for death made gladiators the darlings of the people – superstars idolised by the masses and courted by the aristocracy. Quite how and why this graffiti came to be scratched on the peristyle wall of this rather grand house is something of a puzzle. The house seems to have been undergoing conversion work when the volcano struck, so the graffiti might have been scrawled by one of the builders who knew that all would soon be plastered over. I study the names and crude sketches – they look amazingly fresh, as if made just before all was buried in ash. Surely this is the work of a chap telling his workmates about the gladiators who would soon be appearing in the city's vast amphitheatre.

There is one other building within the walls of Pompeii that I must see, one that offers extraordinary insights into life in the city 2,000 years ago. It's a lupanare, where those who felt inclined could meet a she-wolf, as female prostitutes were called in Roman times. I head towards the narrow streets and winding lanes near the forum to see what is the only known purpose-built brothel from Roman times. I enter and find myself in a strange and intimate world. There is a central corridor off which are five small cubicles and above the cubicle doors is a series of frescoes showing naked men and women indulging in different types of amorous activity. They are rather like the images in the House of the Vettii and not as explicit and bizarre as those in the Suburban Baths. It's assumed that these images were intended to show customers what was on offer, or at least titillate them. I enter a cubicle; at one end is a stone couch and stone pillow and the wall is covered with graffiti – presumably commendations from satisfied customers. I return to the central corridor and walk to the end – tucked behind a low wall is a latrine.

It's time to leave this spectral city in which the ancient dead can suddenly seem so much alive. I leave through the Porta di Ercolano, walk between tombs, and arrive at one of the most moving of Pompeii's monuments – the Villa of Mysteries. I walk inside to see one of the most enigmatic – and visually striking – rooms from the ancient world. This was a triclinium and three of its walls are covered with a richly coloured and beautifully painted cycle of frescoes that date from around 50 BC, with the fourth wall taken up by a large opening that allowed guests and servants carrying food easy access. Few agree about the meaning of these paintings, or even whether or not they are an original composition or based on a now lost Greek original.

But what seems certain is that the cycle is to do with initiation into a sacred mystery with insights being gained through the stimulation – the liberation – of the senses. There are scenes showing music and dancing, wine is being consumed to allow release from the bridle of convention through intoxication. There is a sexual element – one of the participants is about to unveil a phallus, shrouded in purple fabric, to symbolise the revelation of new knowledge – and there is pain with one of the initiates being flagellated.

Presiding over all of this is Dionysus, the god of wine and intoxication, and his presence suggests to me that this fresco has much to do with Pompeii 2,000 years ago. The slopes of Vesuvius, where vines flourished in the mineral-rich soil, were sacred to Dionysus who, as the god of wine, of pleasure, was much loved in this wine-making city of pleasure. This was his land and Pompeii his city.

8

Power

Urban inspiration for the New World
Santo Domingo, Dominican Republic

We arrive at the airport near Santo Domingo, the capital of the Dominican Republic, and drive along the coast road into the city. All appears neat and tidy, with an increasing number of hotels and bars as we get nearer the centre. One building is embellished with a huge image of a cavorting naked lady. This is clearly something of a holiday destination, a place of leisure. The Dominican Republic now shares a large Caribbean island with Haiti. But these neighbours exist in strange contrast. Haiti is notorious for its poverty and social chaos while the Dominican Republic, well ordered and safe, has become a playground for tourists from Spain and the United States.

Santo Domingo is now a backwater where life is slow and peaceful. But 500 years ago all was different for, with dramatic speed, this small island became one of the most important places on earth. Christopher Columbus – on his quest for riches and territorial conquests for Roman Catholic Spain – landed on the island in 1492. He was the first European to do so and, to honour his sponsors, named his discovery La Isla Española – the Spanish isle. This name was soon corrupted to Hispaniola, the name by which the island was known for the next 300 years or so. Realising the commercial and political potential of the island, Columbus established a small outpost, which he named La Navidad, on its north coast.

When Columbus returned the following year with 1,200 colonists he found no trace of the 39 men he had left. Presumably they had died from disease or been killed by the native islanders.

So a new colony was founded 200 miles further east on the north coast. This settlement was La Isabella – this time to flatter the Spanish queen – and Columbus's brother Bartholomew was left in charge. Conditions on the north coast were far from healthy – yellow fever was rife – and things came to a crisis in La Isabella when gold was discovered on the south coast of the island. In 1496 it was decided to abandon this second city. The population moved en masse to the south of the island and a third settlement was founded on the coast, just to the east of a small river that was named the Ozama. This new settlement was called Santo Domingo in honour of the Dominican monastic order that was playing a key role in the conquest of the New World by giving empire an ethical basis through the conversion of natives, forcibly or otherwise, to Roman Catholicism.

But within a few years, and for reasons that are now mysterious, the settlement moved yet again, but this time only across to the west bank of the Ozama. This move, which took place in 1501, was organised by the island's dynamic first governor, Nicholas de Ovando. He clearly had great ambitions. This new foundation was to be more than a mere settlement – it was to be a walled city organised around a regular right-angular grid of streets with handsome and strong public buildings, private mansions and storehouses built of stone, and designed with almost metropolitan grandeur. Ovando's project achieved rapid success. In 1504 Santo Domingo became the seat of a bishop, and before the decade was out it had the rudiments of a city wall and gates and a number of fine mansions, including Ovando's own palatial home located to overlook the mouth of the River Ozama. By the time Diego Columbus – Christopher's son – arrived in 1509 as the Spanish Viceroy, Santo Domingo had become the first European city in the New World.

Shortly after Diego arrived Santo Domingo was declared the capital of the viceregal empire of New Spain, and from here

Spain's great imperial adventures were launched. Santo Domingo was the springboard for Hernán Cortés's conquest of Mexico in 1518, and a few years later Francisco Pizarro sailed from this island on the fateful voyage that ended with the destruction of the mighty Inca Empire in 1533 and the subjugation of much of South America. Perhaps more important for Hispaniola – and for the Columbus clan that ran the place in the name of Spain – is the fact that much of the vast treasure looted from Peru and Mexico passed through Santo Domingo on the way to Spain.

What intrigues me is the city that Ovando initiated – what he created here became an urban inspiration in the Americas for centuries to come. I want to find out more about the way in which one small city and a mighty dream of empire were ultimately to determine the architectural future of a whole continent. I'm in a high state of anticipation as my car nears the old city that now forms the heart of the large and sprawling modern city of Santo Domingo. I've left the glittering high-rise hotels and bars behind. Now I'm passing through a regular grid of narrow streets lined with terraces of one- and two-storey buildings. It's dark now, but these buildings are stone-built and evidently old. The streets all seem to meet at right-angle junctions and each offers a long vista across the city, the perspective view disappearing into the gloom, into infinity. It's all strangely, geometrically, satisfying – like driving through a giant chess board.

Now we turn left and enter a street wider than the rest. This is the Calle de las Damas – the street of the ladies, and was the first street laid out by Ovando. It gets its name from the gaggle of ladies who would accompany Ovando's wife, Maria de Toledo, as she went to church each Sunday. This was the place of parade in the new city – the place in which to be seen – and now I arrive outside the Ovando house. By strange chance, this is the house I'm going to occupy while in Santo Domingo. It's a large, low affair, strong – almost fortified – in appearance. Stone-built, its external details are robust and simple – with the exception of carvings over one of the doors. These are delicate and incorporate Gothic tracery within a large drip mould of curiously stepped design. This reminds me how early Santo Domingo is – the city was built when the traditional Gothic style was still alive in western Europe and when Renaissance thinking – inspired by a new appreciation and knowledge of ancient Greece and Rome – was emerging as an artistic force.

I contemplate the street – it's amazing, really a street of urban palaces and public buildings. At one end, to the west, is the Fortaleza Ozama – the city fortress – that was started in 1502 and built by the Spaniards to safeguard their new possession. At the other, eastern, end of the Calle is the Casas Reales, a large and handsome structure – built between 1503 and 1520 – that was the administrative centre of New Spain and housed the royal court, treasury and office of the governor. It's simple and restrained in design, its stone elevation simply punctuated by two storeys of square windows and topped by a cornice of bold design. Beyond the Casas Reales I can just make out an open space; it's the heart of the old city – the Plaza España – and here was built the palace of the first Viceroy, Diego Columbus.

But now I enter the hotel. Inside all is cool and shady, and beyond the large entrance hall I see an arcaded loggia with a patio beyond. This is the perfect architecture for a hot climate – small windows to exclude the scorching sun, thick stone walls to keep the interior temperature cool, and pleasant shaded terraces in which to catch the sea breeze. Most of the conquistadors came from hot southern Spain – from Andalusia – and this is no more than their native architecture from the Old World transplanted in the New. I walk through the loggia to the patio. From here the view is magnificent. Due to the dramatic fall of the land from the Calle to the river I find myself perched high, at the top of the city wall in fact, with a commanding view of the sea and the

Ozama. From here Ovando would have watched the treasure ships entering his new city, laden with plunder from Mexico.

From Ovando's mansion I walk to Plaza España. I want to get the feel of this pioneering place, of the first bastion of European civilisation in the New World. I enter the Plaza España and all seems strange – or rather strangely familiar. Of course, it's like the plaza in any Spanish or European Renaissance city. But there's more. I suddenly see the whole creation of Santo Domingo as a monstrous – if weirdly well meaning – experiment. The city's plan – with its gridiron streets and great plaza – is inspired by ancient Greek or Roman cities with their chequer-board pattern of streets, agoras and forums. And the fact that the economy and society of Santo Domingo was based on slavery – on the concept of a race of elite masters using and abusing a race of slaves – is rooted in antique precedent. Historically, slaves have been members of conquered peoples, the underclass or criminals, races that were one way or another seen as inferior and legitimately the subjects of the strong, the powerful, the dominant. Slavery played a fundamental role in the inspirational civilisations of Greece and Rome; slavery is accepted in the scriptures of the Old and New Testaments. Historically there is, before the late 18th century, little moral condemnation of the practice. Slavery in the ancient world was accepted as a fact of life – of creation. So why should 16th-century Spaniards have seen the institution as morally repugnant when it seems few had before them? Here the Spanish created a society and economy based on the old and pernicious principles of slavery – once the native population had been worked to death, they imported slaves from Africa.

I walk across the plaza and stand in front of the building from which this deeply flawed society was run. It's the Alcázar de Colón, the viceregal palace of Diego Columbus, built between 1510 and 1513, and like so much of old Santo Domingo it possesses a charm that distracts attention from the troubling origins of the place. Age and beauty are, indeed, an intoxicating mix that can conceal even the darkest past. The palace is not large, it's only two storeys high, but it has a powerful presence – the first piece of major European-style public architecture in the Americas. All is built of stone and sparingly detailed; it seems to epitomise the taste, austerity and pride of the Spanish conquerors who first occupied it. In the centre of the ground-floor loggia is a large door. I enter and discover the domestic world of the Columbus clan – there is a large central Great Hall where the family would have lived and dined. This is the informal, private portion of the palace. I want to see its public aspect. I return to the loggia and spy a staircase in one of the end pavilions. I mount the stair and, by means of its majestic steps, arrive at the first-floor loggia. This is where all with official or state business in the early years of New Spain would have found themselves. I walk into the loggia, past windows ornamented with Moorish-style, almost Gothic details in the Isabelline style that was fashionable in Andalusia in the very early 16th century. By its plan and details it's evident that this is no mere utilitarian and provincial building. Diego Columbus obviously wanted up-to-date architecture, something that would impress his visitors and proclaim the achievements, power and cultural aspirations of the blossoming empire of New Spain. The designer of the alcázar – a Spanish term of Andalusian Arab origin meaning castle – is unknown, while what is known about its construction seems chillingly symbolic of the imperial adventure in the Americas. Works were overseen by Spanish masons but all the heavy work undertaken by a workforce of around a thousand local Taino Indians, who had been effectively enslaved by the European settlers. So this first great European building in the New World is a monument not only to Spanish enterprise and ambition, but also to the institution of slavery. For over 350 years things were to continue as they started. I step from the loggia into the main first-floor room – the Great

Chamber or Court Room – and beyond I see another loggia, this one overlooking the Ozama. The palace is a brilliant design, for this pair of two-storey loggias not only create shade but allow air, cooled by the river, to blow abundantly through the building. I stand in this comfortable, naturally ventilated room and ponder. Amazing, this was the epicentre of power. For a short while the whole Spanish Empire in the New World was ruled from here. What a momentous room. Decisions were taken here that were to change – to define – the world.

I leave. I've seen what was the political heart of Santo Domingo; now I want see its soul, so I head towards the cathedral of Santa Maria. On the way I begin to get a better sense of the way in which the city was originally occupied, because many early houses survive. It's obvious that initial aspirations – and expectations – were high. The very earliest houses – always well built in stone, sometimes with telling touches of late Gothic detail – were generally two storeys high, occasionally with squat corner towers and generally with stone construction, if of coursed rubble, covered with colour-washed lime render. But by the 1540s things had changed. The houses are still stone-built but details are now uniformly classical and most houses are only one storey high, sometimes raised on a high half-basement level. It seems that the population of the city did not grow as expected. Even at this relatively early date things were starting to go wrong for Santo Domingo. Quite simply the cities and colonies that had sprung from it – in Cuba, Peru and Mexico – were increasingly and remorselessly becoming its competitors for trade and investment.

Soon I arrive at another plaza – slightly smaller than the Plaza España. This is the cathedral square – and there the building stands, a large, low, stone-built structure that spreads all along one side. Since Santo Domingo was the first major European-style city, its buildings score lots of firsts – the first stone-built fortress, the first monastery, the first hospital, the first university, and this, obviously, is the first Christian cathedral constructed in the Americas. Work started in 1512 but the first stone was not laid until 1521 with all completed by 1541. I enter through the north porch – dated 1527 – and I am amazed. This porch, the interior nave and aisles are in full late-Gothic manner with pointed arches and rib vaults. Each side of the aisles are small chapels, some of which contain majestic yet mouldering tombs of long-forgotten conquistadors. It's all so evocative and distinctly melancholy, the mortal remains of a great adventure that shaped the world and had consequences far beyond the wildest imaginings of these once haughty fellows. Did they come here primarily for personal wealth and power, or was it for the glory of Spain and the Roman Catholic Church? In this moving space – once the Christian heart of an entire continent – it's just possible to think the best. And what a shocking place this cathedral must have been when new; a huge, modern and sophisticated engineered structure rising high and perfect in a remote and primitive world. And that was half the point of course – it was intended to awe the native population, to impress them with the power of the white invaders, and made it clear that these strange men, with steel armour and explosive sticks firing deadly missiles, were here to stay. This building had spiritual aspirations but was clearly a powerful piece of political, imperial, rhetoric.

As with cathedrals built in Europe, construction here started at the east end, so that the high altar could be up and running as quickly as possible, and ended with the west door. So I walk from east to west to see the last part of the cathedral to be completed. As I suspect, the contrast between the first and last portions is dramatic and shows what a difference a few years can make in architecture. The Gothic spirit is entirely absent from the west front that was built in 1540 – here all is classical and in a style called plateresque that was fashionable in early

16th-century Spain. The surface treatment was inspired by the design of silver plate and is rich in lively detail and texture – and some of this ornament is very informative. A classical frieze along the top of the elevation illustrates the journey to the island, and is complete with images of the sea monsters and low and tempting women – like sirens I suppose – who the conquistadors were obliged to resist on their journey from Spain. What, I can't help but wonder, would be the current condition of the world if these early explorers had been less strong-willed?

What I find pleasurable in the city – its sense of order, the combination of intimate streets and generous plazas all contained within a protecting wall – obviously appealed deeply to the early Spanish colonists. In 1573 the type of plan pioneered by Santo Domingo was refined, codified and promoted by Phillip II of Spain in a document called the Laws of the Indies. These laws, based on rudimentary urban codes that had evolved during the previous 60 years, and informed by Roman texts such as that written in the 1st century BC by Vitruvius, and by Renaissance theories, sought to govern Spanish behaviour in the New World. The laws, organised as 148 ordinances, dealt with issues ranging from spiritual, political and economic matters to architecture, town planning and the distribution of building lots. These laws were intended to create ideal urban centres that would strengthen Spain's hold on its possessions in the New World – and this was to be achieved by displaying both physical strength and spiritual power. These cities were to be fortified, garrisoned, organised for trade and defence, but they were also to be magnificent and ornamental. They were to be well-ordered and handsome creations, with refined and generally uniform architecture, calculated to impress the native people with the permanence of Spain's presence and the superiority of its civilisation – to be tools in the winning of souls.

The pattern was applied with ruthless regularity, and from

the late 16th century every major town or city in the Spanish possessions – stretching from central and western south America, through Central America to the southern portions of North America, including California, Florida and New Mexico, and in Caribbean islands such as Cuba – was created in the image of Santo Domingo. As in Roman gridiron cities, the relationship between different streets and open spaces was subtle but significant, reflecting a social and functional hierarchy. Not only were major public and ecclesiastical buildings gathered on the main plazas, but the major mansions were grouped on the longest and widest streets with humble houses, shops, warehouses and factories located on narrower and relatively minor streets farther from the city centre. The ordinances of the Laws of the Indies reveal that the early town builders were concerned not just to express the power of state and Church but also to respond thoughtfully to site and climate. And, in the spirit of the Renaissance, ratio and proportion were seen as reflections of divine beauty and order based on nature.

Through these dictates the beautiful, functional, rational and harmonious classical gridiron city was established as the basic urban form in the New World. It became the norm, and although other influences were to confirm the advantages of this plan-form, it's safe to say that the grid of Manhattan has its roots in the diminutive colonial city of Santo Domingo. Quite simply, the Laws of the Indies formed the most influential and far-reaching city-planning document ever created.

Tonight there's a fiesta in full swing, the plaza is packed with citizens. With them, I dance the merengue, a sensuous marriage of Spanish and African cultures. There is much stamping of feet and majestic swaying of body. Santo Domingo, the first European city in the New World, is very much alive and – in its urban quality, beauty and joy of life – still has many lessons to teach its teeming progeny.

Monstrous symbol
of a despotic ruler
Ceausescu's Palace, Bucharest, Romania

Bucharest, the capital of Romania, was known as the Paris of the Balkans and it's still possible to see why. It retains a distinctly cosmopolitan character, even has its own Arc de Triomphe erected in 1935 to commemorate the unification of Romania, and there are boulevards lined with Parisian-style apartment buildings, picturesque streets of late 19th-century villas and the occasional, bold 1930s apartment block of avant-garde design. Walking through parts of Bucharest you'd hardly believe that the city was the target of the most concentrated and vicious attack on architecture and history that has yet been seen in post-Second World War Europe – an attack that was provoked by an obsession to express power and to exercise control.

The history of Romania is bizarre. It has existed as a nation only since 1862 and before that was a series of principalities forming, in the late Middle Ages, the embattled frontier of Christian Europe with the increasingly threatening Muslim Ottoman Empire. The most famous of its medieval princes, ruling part of Wallachia and Transylvania and locked in constant conflict with marauding Islamic forces, was Vlad the Impaler – called Dracula, meaning the son of the dragon – who made a habit of impaling his conquered foes on wooden stakes. Despite his drastic techniques of terror Vlad could not stop the Muslim invaders, and Transylvania fell under Ottoman rule. But the gradual erosion of Ottoman power from the late 16th century onwards changed the political complexion of southeast

Europe. By the end of the 19th century Romania was enjoying an economic and cultural boom and had increased in size to become a major Orthodox Christian nation with much coveted access to the Black Sea. But Transylvania – at the heart of Romania – was still ruled by the Austro-Hungarian Empire and so when the First World War broke out in 1914 Romania soon joined the side of the Triple Alliance (France, Britain and Russia) in their conflict with Germany, Austro-Hungary and Turkey. The prize for Romania was Transylvania, which it acquired in 1918. But during the next great worldwide conflict Romania was not so lucky. By 1941 it had became a Fascist dictatorship ruled by General Ion Antonescu who retained the king as a token head of state, and joined Nazi Germany's disastrous adventure against Soviet Russia. The consequences for the country and its people were catastrophic. Tens of thousands of Romanian soldiers were ultimately killed or captured in the Soviet Union, and 400,000 Romanian Jews and 36,000 gypsies were murdered in Nazi concentration camps. The country survived as an independent nation after the Nazi defeat of 1945 because it had changed sides in August 1944 and fought successfully with the allies against Germany and Austria. More importantly it suited Soviet policy that Romania remain an independent nation, in theory at least, although under total Soviet political control. And in these circumstances Nicolae Ceausescu – the despot responsible for the sack of his own capital and country – eventually came to power in 1965. Ceausescu started as a mere creature of the Soviet Union, but his ignorance, stupidity and cruelty were matched by ambition and greed. His regime was megalomaniac in its action, deeply corrupt and shamelessly nepotistic.

By 1974 when the post of president was created for him Ceausescu's grip on power – maintained through terror, secret police and a network of informers – was absolute. As far as Ceausescu was concerned, Romania and its people would not only have to put up with his despotic regime but also pay for it, and increasingly he siphoned off national wealth to finance self-aggrandising schemes. One of them was the construction in Bucharest from 1981 of his vast People's Palace – in floor area the second largest building in the world after the Pentagon. Others included the huge and ill-conceived Danube Canal and the 'systemisation', control and destruction of rural communities by resettling villagers in clusters of badly built concrete towers and apartment blocks. Ceausescu crippled the economy of his country and utterly abused and alienated its people. But in the late 1980s things at last started to go wrong for Ceausescu and his clique – terminally wrong as it turned out.

I walk from my hotel in the city centre towards Ceausescu's People's Palace. I have come here to see it, and the setting created for it, because in its design and scale this ensemble is the ultimate expression of an architectural dream – the dream of power made manifest – that has haunted the imagination of megalomaniac despots for the last 2,000 years. Soon the pleasant streets of classical villas and apartment blocks give way to wide and Stalinist-style avenues lined with tawdry slab blocks. All is most depressing but this is just a prelude. I get to a large roundabout and find myself in the proximity of Ceausescu's greatest folly. It's the Boulevard of the Victory of Socialism and was cut through the centre of the city during the 1980s to provide Ceausescu with a suitably impressive triumphal route to his palace. Inspired by the Champs Elysées in Paris – but longer – the boulevard is 90 metres wide and runs for 3.2 kilometres. At one end is a huge circus lined with dreary high-rise concrete slabs, while at the other is the dominating bulk of the palace, set within the ill-designed fragment of a park that looks more like a stretch of wasteland or a vast building site. It's extraordinary the way long, straight roads are timeless symbols of order, control and power.

Full of gloom I start to walk down the boulevard, towards the distant and lowering palace. On each side of the boulevard – really a six-lane urban motorway – are ugly apartment blocks, offices and government buildings. It's appalling. Firm facts remain hard to establish, but it's generally agreed that well over 9,000 housing 'units' and 13 historic churches were destroyed for these works, a quantity of destruction that some authorities say represented a fifth of the city. Protests were in vain. An estimated 40,000 people were turned out of houses their families had perhaps owned and occupied for generations and made homeless, or they were dispatched to distant suburbs to live in tiny apartments in poorly built housing blocks. How, I wonder, can this city ever recover? Not only has it lost history, beauty, a sense of continuity and memory, but has been damned with acres of roads and buildings that are utterly banal, ugly and soulless. Since Ceausescu's fall and execution, along with his wife Elena on Christmas Day 1989, there has been little restitution. Democracy has returned to Romania but, in a sense, not justice, with many who were part of the old regime still in power. Without profound change, without justice, surely many must remain bitter and feel cheated. In these circumstances how can the wounds ever heal?

Finally I arrive outside the palace. It rises high above acres of tarmac and scrubby planting – the setting's rough but not as rough as the architecture. The palace is conceived as a vast Renaissance classical composition and, in this sense and in its oppressive scale, has much in common with the neo-classical architecture conceived just before and after the Second World War for two other great totalitarian rulers of the 20th century. Adolf Hitler and Joseph Stalin both valued overblown classical design as the best way of giving their power pedigree and tangible expression. Their architecture may have been terrifying and mechanistic but at least it was well executed. I contemplate

Ceausescu's confection. The commission was won via an architectural competition but the design was tinkered with endlessly by Ceausescu – even during construction – as he sought to speed completion and make his palace ever larger and grander. This constant interference, combined with Ceausescu's passion for gigantism and his banal taste, explains much of the palace's awfulness and its dire execution. This building fails to hit the mark at every level – or rather every level except one. If the intention was to create architecture that is menacing and threatening then, it must be admitted, the palace is a brilliant success.

I stand and stare at the mountain of stone, concrete and glass erupting in front of me – and it stares back. There are tiers upon tiers of windows, hundreds of them – like eyes. They make the building seem omnipotent. The very image of George Orwell's 'Big Brother' regime in *1984*, the palace is watching, keeping the city and its citizens under surveillance. It was clearly a key part of a mechanism of control and terror and now it's a place rich in ironies. When the ghastly pile was started during Ceausescu's regime it was, painfully and euphemistically, called the People's Palace. Now it's known as the Palace of the Parliament, for this powerhouse of a despot, the epicentre of a totalitarian regime, is the home of a democratic government. This is a triumph. Romania may now be one of the poorest and most deprived countries in Europe, where organised crime is an increasing problem, but it's politically free and its elections deemed to be fair and open. In the historical circumstances, these are no small achievements.

I enter the palace and walk to an inner hall. The place is cavernous, ghastly and funereal in feel with its abundance of pale, polished, expensive marble cladding on walls and floors; its detail is crudely executed and repetitious. From where I stand a series of long vistas stretches before me and, with doors opened and aligned, I can see the full depth of the huge building. It's daunting – this is power personified. Indeed the interior reads like a road map to oppression for it offers different routes, each with a story to tell about Ceausescu and his ignoble ambitions. I choose a route and follow it to discover how the building works, to see how absolute, arbitrary and corrupting power expresses itself. I ascend one of the mighty marble staircases and head to the first floor. It's scaled to make me feel small, insignificant, manipulated and observed. The architecture on the first-floor landing directs me to a huge door. I enter what, during Ceausescu's reign, was known as the Document Signing Room. This is the climax of the parade of power – it was in this gigantic hall that Ceausescu was to sign documents of state and receive his grovelling and greedy courtiers. I walk across it. If left in any doubt that they were in the grip of a man of power his courtiers had only to take a look through one of the windows in the hall. I do – and it's like being kicked in the guts. The centre window is set on an axis with the Boulevard of the Victory of Socialism – there it is stretching over three kilometres into the distance. The very city seems an extension of the route through this building, a mere annex to Ceausescu's palace and power base. This room has the biggest view in the palace – but it's not the biggest room. I now make my way back to the ground floor to see Ceausescu's pride and joy – his state ballroom, now named the Union Hall. It's set at the end of a dramatic axial route through the building and is a massive and high-ceilinged hall with giant columns set along its sides – a place calculated to chill and crush. The empty niches at each end of the room were to contain huge portraits of Ceausescu and his wife, but their fate overtook them before the palace was complete.

There's one more room I want to see. I go to the room in which Ceausescu was to meet heads of state, and in it see seating arranged to face a high dais. This is now the Senate – the upper house of the government. It sums up the dramatically changed role of this building. Designed as a space in which a despot would strut, this room is now at the heart of a new democratic Romania. It almost gives me hope.

I leave the Senate and walk to the main state staircase – a monstrous and extravagant affair of white marble. It reminds me about some of the palace's extraordinary statistics. Over a million tons of marble and 3,500 tons of crystal have been used in its embellishment. It contains 1,000 rooms, has a volume of 2,550,000 cubic metres (2 per cent more than the Great Pyramid in Egypt), and was laboured over by 700 architects and 20,000 workers toiling in shifts 24 hours a day. Its main frontage measures 270 metres, and while parts of it rise up to 13 storeys above ground there are another eight storeys below ground – or so it is said. No one seems to know, but the subterranean part is said to have been intended as Ceausescu's own dark and secure world, complete with bunkers, railway and escape tunnels. All this cost the nation vast sums, and with misplaced patriotism Ceausescu wanted only Romanian materials and workers used. He thought the building would demonstrate that a small socialist republic could match the opulence of a superpower. But, oh dear, at this level alone the project has misfired horribly. Some of the materials are indeed beautiful and valuable, but the detailing and construction are miserably poor and clearly executed under pressure of time and cost. The building really is a chillingly accurate portrait of the regime that created it – pompous, full of bombast and bluster, but empty, tenth-rate, cheap.

To discover more I meet the architect of the palace – Anca Petrescu – who won the commission through a competition in 1981. I ask what it was about her design that appealed to Ceausescu? 'Monumentality,' she replies. What contribution did Ceausescu make to the evolution of the design? 'It was Ceausescu who set the theme of the building.' I ask her what exactly Ceausescu's 'theme' was – simply power? 'No,' she answers, 'he never said "I would like to emphasise power" – this never happened.' I ask how this extravagant project was justified? She answers deftly, 'This was an important project for our country, it created jobs.' Anca is an amazing survivor – she survived Ceausescu's downfall when she was almost arrested because of her role in the creation of this expensive folly, and now she is an MP.

I leave this mega-structure, only 80 per cent complete at the time of Ceausescu's death and now partly a building site again as it's made to serve the needs of the parliament. It's extraordinary indeed to see this huge structure, built to express a dictator's power, being transformed into the home of 'people power'. Like it or not, this must be the case because the palace consumed too many national resources and is just too expensive to demolish. This monstrous devourer of the city has become its emblem; it's what Bucharest is now known for. But what of the building's long-term future? The people are compelled, for practical and economic reasons, to keep and use a building that is a monument to their former oppression, but can it ever be accepted?

Medieval fortress – an expression of power through architecture

Qalaat Marqab, Syria

On the Mediterranean coast of Syria stands Marqab, one of the most architecturally powerful and historically important castles ever built. To understand its reason for being and its ultimate fate is to throw light on the origins of the frictions still dividing the peoples who now occupy this land – land that 900 years ago was the most contested region on earth. I go to Qalaat Marqab to see not only a mighty fortress – a great medieval example of the science of military engineering – but also to discover the nature and motives of the men who made, held and attacked this place.

For hundreds of years after the rise of Islam in the mid-7th century, Christian pilgrims continued to visit sacred sites in the Holy Land. Although Islam had most serious differences of interpretation and meaning when it came to the scriptures, it respected Judaism and Christianity because they were religions of 'the Book', with all three faiths venerating the same prophets and sacred sites. But both Jews and Christians had been shocked by the sudden and dramatic rise of Islam during its early years in the 630s, when Muslim Arabs seized the Middle East from the control of Christian rulers who had been the power in the land since the late 4th century. Despite this dramatic swing in the balance of power, the relationships between the three religions were reasonable and did not start to deteriorate until the 11th century.

The reasons for the change are complex. There was a gradually growing antipathy to Christianity and Christian pilgrims among certain Muslim rulers in the Middle East. And there was a restiveness among Christian feudal lords in the West who wished to expand into new territories, and to demonstrate their military prowess and impose their beliefs on the Islamic usurpers in the Holy Land. A clash was inevitable. It came in the 1090s when a number of men of power, wealth, ambition and religious conviction in the West resolved to launch a crusade to regain the Holy Land for Christendom. The crusade, launched with the Pope's blessing in 1096, caught the then divided and unprepared Muslim world by surprise, and after a series of startling military triumphs took Jerusalem in 1099, leading to the foundation of a Christian kingdom centred on the sacred city.

But from the start fatal flaws among the Western crusaders were exposed. It was soon obvious that this was not so much a holy war as a Western invasion of the Middle East. And there was the cruelty – the bloodlust. The Christian conquest of Jerusalem was a brutal affair involving the massacre of Jews and many Orthodox Christians as well as Muslims.

These events shocked the Muslim world. True followers of Christ – the Prince of Peace, the preacher of love – could not behave like this. To the sophisticated Muslim princes the Westerners were barbarians who had to be expelled at all costs. The sacking of Jerusalem went a long way towards uniting disparate Muslim rulers and made the recapture of the land for Islam a holy enterprise.

So for the next 200 years after the fall of Jerusalem the control of the Holy Land became the primary aim of both Christians and Muslims, with both religions locked in struggle. And during most of this time the castle of Marqab played a crucial role. It was a Christian power base that dominated the coastal road – and so was able to extort tolls from travellers and merchant caravans – and held sway over a vast inland territory. The castle, in its prime, was military power incarnate.

I approach the castle by boat and, landing in the small port of Valenia, see Marqab in the distance. The castle sits high on a hill, rising 360 metres above me, master of all it surveyed. There is nothing fancy about Marqab – no soaring towers, no picturesque silhouette. Instead it is long and low, hugging the contours of its hilltop location. And it is dark – almost black – for its walls are built of immensely hard volcanic basalt. It clearly means business and was built not for show but to fulfil its specific purpose – to hold down territory, to intimidate and extort tribute, to offer security in a hostile land. The immense military power of Marqab was demonstrated during the tumultuous events of 1187 when life in the Holy Land changed forever. In that year Salah al-Din – the greatest Muslim commander during the struggle for the Holy Land and known to the crusaders as Saladin – crushed a mighty Christian army during the Battle of the Horns of Hattin and retook Jerusalem. But even Saladin was daunted by the sight of Marqab and did not attack it.

I walk to the site on which he must have stood – it's on the south side of the castle and the best place to survey its impressive defences. As I stand and look I realise I am being observed. A couple of figures have emerged from nowhere – they are moustachioed and wear bulging leather jackets. Secret police of course – although they are making little effort to be secret. They are reminders that the hill on which the castle stands is still a militarily sensitive site and that modern Syria is an authoritarian state in which the police play a dominant role. I ignore them, and turn my mind back to Saladin and his military tactics in 1188.

Saladin would have noted the strength of Marqab's basalt walls, and the natural strength of its site made stronger still through the castle's design. He would have recognised it as a cutting-edge example of sophisticated military design. The topography of the site dictates the castle's basic form – the high plateau on which it stands is roughly triangular so the outer curtain wall of the castle follows the natural perimeter. Then within this outer curtain wall the designer skilfully integrated several theories of defence. First, he applied the principle of defence in depth. The castle is divided into a series of walled enclosures, or baileys, each a self-contained fortress in its own right. There is the outer bailey containing the castle town, occupied by around 1,000 people in the early 13th century, then there is the citadel and, at its point – at the sharp end of the triangular plan of the castle – is the mighty round keep. An attacker wishing to conquer the castle had to take this immensely strong redoubt – and to do that meant attacking through an outer series of defences, for the designer had also utilised the theory of concentric defence. The outer curtain wall is echoed by a higher inner curtain wall so any attackers who broached the outer wall would find themselves trapped in a killing ground between the outer walls and higher inner wall and exposed to missiles raining down from above.

I walk down from the high land to the south of the castle and approach it from below, on its western side. From here the castle looks formidable indeed. Its curtain walls – strengthened by a series of round towers – rise above me. I walk up steps and enter the main gate. I find myself in the narrow space – the list – between the two curtain walls. I turn right and walk along the killing ground. Yes, this would have been a frightful place for attackers – the high inner curtain wall rises above me, well furnished with arrow slits from which defenders would have fired down, causing huge slaughter among any assault party. Ahead of me is a gate, through the inner curtain wall, leading to the interior of the citadel. I enter, the floor slopes up, there's no obvious entry to an upper floor – at the far side are arched openings leading in different directions. The designer has laid the seed of confusion. For attackers, entering the citadel – the inner world of the castle – was like entering a deadly labyrinth.

I walk on and enter the court of the citadel. All around me are the remains of storerooms, kitchens, barracks, stabling and lodgings. But right ahead of me is a more substantial building – the castle chapel, a simple but superb structure. It rises high, a lofty building wrought of basalt blocks, but with doors on its west and north sides. These are made of limestone that, unlike the vastly hard basalt, can be delicately carved. This pair of doors is stunning – they incorporate pointed arches supported on columns topped by capitals that are carved with bold foliage. This is Gothic architecture of the earliest type. I enter through the larger west door – where the framing columns are missing – and enter the chapel. The experience is breathtaking. Built in about 1190, it's a fantastic example of austere crusader architecture. It's all so beautifully simple, light and spacious – the essence of the Gothic spirit.

I walk through this chapel which was converted to a mosque over 700 years ago and is now a secular space, but which still proclaims the stern beliefs of the crusaders who built it. This chapel is a clue to the meaning and design of this castle; it proclaims that this was not just a great fortress but also a monastery! From 1186 Marqab was possessed by warrior monks, one of the Military Orders fighting in the Holy Land to safeguard it for Christian pilgrims. These were the Knights Hospitaller – the Knights of St John of Jerusalem – whose order had been regulated soon after the conquest of Jerusalem. The aim of the order was to succour and house Christian pilgrims coming to the Holy Land, and the knights were prepared to do this in the most extreme form necessary – they would fight any who stood in their way and they would battle to extend and protect the Christian kingdom of Jerusalem. The men who occupied this castle, which had first been constructed in the early 12th century, and who so brilliantly strengthened and extended it after 1186, were holy men fighting for Christian control of the Holy Land.

I stand in the apse, formed by finely cut limestone blocks, and then enter a small room standing just to its north – this would, I suppose, have been a side chapel or sacristy. The room is now dank, lit only by a small window because it adjoins the inner curtain wall. Then I glance up – and am astonished. On the ceiling, and on part of the west wall, survive substantial portions of a fresco – and it is amazing. It shows the head and shoulders of 12 men looking towards a now much-damaged figure. This figure must be an image of Christ and the faces the 12 disciples. The fresco looks as if it dates from around 1200 and, astonishingly, many of the faces have survived the usual Muslim attack on images of living beings. I stare at the surviving faces. These may have been intended to represent holy men but they are more – the faces are stern of aspect and military, and they are individual. Surely these are portraits of holy warriors, of the knights who built the chapel and extended the castle.

I enter the Great Hall of the knights. This is the place where they and the garrison would have gathered to dine – it was a convivial place, but even it is part of the fighting machine. Holes in its floor lead to vast storerooms holding victuals to withstand a siege, and nearby are huge cisterns that collected rain water to supplement the wells in times of crisis. Adjoining the Great Hall is the castle's ultimate fighting position – the keep. It is tall, round, with walls up to five metres thick, and sits at the southern end – the sharp end or spur – of the castle's defensive plan. On the top floor a deep vaulted recess is set off the main room. I explore it and discover a garderobe located in a small cubicle. I contemplate the recess – at a high level there is a window – suddenly I realise what this was. At the top of the keep, in the most secure part of the castle, and separated from the adjoining room by a timber screen, was the cell occupied by the commander of the castle, as safe as possible from attack by assassins. I look around the room of the castellan, with its thick walls and narrow window commanding the surrounding land. It's a deeply melancholy place because it is a stark reminder that, ultimately, all this vast physical strength could not save the castle or the Hospitallers from their fate. And the irony is, when the final attack came it was focused not on these tremendous walls that could withstand almost any amount of punishment – it came from below. But, I reflect, perhaps the real cause of the eventual fall of the castle had little to do with physical assault but was really to do with a spiritual crisis.

After the loss of Jerusalem in 1187 the story of the Christian state in the Holy Land is one of gradual and remorseless decline. It's true that Jerusalem was recovered briefly – in 1229 – but that was through treaty, and it was taken again by the Muslims 14 years later. Little by little and one by one, territory and castles were lost to various Muslim forces. The soul went out of the crusading movement, fewer and fewer volunteers arrived, and in Europe dismay at the losses was replaced by resignation and then by disinterest. In 1272 the great Hospitaller castle of Krak des Chevaliers – just 60 kilometres inland from Marqab – fell. But Marqab itself, and its dwindling territory, survived – an increasingly isolated Christian bastion in an ever more powerful and expanding Muslim realm.

Marqab inevitably became the prime target for Muslim aggression. In 1284 Sultan Qala'un, intent on driving Christian forces out of the northern Holy Land, now focussed on Marqab. Qala'un arrived in front of Marqab on 17 April 1285, established his camp on the slopes of the hill to the south where he could best observe the castle, and opened his attack on its vulnerable southeastern side. The initial phase was to bombard the castle with huge stones hurled from catapults. The castle was designed to withstand this type of assault and returned fire from catapults mounted on its flat roofs and tower tops. But this seems to have been little more than a diversion and covering fire for the Muslims who, having forced their way into the ditch, had tunnelled below the Tower of the Spur just to the south of the keep. Undermined, the Tower of the Spur collapsed on 15 May and an infantry assault followed immediately. This was beaten off, but the Muslims continued to tunnel below the keep and on 28 May the great castle of Marqab surrendered.

Marqab is a dramatic example of the power of an idea – an ideal – expressed through architecture. It was created to promote and protect Christianity, to claim and hold the Holy Land. When it fell, the last great inland Christian fortress, the dream of a Christian state in the Holy Land was over. It's a powerful and sombre monument, this black stone castle, which as I stand on its high keep is being enveloped in shadow below. The sun is setting; I must leave. I am followed, with little discretion, by my pair of burly secret policemen – they even nod their moustachioed faces in farewell. I climb into my vehicle, they into theirs, and we disappear together into the gloom.

Palace with a secret at its heart

Topkapi Harem, Istanbul, Turkey

I've come to Istanbul in Turkey to explore an institution of the former Ottoman court which, in the West at least, is reviled and misunderstood. It was a place where, it is said, men exercised absolute power over women and where the system of domination was enshrined in the architecture. My destination is the harem of the sultans, and despite the fact that the last harem in Turkey closed 100 years ago, its history remains controversial, contested and also – to a strange degree – secret.

The Christian city of Constantinople, which was the capital of the eastern Roman Empire and then of the Byzantine emperors, was seized by Islamic Ottomans in 1453 and renamed Istanbul. The city became the capital of the Ottoman sultans and during the height of their rule in the 16th century it was the prosperous heart of the most technologically advanced and powerful state on earth. Istanbul was also a hugely important spiritual centre because the sultans were the head of the Sunni Muslim faith and claimed to be the divinely appointed leaders of the Islamic faith.

I make my way to the Topkapi Palace, which was built from 1460 and was the power base from which the sultans ruled their empire. I pass through a fortified gate and enter a large walled garden. Beyond is another gatehouse and within it are the main buildings of the palace in another generous garden. I look around – this is a self-contained, fortified town set within the sprawling city of Istanbul. With its trees, plants and views over the waters of the Golden Horn and the Bosphorus it's an image of paradise.

The Topkapi, one of the greatest royal palaces on earth, holds vital clues to the secrets of the Ottomans, for it contains the imperial harem. This occupies more than a quarter of the area of the inner court, and it's also a walled and secure world. Extraordinary – this is like penetrating a Russian doll. The harem is a fortress, within a fortress, within a fortified city. This high level of security alone reveals the importance of the life within it and of the secrets it enshrined. Over the centuries, ambassadors, men of power and foreign princes entered the grounds of this palace, heading for an exquisite audience chamber which stands within this inner garden court. But none of these men would have been allowed to visit the secluded world of the harem that now stands before me; the full delights of this place were reserved for one man only – the sultan. Here, the sultan lived with his family in high security and privacy. Here, in a most ritualised manner, he could enjoy both intellectual and physical pleasure, all his senses could be aroused and satisfied and the survival of his dynasty could be assured. The harem, in its political complexity, was an astonishing institution. Within its walls imperial policy was decided, power exercised and – at a more basic level – the sultan was provided with an adequate supply of healthy male heirs, thanks to his own often strenuous efforts.

The close relations between the governance of the empire and the harem is revealed most succinctly by the fact that the Supreme Court, set beneath the mighty Judgement Tower, abuts one of the outer walls of the harem, and set high within this wall looking down into the court is a window defended by a gilded grille. Sitting behind the grille, and within the harem, the sultan could supervise the far-reaching decisions made in the court below. Without even leaving the harem he could control his vast and far-flung empire.

I enter the gate to the harem and find myself in a dark chamber, its walls lined with stone seats. For more than 400 years the harem was the most fiercely guarded of all the Ottoman Empire's institutions, and this was the first point of exclusion. This gate was guarded by the harem's famed black eunuchs. These eunuchs were selected from young slaves acquired in North Africa and Egypt who were castrated on the journey to Istanbul – brutal indeed. It's typical of this strange institution that these young men, who were physically and no doubt psychologically damaged, were put in charge of the most precious possession of the man who was ultimately responsible for their mutilation – the harem with its beautiful women.

I walk from the entrance chamber into a narrow court. On each side are the lodgings once occupied by the eunuchs, and the walls are decorated with beautiful polychromatic Iznik tiles, inspired by imported Chinese porcelain. The tiles, in accordance with Islamic beliefs, show no images of living beings. This was thought to be idolatrous. Instead there are texts from the Koran, wishing fertility and health, and images of flowers, especially tulips. Flowers in general evoked thoughts of the gardens of paradise, but the tulips have a more specific meaning. It was from the Ottoman Empire that tulip mania spread to Europe, particularly to the Netherlands, and one of the reasons tulips were much loved by Muslim Turks is because they were a symbol of Allah and a way of referring to the deity when it was unlawful to show his image. The connection between Allah and tulips is direct. The name of the tulip, when spoken or written, is the opposite sound and script to Allah. So in large tile roundels and in small tile borders are images of tulips, each an evocation of god. It's beautiful and subtle but, standing in this narrow court, I can't believe this was a happy place. Rather I imagine the fury and frustration that must have haunted the palace, generated by these woefully mutilated men who were forced to work for the very power that was their undoing.

I turn to my right and climb the Judgement Tower to get an

overview of the Topkapi and its harem. Its large size is obvious – around 400 rooms – and I can see that it's a labyrinth, and for good reason. This complex form made it difficult for intruders to penetrate, and easy for the eunuch guards to defend. It also made it easier for the eunuchs to isolate different parts of the community living here – women could be more effectively secluded and kept apart if necessary. All has to do with control. This really is the architecture of power. The hierarchy of the harem is also apparent. Below me are small buildings, courts and yards which are the realm of the more lowly occupants of the harem, including the eunuchs. In the distance the buildings and spaces get larger, and this was the world of the sultan and his family.

Much of the harem dates from the mid- to late 16th century, its Golden Age, when at least 200 women lived here, although some sources say more than a thousand. The man responsible for expanding this harem and increasing its power in the complex world of Ottoman politics, and who remodelled many of its interiors, was Murad III. He reigned from 1574 to 1595 and presided over an empire at the height of its power. The harem was at its centre. Virtually all the women in the harem at this time were slaves, captured in raids, bought from slave markets or presented as gifts. Since Islamic law forbade the enslavement of Muslims, these women were normally Christian or Jewish in origin with blonde-haired and blue-eyed Circassians – Chechens and Georgians – being particularly prized. Most of these girls would have been selected or approved for service in the harem by the sultan's mother – in Murad's time, the powerful and scheming Nur-banu. She was a beautiful Venetian Jewess of noble birth who had been captured in 1537 and brought to the harem when 12 years old. Nur-banu ensnared and retained the heart of Sultan Selim II and created the powerful role and official title of valide sultan – the queen mother.

I continue my journey into the heart of the harem and reach a central vestibule from which several routes radiate. One is called the Golden Way, and must have been heavily guarded in the past for it led to the quarters of the royal family. Another leads to a large courtyard, with an arcade down one side and its walls decorated with beautiful 15th-century polychromatic tiles showing the flowers of paradise or emblazoned with poetic Koranic texts. This is the courtyard of the valide sultan and was the centre of her court within the harem. But I follow a third route that leads into the food-tasters' corridor, lined with stone tables on which the products of the kitchen were subjected to careful scrutiny. This corridor alone reveals the air of suspicion that must have hung heavy within the closed world of the harem.

At the end of this corridor is the courtyard around which the young concubines were lodged. These girls were all virgins and no older than 12 when they arrived here. All would have been educated within the harem and all would have been converted to Islam. Above the arcades around the court are large dormitories, and in these the girls slept, overseen by a matron who would offer guidance, impose discipline and prevent any Sapphic activity. It's easy to see the harem as a curious cross between a finishing school and a convent. But there was, of course, much more to it. These girls were concubines and so were also taught various 'harem skills' that would please their master – the sultan – but few, it seems, ever had the chance to test these on this exulted personage.

Most of the girls would become no more than rather grand domestic servants or eventually rise through the harem to become mentors to younger girls and matrons. But a few would be selected to become 'favourites' and deemed as suitable to have sexual relations with the sultan and bear his children. If you were chosen as a favourite your power, prestige and influence increased, quite literally, overnight. You were moved to a larger and grander court in the family portion of the harem, had an increase in your allowance and were provided with your own bedroom, servants and even a personal eunuch. Mostly these favourites were selected by the sultan's mother and all had the possibility of greatness. If they bore the sultan a son, that son could perhaps one day become sultan, and his mother the valide sultan – the most powerful woman in the Ottoman world. But despite this heady promise of potential power these women – while they remained one favourite among many – also remained slaves and were denied the basic dignity of freedom. It is possible that the sultan would, eventually, choose a favourite as a wife but this did not always happen. If it did, the system could become compromised for if a wife had a son it could be assumed that this son would inherit, and this might not be best for the future security of the empire. What was required was for the most able of the sultan's sons to succeed him.

One of the mysteries of the harem is how succession was established, how the victor won the ruthless battle for survival. In theory, all sons had an equal right to the throne. It was assumed that from among this brood of equals the most able would rise to the top and rule. He who was able to survive harem intrigues would also probably survive intrigues in the court. What this meant, in fact, was years of infighting and backstabbing between different cliques in the harem, each led by a mother of one of the sons. All manner of ruthless behaviour was justified because the stakes were incredibly high. Not only would the winner rule the empire, with his mother becoming one of the most powerful women in the Muslim world, but the losers would meet a most dismal fate. At best they could expect exile or imprisonment, and at worst execution. Indeed, upon coming to the throne it was the custom until the early 17th century for the sultan to execute his brothers – even if he loved and trusted them. It was thought simply too risky for the stability of the empire to leave alive men who had an equal claim to the throne as the ruling sultan. At any moment they could – even against their will – become embroiled in an intrigue and become a rallying point for a coup. All such disruptions within the ruling house risked weakening the Ottoman Empire and made it potentially vulnerable to invasion from without.

Adjoining the Concubines' Court are the quarters of the valide sultan. The main reception room is decorated with gorgeous tiles and frescoes with, like most important interiors in the palace, a small fountain set in one wall. The water for this was stored in a large cistern secreted in the thickness of the wall and this would have been fed by conduits or by a constant relay of slaves feeding buckets of water into an orifice located in a nearby but discrete service corridor. The grandeur of this room instantly reveals the privilege and prestige of the valide sultan. Along one wall is a large divan, raised on a dais and set within a deep alcove. This is the valide sultan's throne and from here, sitting in the centre of the harem, she would have controlled all. She would have inspected concubines paraded before her, selecting 'favourites' for her son, and here, while visiting his mother, the sultan would also have chosen a favourite for an assignation by placing a handkerchief on her shoulder. Adjoining the valide sultan's reception room are her private rooms. I stoop to pass through a low door and find myself in her bedchamber. It's dark, lit only by borrowed light passing through a grille from an outer room. On one side is a raised platform on which the bed would have been placed and the walls of the room are covered from floor to ceiling with tiles showing flowers and plants, so she slept within an image of the gardens of paradise. The next room, with the grille forming one of its walls, is the valide sultan's prayer chamber – the mihrab or niche towards which she prayed. This orientated her in the direction of Mecca and is embellished with tiles showing the sacred mosque of Mecca with the cubical al-Ka'ba at its centre. It's very charming. It's amazing to think of the plots that must have been hatched here, stratagems that in the late 16th century would have affected a large proportion of the civilised world.

I now go to see the quarters inhabited by Murad III. I leave his mother's apartment and pass along a light-bathed corridor off which are located various domed and top-lit bathrooms and lavatories. These are the valide sultan's baths and the Imperial baths, and very handsome they are. The large number of bathtubs and basins and the amount of water they would have consumed reveals the wonders of the plumbing arrangements in the harem in the mid-16th century, when these baths were constructed. They also say much about the atmosphere of fear. In several of the steamrooms basins are protected by gilded grilles so that the sultan, when vulnerable with head immersed in water and shrouded in steamy mist, could feel safe from being stabbed in the back. The corridor terminates at a particularly well-appointed lavatory, and then I find myself in Murad III's mighty, domed, throne room. This is the epicentre of power in the harem – in the Topkapi Palace really. Of course, no male outsiders could enter this room – no Muslim princes, no foreign ambassadors – but from here the sultan, surrounded by his large and multi-layered family, ruled his empire. I stand by the couch-like throne on which he would have reclined and reflect on the paradoxical Ottoman world – here was an exclusive monarch, claiming divine authority for his rule, and the self-proclaimed head of the Islamic faith, yet the son of a mother who had been a slave and who had almost certainly been born a non-Muslim. A peculiar institution indeed as the sultan, apart from anything else, was perhaps the product of generations of Circassian mothers and so ethnically far removed from the Turkish people he ruled.

Beyond the throne room is Murad's Privy Chamber. It retains

its late 16th-century tile decoration, incorporating texts from the Koran, and against one wall is a large water basin. When the sultan wanted a private conversation he would increase the water-flow in the fountain so the sound of water trickling from basin to basin would conceal his whispered words. The harem was full of stealthy eavesdroppers – here knowledge, especially of the sultan's plans, was power. Murad would also sometimes use this chamber as a bedroom. He would repose in one of the divans and a favourite would approach – showing great humility by entering the divan inch by inch. And as the sultan and the favourite coupled they would be observed, for this was more an act of state than an act of love. It is said that every potentially procreative moment enjoyed by the sultan was recorded, along with the date and the favourite's name, to establish the legitimacy of any resulting offspring.

I leave Murad's Privy Chamber, cross a tile-lined vestibule and arrive at one of the most mysterious apartments in the harem. Much of Ottoman history remains shady because in modern Turkey there is a reluctance to discuss openly many key aspects of harem life. The fact that women were kept in bondage all their lives now causes embarrassment, but this pales to insignificance when the subject of fratricide is raised. Fratricide was the way in which the Ottoman Empire retained its stability; it was the accepted modus operandi of dynastic succession. Murad III – mild sensualist that he was, more interested in women and poetry than politics – still contrived to have all of his brothers murdered lest one might rise to challenge his rule, while Mehmed III had all 19 of his brothers strangled by deaf-mutes and all his sons confined.

The apartment I now enter is one part of the palace used for the confinement of princes. They are beautifully appointed rooms, and they look onto the court around which the favourites lodged so the young men in here could ogle the beautiful women who were the property, the sexual objects, of their brother or father – also their gaoler. These rooms are now described by the Topkapi Museum authorities as the apartment of the Crown Prince but, if ever the case, this could only have been the apartment's function from the 18th century. It was originally a gilded cage in which, putting it at its most charitable, the inmates were kept in protective custody, perhaps for decades. When the sultan died all could change. One of the young men in the cage could suddenly be elevated to the throne, while the women of the harem would be dismissed from the Topkapi – married off or sent to the Old Palace – and a new harem formed by the new valide sultan.

The harem in the Topkapi closed in the 1850s, but the institution of the harem remained legal in Turkey – even common – until the early 20th century. The true history of the harem is now almost lost in romance, secrecy and misinformation, but what is certain is that power, in this architecturally exquisite world, was achieved and maintained at a tremendous human price. It's true that within the harem slaves were educated and could even rise to heady power within the empire. The harem system was in a sense a meritocracy; but it was also a world in which girls were enslaved and trained so as to be a source of pleasure for one man, where these girls were guarded by male slaves who, because of harem rules, had been castrated, and it was a place in which fratricide was regarded as an acceptable tradition. The harem may have been a beautiful, complex and efficient machine of state, but ultimately it was a terrifying, and very deadly, place.

Classical beauty with a dark and troubling heart

Evergreen Plantation House,
New Orleans, USA

I fly into New Orleans in November 2006. I'm here to see a building that gets to the very heart of the complex nature of American society. It's a fine house built in the 1830s, and I hear it's a beautiful and serene piece of classical architecture on a large and once very profitable sugar cane plantation. But this house was part of a paradise born under an evil cloud. All was created and maintained by the dark and troubling institution of slavery. And slavery in the States is not just a memory; it remains a livid scar, a cause of festering fury that continues to divide the nation. I'm reminded of this as I enter the historic centre of New Orleans. Hurricane Katrina engulfed the area only 14 months before, and as it stormed through the city it stirred up painful and poisonous memories of oppression, revealing that in the southern states the legacy of slavery – poverty, anger, injustice and prejudice – is still a potent force in society.

It's the remains of this deeply disturbing world – in which the evil of slavery was practised by freedom-loving men – to which I speed along the River Road that leads out of New Orleans and along the banks of the Mississippi. I'm heading towards the heartland of a Louisiana plantation house, part of a way of life that was eventually to divide the United States and which stained the early history of a great nation.

Once the River Road was lined with plantation houses, each

simultaneously the hub of elegant life and of a blood- and sweat-stained industry. The profits from this slave-powered rural industry were massive – the River Road was early 19th-century America's Millionaires' Row – and Evergreen is one of the last plantation houses to survive on the road and the only one to remain involved with sugar cane production. On the River Road I pass the wrecks of several mansion houses and then, quite suddenly, I am at the Evergreen plantation. I'm puzzled. There are two drives – one leading through a set of gates to a fine-looking, white-painted classical mansion, and another leading to an avenue of aged oak trees. Because this gate is open I drive in towards the oak avenue and, without realising it, I have entered the parallel worlds of the Evergreen Plantation.

Plantation houses along the River Road had evolved an optimum estate layout by the 1830s. The mansion stood some way back from the road, with gardens in front and behind, and functional buildings such as kitchens and house-slaves' quarters disposed about it in a loosely symmetrical and ornamental manner. Adjoining this idyllic-looking world was the working world of the estate – reached by a drive like the one on which I'm now standing. Disposed along this rough road were the cabins of the field slaves and, beyond these, the steam-powered mill that processed the sugar cane before it was carried up to the River Road and loaded on ship to take it down to New Orleans.

I decide to look first at the mansion, which looks splendid in the frosty morning light. In about 1830 the estate came into the hands of Pierre Clidamant Becnel, whose family had owned the land since the 1760s. Pierre inherited a modest house, built in the 1790s in a simple vernacular manner, but he had grown up in a changing world, one that was becoming increasingly sophisticated and cosmopolitan. The Americans, who had flooded into Louisiana after the territory had been purchased from France in 1803, brought not only energy and commercial ruthlessness but also new artistic tastes. Young Becnel was entranced by the fashion for the grandiose Greek Revival architecture favoured by prosperous planters in neighbouring states and along the east coast, and resolved to transform Evergreen. To the entrance front of the modest one-room-deep house Becnel added a row of giant Doric columns supporting a cornice and incorporating a pedimented portico, into which rises a curving staircase leading to a spacious first-floor veranda. This is the ambitious composition that confronts me now. The house is a mighty mansion, but in miniature. The giant order of columns, rising from ground to eaves, increases the sense of scale and importance of the place, and the pair of curving staircases is most theatrical – but all is on a charmingly intimate scale. I climb the stairs to the first floor and approach the main door. It has delicate Greek Revival detail that was the height of fashion in Europe and in the United States during the early 1830s. It's curious the messages this neo-Greek architecture carried. For some it symbolised revolution, freedom and national identity, for it echoed the ferocious pride and independence of ancient Greece and was steeped in republican and democratic virtues. But here this fresh and lively Greek detailing cloaks a predatory and exploitative society. It's most disconcerting. I enter the house. It's very simple – the large central hall is flanked by smaller rooms and leads to what was originally a second open veranda looking onto the rear garden. There is delicate internal detailing – cornices, architraves and fire surrounds. So this is the favoured world of the early 19th-century slave-owning southern aristocracy. The main house itself forms only the centrepiece of a symmetrically arranged family of buildings that, in its rigid mirror-image planning, seems to be striving to impose order on an ancient, unruly and menacing landscape. On each side of the main house is a pair of detached and identical garçonniers in which, according to the custom of Louisiana, the young men of the family would live. Behind these – one on each side of the rear garden – is a pair of pigeonniers in which edible fowls were raised, then another pair of matching pavilions, one of which contained the quarters of house-slaves and offices. The other was the kitchen – isolated as a fire precaution and because the kitchen was the domain of the slaves, who were, as far as possible, to be kept out of the main house.

I leave this visually attractive world and walk to what is the true wonder of the Evergreen plantation. Where plantation houses survive in the south, the complex world that supported them – industrial and agricultural buildings, slave quarters and all the deeply troubling paraphernalia related to the slave regime such as auction blocks – has generally disappeared. But not at Evergreen. Here the slave quarters still stand each side of the road that runs parallel to the main drive but set some way back. There are 22 virtually identical single-storey cabins, all now deserted, slowly disintegrating, and haunting. The cabins are slightly built, with timber-frame construction and thin outer walls of horizontally nailed planks, with their ground floors raised on stumpy brick piers. Each cabin incorporates an entrance veranda, and it's here that the slaves would have snatched moments of rest and relaxation between long periods of hard, enforced toil – a regime that would continue year after year, with no hope of change, until death or – perhaps worse – until sold to another estate. The uniformity of the cabins, the fact that all the open verandas can be observed – can be policed in fact – from one point reveals the ruthless and heartless nature of the place. And that's why it's familiar – it's like an image of any concentration camp or prisoner-of-war depot. The picturesque avenue of oaks that now looks so beautiful has grown here after slavery was finally abolished in 1865 at the end of the Civil War. When these cabins were made, the road they were built along was no finely planted avenue. It was a bleak industrial road leading from the steam-powered sugar cane mill at one end – with a tall brick chimney puffing fumes and smoke over the cabins – and a river wharf at the other. I climb onto a veranda and look inside the cabin. It appears authentic. The spindly timbers are pegged together, the cladding of planks is woefully thin and in the centre is a brick-built chimneystack with fireplace openings on each side. I try to image the scene, the noises, the smells, the crowded conditions. It's hard to say how many people would have lived here, but there are accounts from other plantations of several families being crowded into each living space – there could have been up to 20 or so people in each cabin. It's disheartening to imagine these people with so little, compared with the opulence at the big house. At Evergreen it is still possible to populate the cabins with real people because an inventory survives from 1835 listing Becnal's property and this, naturally, includes his slaves. It reveals that there were then 57 on the estate and gives their names, ages, occupations and value. For example, the senior slave was named Rançon, aged 37, described as a 'Commander capable of directing the work of the plantation', and valued at $1,200.

The origin of the Civil War – a struggle that would eventually end the evil of slavery in the United States – had little to do with slavery. Abraham Lincoln declared, 'My paramount object in this struggle is to save the Union, and is not either to save or to destroy slavery. If I could save the Union without freeing any slave, I would do it; if I could save it by freeing all the slaves, I would do it; and if I could save it by freeing some and leaving others alone, I would also do that.' This was the public voice of Lincoln, the canny and pragmatic politician fighting by any and all means for the survival of the Union. But Lincoln was, privately, a deeply committed abolitionist tortured by the evil of slavery that he believed was gnawing at the soul of the nation. In September 1862, when he believed Union forces might at last be on the road to victory, Lincoln finally took the plunge and made his personal loathing of slavery into government policy. On 22 September Lincoln issued the Emancipation Proclamation. It stated that: 'On the first day of January, in the year of our Lord one thousand eight hundred and sixty three, all persons held as slaves within any State, or designated part of a State, the people whereof shall be in rebellion against the United States, shall be then, thenceforth, and forever free.' This was a tricky and cautious act – some might say cynical – freeing slaves in rebel territory that Union forces did not control while allowing slavery to continue in states loyal to the Union – but it was a move in the right direction. It made slavery one of the big issues of the war and its abolition a declared Union cause.

By the time this proclamation was made, the fate of New Orleans – and the plantations such as Evergreen along the River Road – had already been settled. In April 1862 a Union fleet seized New Orleans and then sailed up the Mississippi – past Evergreen – and in May captured the important river port of Baton Rouge and pressed on to Vicksburg. So, effectively, for Evergreen the war was over by the spring of 1862. The plantation had been forcibly returned to the Union, which was architecturally most fortunate because the house and its subsidiary buildings consequently escaped the fiery fate that befell many southern plantations later in the war as the confederacy was ravaged by Union troops.

As for the Becnel family, one of Pierre's sons never saw Evergreen again – he was killed near Atlanta while campaigning with the Confederate army – but his brother, Michel Alcide, returned to New Orleans and, despite his rebel track record, recovered Evergreen and made it, once again, into a going concern. It is likely that most of the slaves, although freed by 1865, continued to live at Evergreen, in the same cabins. Where else were they to go? This was their home and had, in some cases, been so for generations. Conditions probably stayed much the same, only they now had some form of wage, no doubt minimal, and – most important of all – they had their freedom. Michel Alcide lived until 1893, when the plantation was sold to a family who plunged into debt during the recession when sugar prices plummeted, with the house being forfeited to a bank in 1930. The plantation lay abandoned for 14 years until purchased for careful preservation and restoration by an oil heiress.

Evergreen survives as a memorial to a turbulent and contradictory period in the history of the United States, when beautiful architecture was created within a society that harboured a dark seed of evil. I return to the slave quarters, sited in their now deceptively tranquil forest glade. The rare survival of these modest and fragile structures is what makes Evergreen a place of international importance. To some, these potent structures may be an embarrassing reminder of a period best forgotten. But it is good they survive, good that they retain the power to shock, to anger, to shame, to remind. Forgetfulness is the great enemy. We need reminders of the evil that comes when man has power over man, of the evil of selfish exploitation, of ignorant bigotry. Only when memory survives is there any chance that these evils can be eradicated.

Further reading

Publications consulted during preparation of *Adventures in Architecture* series for BBC2 and for this book, and which provide useful further reading.

Beauty

The Indians of Canada, Diamond Jenness, Toronto, 1986
Eskimo Architecture, Molly Lee, Andrew Toovak Jr and Gregory A. Reinhardt, Alaska, 2003
A History of Russian Architecture, William C. Blumfield, 1993
St Petersburg: A History, Arthur and Elena George, London, 2004
The Romanovs, W. Bruce Lincoln, 1981
The Three Empresses, Catherine, Anne and Elizabeth of Russia, P. Longworth, 1972
The Hammer of the Inquisitors, Alan Friedlander, Leiden, 2000
Massacre at Montsegur, Zoe Oldenbourg, London, 1961
The Yellow Cross, René Weis, London, 2000
The Perfect Heresy, Stephen O'Shea, London, 2000
Albi Cathedral and British Church Architecture, John Thomas, London, 2002
Brick: a World History, James W.P. Campbell and Will Pryce, London, 2003
The Gothic Cathedral, Wim Swaan, London, 1984
The Art and Architecture of the Indian Subcontinent, J.C. Harle, 1994
Hindu Mythology, W.J. Wilkins, 2006
Konark: Monumental Legacy, Thomas E. Donaldson, Oxford, 2003
Black Pagoda, Robert Ebersole, University of Florida Press, 1957
Tantra and Sakta Art of Orissa (3 vols.), Thomas E. Donaldson, New Delhi, 2002
Mysterious Konarka, R.K. Das, 1984
Gods and Goddesses, T.C. Majupuria and Rohit Kumar, Bangkok, 1998
The Essence of Buddhism, Jo Durban Smith, 2004
The Art of Tantra, P. Rawson, London, 1973
Erotic Sculpture of India, D. Desai, 1975
Pauranic and Tantric Religion, J.N. Banerjea, 1966
Symbols and Manifestations of Indian Art, ed. Saryu Doshi, 1984
Secrets of Mary Magdalene, ed. Dan Burnstein and Arne J. De Keijzer, London, 2006

Connections

The Rise of the Skyscraper, Sarah Bradford Landau and Carl W. Condit, New York, 1996

Skyscraper: the search for an American style 1891–1941, ed. Roger Shepherd, 2003

The City Observed, Paul Goldberger, 1979

The American Skyscraper, ed. Roberta Moudry, 2005, essay by Carol Herselle Krinsky: 'The skyscraper ensemble in its setting'

Damascus: a historical study of the Syrian city-state from the earliest times until its fall to the Assyrians in 732 BCE, Wayne T. Pitard, 1987

Mirror to Damascus, Colin Thubron, London, 1967 (1988 edition)

Damascus: Hidden Treasures of the Old City, Brigid Keenan, 2000

A Short Account of Early Muslim Architecture, K.A.C. Creswell, 1989

A New Old Damascus: authenticity and distinction in urban Syria, Christa Salamandara, 2004

Damascus and its people, Mrs Mackintosh, 1883

The Damascus Chronicle of the Crusades, trs. from the chronicle of Ibn Al-Qalanisi (1097–1159), H.A.R. Gibb, 1932

Damascus, Palmyra, Baalbek, Rouhi Jamil, 1941

The Travels of certaine Englishmen into Africa, Asia, Troy...and...into Syria... Mesopotamia, Damascus...Palestina, Jerusalem, Jericho.... Begun in the year 1600, and by some of them finished this yeere 1608...very profitable for the use of Travellers, 1609 (William Biddulph)

Great Mosque of Damascus, Finbarr Barry Flood, 2000

Studies in Medieval Islamic Architecture, vol. I, Robert Hillenbrand, 2001

From Damascus to Palmyra, John Kelman, 1908

Monuments of Syria: an historical guide, Ross Burns, 1992

Early Muslim Architecture: Umayyads AD 622–750, K.A.C. Creswell, Oxford, 1969

Two Brazilian Capitals, Norma Evenson, New Haven, 1973

Death

Il Cimitero Monumentale di Staglieno a Genova, Franco Sborgi, Genoa, 2003

The Architecture of Death, Richard A. Etlin, 1984

Death and Architecture, James Stevens Curl, 2002

Art and Architecture of Ancient America, George Kubler, London, 1984

A Survey of Maya State, Religious and Secular Architecture, James MacKeever Arnold and James Robert Moriarty III, 1971

Living Architecture: Mayan, Henry Stierlin, London, 1964

Memoirs of Toebart Maler, The Peabody Museum of American Archaeology and Ethnology, Harvard University, 1908

Breaking the Maya Code, Michael D. Coe, London, 1992

The Ancient Maya, Robert J. Sharer, Stanford, 1994

The Days of the Dead, John Greenleigh and Rosalind Rosoff Beimler, San Francisco, 1991

The Day of the Dead, Haley and Fukada, 2004

Hatshepsut the Female Pharaoh, Joyce Tyldesley, London, 1996

Ancient Records of Egypt, James Breasted, Chicago, 1907

Ancient Egypt, Delia Pemberton, London, 1992

Hatshepsut: in search of the woman pharaoh, H.E. Winlock, London, 2001

Eternal Egypt, Pierre Montet, London, 1964

Rewriting Bible History, Charles Taylor, 1985

The Complete Temples of Ancient Egypt, Richard H. Wilkinson, 2000

A Test of Time, David M. Rohl, London, 1995

Disaster

The Road to Oxiana, Robert Byron, London, 1934

Afghanistan, Louis Dupree, 2002

The Minaret of Djam: an excursion in Afghanistan, Freya Stark, 1970

Islamic Art and Architecture, 1999, and *Islamic Architecture: form, function and meaning*, R. Hillenbrand, 1994

Studies in Islamic Art, London, 1985, VII – 'The Minaret of Mas'ud III at Ghazni', Ralph Pinder-Wilson

Ghurid Monuments and Muslim Identities: epigraphy and exegesis in twelfth-century Afghanistan, Finbarr Barry Flood, 2005

Cairo to Kabul: Afghan and Islamic studies, ed. Warwick Ball and Leonard Harrow, London, 2002

Gertrude Bell, H.V.F. Winstone, 2004

Le Minaret de Djam, La découverte de la capitale des sultans Ghorides (XIIe–XIIIe siècles. Mémoires de la Délégation Archangélique Française en Afghanistan, A. Maricq and G. Wiet, Paris, 1959

Traditional Architecture of Afghanistan, Stanley Ira Hallet and Rafi Samizay, New York & London, 1980

Afghanistan: an historical guide, Nancy Hatch Dupree, Kabul, 1977

Monuments of Central Asia, Edgar Knobloch, London, 2001

Palmyra, Iain Browning, London, 1979

Report on a Voyage to Palmyra, Dr. W. Halifax, Philosophical Transactions of the Royal Society, London, 1695

*A Compendium of a Journey from Aleppo to Jerusalem by Henry Maundrel,
The Travels of Dr. Thomas Shaw, F.R.S. and A Journey to Palmyra*
(London, undated)
The Ruins of Palmyra, otherwise Tedmor, in the Desert, Robert Wood, 1758
Dresden: a city reborn, ed. Anthony Clayton and Alan Russell, especially
chapters by John Soane on 'Destruction and rebuilding', and
'Dresden's renaissance after 1985', Oxford, 2001
Dresden: Tuesday, February 13, 1945, Frederick Taylor, 2004
The Revival of Dresden, ed. W. Jager and C.A. Brebbia, 2000
Firestorm: the bombing of Dresden 1945, ed. Paul Addison and
Jeremy A. Crang, 2006

Dreams

Discovery Guide to Yemen, Chris Bradley, London, 1995
'The world's most influential prison', Norman Johnston, *The Prison
Journal*, vol. 84, No. 4 December 2004
A History of Building Types, Nikolaus Pevsner, London, 1976

Paradise

Sri Ranganathaswami, Jeannine Auboyer, Paris, 1969
Suleiman the Magnificent, André Clot, 1992
Gardens of Paradise, John Brookes, London, 1987
Architecture in Wood, William Pryce, London, 2005
Wooden Churches of Eastern Europe, Edward Buxton, Cambridge, 1981
The Wooden Architecture of Russia, Alexander Opolovnikov, London, 1989
The Church of the Transfiguration, Valerie Zalessov, 2001

Pleasure

The Amazon Rubber Boom: 1850–1920, Barbara Weinstein, Stanford, 1983
The Commerce in Rubber: the first 250 years, Austin Coates, Oxford, 1987
Brazil and the Struggle for Rubber, Warren Dean, Cambridge, 1987
Bombay: the cities within, Sharada Dwivedi and Rahul Mehrotra, Bombay,
1995
Neuschwanstein, Peter Kruckman, 2000
Neuchwanstein, The King and his Castle, Peter Kruckmann, 2001
Neuschwanstein, Gottfried Knapp, 1999
The Mad King: the life and times of Ludwig II of Bavaria, Greg King, 1997
The Dream King: Ludwig II of Bavaria, Wilfred Blunt, 1973
The Swan King: Ludwig II of Bavaria, Christopher MacIntosh, 2003
Pompeii: the living city, Alex Butterworth and Ray Laurence, London, 2005

Roman Pompeii: Space and Society, Ray Laurence, London, 1994

Priapeia, L.C. Smithers and Sir Richard Burton, 1890

Pompeii: the living city, A. Butterworth and R. Laurence, 2005

The Days of the Dead, John Greenleigh and Rosalind Rosoff Beimler, San Francisco, 1991

Power

The Queen's Pirates, Derek Parker, London, 2004

Sir Francis Drake's West Indian Voyage, 1585–86, ed. Mary Frear Keeler, The Hakluyt Society, London, 1981

Art and Architecture in Spain and Portugal and their American Dominions, 1500–1800, George Kubler and Martin Soria, Harmondsworth, 1959

Spanish City Planning in North America, Dora Crouch, Daniel Garr, Axel Mundigo, Cambridge, 1982

The Making of Urban America: a history of city planning in the United States, John W. Reps, New Jersey, 1965

Architecture and Town Planning in Colonial North America, 3 vols., James D. Kornwolf, Baltimore, 2002

The European City, Leonardo Benevolo, Oxford, 1993

The Colonial Spanish-American City, Jay Kinsbruner, Austin, 2005

Sensuous Worship, Jesuits and the Art of the Early Catholic Reformation in Germany, Jeffrey Chipps Smith, Princeton University Press, 2002

The Jesuits and the Arts, ed. John W. O'Malley, S.J. and Gavin Alexander Baily, Saint Joseph's University Press, 2005

The Imperial Harem: Woman and Sovereignty in the Ottoman Empire, Leslie P. Peirce, Oxford, 1993

The Topkai Saray Museum, ed. J.M. Rogers, London, 1988

Architecture: Ceremonial and Power, The Topkapi Palace, Gulru Necipoglu-Kafadar, Cambridge, 1991

Back of the Big House: The architecture of plantation slavery, John Michael Vlach, 1993

Slavery and Freedom, James Oakes, New York, 1990

The Peculiar Institution: Slavery in the Ante-bellum South, Kenneth M. Stampp, 1956

The Slave Community: Plantation life in the Antebellum South, John Blassingame, 1972

Life and Times of Frederick Douglass: His early life as a slave, his escape from bondage, his complete history, Frederick Douglass, 1892

Plantations of the Carolina Low Country, Samuel Gaillard Stoney, The Carolina Arts Association, 1938

Plantation Houses and Mansions of the Old South, J. Frazer Smith, New York, 1993

Acknowledgements

I would like to thank Roly Keating, Controller of BBC2, and Adam Kemp, Controller of Commissioning Arts, for commissioning the *Adventures in Architecture* series of which this book is a record. Also from the BBC, Mark Harrison, former Creative Director of Arts for supporting the project and – in particular – Basil Comely, Executive Producer for the series and the BBC's Acting Head of Arts for the energy he has expended and time he has committed to developing the initial idea, discussing locations, working on the scripts and supervising the edits. Critical to the production of the series and this book have been the directors and assistant producers: John Hay, Andrea Illescas, John Mullen, Helen Nixon, Nicola Seare, Graham Cooper, Jon Morrice, Anya Saunders and Anthony Barwell. Also many thanks to the production team under production managers Emma Fowler and Deborah Long and production co-ordinators Cara Gold, Emma Fletcher, Tallulah Capaldi and Alice Barnard, that organised often complex logistical matters in a most deft manner and – perhaps more difficult – ensured that the series was produced reasonably within budget and on schedule. For additional support and research thanks to Suniti Somaiya and Mariana Ziadeh and Sophia Luzac. For their tireless and energetic work on the series I am deeply grateful to the crew members who have worked on the series over a ten-month period. My special thanks goes to cameramen Mike Garner and Patrick Acum and sound recordists David Williams and Stuart Thompson who were amongst the longest serving members of the team that zigzagged with me around the world. But also many thanks for their outstanding work and stamina to cameramen Hugh Hughes – who joined me on a BBC Hostile Environments refresher course and then in the late summer of 2007 travelled with me happily into the unknown perils of central Afghanistan – to Ben Joiner, Richard Numerov and to always energetic Will Edwards. Also thanks to old friend Simon Parmenter who recorded sound during the last locations filmed and to Jeff Colon and Sean O'Neill. I would like to give my thanks to the home team that worked tirelessly and creatively in the edit suite to mould the material into a respectable and coherent series: Andrea Carnevali, Mark Townsend, Jan Cholawo, Joanna Crickmay, George Cragg, Andy Linton and Angus Sutherland. Also thanks to Stephen Ryan and Colin Pereira of the BBC High Risk team and to David Holley, BBC security consultant, who joined and oversaw the foray into Afghanistan and ensured that we got our material and all returned safely. Essential to the completion of a series involving filming in many foreign and remote locations are the local fixers, translators and drivers. I am delighted to thank the following people for their much valued help: Abdujalil Abdurasulov (Kazakhstan), Martin Asturias (Guatemala), Carlos Batista (Santo Domingo), Gideon Boulting (Brazil), Karma Choden (Bhutan), Maria Laura Frullini (Genoa), Mujahid al-Hashidi (Yemen), Mohamed Hawash (Egypt), Qian Hong (China), Vit Kolar (Czech Republic), Rino Piccolo (Pompeii), Mihai Radu (Romania), Renga Rajan (Srirangam, India), Razan Rashidi (Syria), Magdy Rashidy (Egypt), Tshewang Rinchen (Bhutan), Jason Roberts (Greenland), Rudi (fearless dog-sledge handler in Greenland), Hanif Sherzad (Afghanistan), Lina Sinjab (Syria), Toby Sinclair and his most able son Oliver (India), Elena Smolina (Russia), Philipp Steglich (Dresden), Frank Stucke (Bavaria), Zeynep Santiroglu Sutherland (Istanbul), Amit Vachharajani (Mumbai), Migde Velazquez (France). At the publishers I would like to thank: Michael Dover for commissioning the book, Susan Haynes, Editorial Director, and Jinny Johnson for turning a vast and tortuous text into a publishable proposition, and to David Rowley, Design Director, and Clive Hayball for their visual flair. I would like to thank the following for the use of their photographs: Anthony Barwell, Graham Cooper, Marenka Gabeler, Mike Garner, Andrea Illescas, Jon Morrice and David Williams.

I would also like to thank Charles Allen and Sharada Dwivedi for allowing me to use the manuscript of their unpublished book on the Taj Mahal Hotel, Bombay. And last, thanks to the following for information, advice and valuable contributions: Richard Allen, Christopher Benninger, Sandra Berresford, Owen Bissel, Jane Boddie, Roger Bowdler, Michael Brey, Professor Andrea Bruno, Diamente Luling Buschetti, Centro Internazionale di Studi Architettura Andrea Palladio, Pascole Chabiron, Chris Chanda, Sidney Dukes, Kate Fleet, Todd Longstaff Gowan, Paul Goldberger, Peter J. Johnson, Gülru Necipoglu-Kafadar, Sean Kelley, Alistair Leithead, Wes Neighbour, Bart Ney, Vishnu Dott Pandey, Avril Price, Rachel Reid, Bart Robertson, Bill Richards, David Rockefeller, Professor Franco Sborgi, Professor Nicholas Sitar, David Smith, Brooke Smy, John Soane, Dr David Thomas and the Minaret of Jam Archaeological Project, and John Michael Vlach. Finally, thanks to my agents Charles Walker and Lydia Lewis for sound guidance and for ensuring that the idea of this television series and book has become reality.

Index